Fiction and the Unconscious

For Berta, Peter, Mary, little Simon
Surprised, the sceptic heart encounters joy . . .

FICTION
AND THE
UNCONSCIOUS

BY

SIMON·O·LESSER

WITH A PREFACE BY ERNEST JONES

VINTAGE BOOKS

A DIVISION OF RANDOM HOUSE

NEW YORK

First Vintage Edition, September, 1962

VINTAGE BOOKS

are published by ALFRED A. KNOPF, INC.

and RANDOM HOUSE, INC.

MANUFACTURED IN THE UNITED STATES OF AMERICA

Preface

When one reflects on the enormous part fiction in its various forms, verbal and written, has played in all ages it is remarkable that we have had to wait so long for a comprehensive study of its function and mode of operation such as Mr. Lesser has provided us with in this fascinating book. He has evidently pondered deeply and long on the many problems the word "fiction" gives rise to, and he wears his learning so lightly that the book is a pleasure to read in its easy and attractive style. I would specially commend the Appendix on the use of scientific psychological knowledge in literary study. I do not know a more balanced pronouncement on the value of such assistance and on its frequent misuse; it should be of special interest to literary critics. I can only hope that the book will meet with the wide success it assuredly deserves.

ERNEST JONES, M.D.

Acknowledgments

A book is a dream to which one attempts to give substance in the recalcitrant materials to which one is limited when awake. Since dreams are gliding and effortless, and yet sometimes convey an impression of beauty, of something rounded and perfectly wrought, the translation of dreams into words, the writing of a book, is bound to seem onerous and disenchanting. There is some wisdom in one's tendency to postpone the task, whose frustrating quality one divines, as long as one possibly can; nor is it unnatural that one recoils in disappointment from one's first attempts and seeks further excuses for delay.

To write a book on a difficult subject, therefore, one needs all the help and encouragement one can get. Particularly is this so if valid external excuses present themselves so that many years elapse between the time a book is conceived and work on it begins; then there is grave and increasing danger that the book will remain nothing but a roseate but private dream. I therefore feel an especially keen sense of gratitude to the American Council of Learned Societies, which will always be personified for me by the late Donald Goodchild, for having had sufficient faith in me to award me a fellowship in 1948. The fellowship helped to make it possible for me to resume the studies on which this book is based, but perhaps more important still it provided the psychological stimulus I needed to resume them—to overcome the temptation to stretch what was initially a stint of wartime service in government into a comfortable career.

The writing of *Fiction and the Unconscious* proved so much more difficult than I had anticipated, however, that I would not have proceeded far without additional help. I

Acknowledgments

quickly found that progress was slow, and sometimes non-existent, when I tried to combine work on the book with graduate study or teaching. In 1951 the Rockefeller Foundation awarded me a most generous grant, which was twice renewed, which enabled me to devote my full energies to work on the book; and simultaneously the University of Chicago appointed me a Research Associate, with no other responsibility than that of pressing forward with the study on which the book was based. My gratitude to the Rockefeller Foundation and the University is profound; *Fiction and the Unconscious* owes its existence in part to their helpfulness. I wish to express my thanks to all four of the men who then constituted the Humanities Division of the Foundation, Messrs. Charles B. Fahs, John Marshall, Edward F. D'Arms and Chadbourne Gilpatrick. I was heartened by the feeling that each of them was personally interested in the way the study developed. To Mr. D'Arms, and to Mr. Ralph W. Tyler, then of the University of Chicago, the two men who followed the progress of the study most closely, I feel an especially deep sense of appreciation. Their confidence was a constant inspiration to me to try to produce work which merited it.

I am also grateful to many of my teachers at Columbia University, both for their interest in my study, which is not altogether typical of those undertaken by students of English, and for many helpful suggestions. In particular, I should like to express my thanks to Messrs. Mark Van Doren and Richard Chase.

Several members of the New York Psychoanalytic Institute also showed an interest in my study and took time out from impossibly crowded schedules to give me various kinds of help. Some discussed the study with me in its earliest phases, giving me suggestions which proved of the greatest value and directing my attention to psychoanalytic references whose relevance for my own work I might not otherwise have dis-

Acknowledgments

covered, at any rate until much later on. Then and later some were kind enough to give me case material which bore on response to fiction, and while in the aggregate the amount of such material was not great, its value, in clarifying and confirming some of the ideas about unconscious response then shaping themselves in my mind, was incalculable. Several analysts also read parts of the manuscript critically. I should like to express my thanks to Doctors Gustav Bychowski, Charles Fisher, Mark Kanzer, Ernst Kris, Margaret Mahler and Sidney Tarachow, all of whom helped me in more than one of the ways I have mentioned and many less tangible ways besides. My sense of obligation to Dr. Kanzer is particularly great. Though his own program of activities would exhaust anyone less well adjusted and less gifted, he took a continuous interest in my study, gave me prompt and detailed criticisms of the chapters as they were drafted, put unpublished as well as published material of his own at my disposal, and, in general, gave me the kind of help and encouragement which one can only hope to experience when one has the rare good fortune of discovering someone who shares one's interest in a subject, knows it thoroughly, and is at the same time generous and selfless. I should also like to take this opportunity to thank Dr. Edwin R. Eisler of the Chicago Psychoanalytic Institute who taught me much of what I know about psychoanalysis and laid the groundwork for all that I subsequently learned.

Since publication is a potent form of encouragement, I also have a feeling of gratitude to Philip Rahv and William Phillips, editors of *Partisan Review*, Dr. Mabel Blake Cohen, editor of *Psychiatry*, Leonard Manheim, editor of *Literature and Psychology*, and Maurice Beebe, managing editor of *Modern Fiction Studies*, for wanting to bring portions of *Fiction and the Unconscious* to the attention of their readers.

There is a growing body of empirical material bearing on response to fiction which I was of course eager to sample as

Acknowledgments

part of my preparation for writing this book. I am grateful to the following people for making material available to me: Mrs. Marie H. Briehl, a child analyst now living and practicing in Hollywood, California; Eliot Freidson of the University of Illinois; Carl R. Rodgers, executive secretary of the Counseling Center, University of Chicago; Oscar Katz, then Research Director, and Tore Hallonquist of the Research Department of CBS-Television; and Mrs. Harriet B. Moore of Social Research, Inc.

In writing a book one quickly discovers that not all of one's friends share one's own passionate interest in the subject, the details of one's progress, or even the trickle of typed pages which, despite all obstacles, miraculously materialize. The interest of those friends who *are* interested is, however, a constant source of encouragement. Contrary to the general impression, furthermore, friends do not simply bestow praise; they are sometimes less hesitant than those with whom one is on more formal terms about offering criticisms and suggestions. I have profited in more ways than I can possibly indicate from the comments of various of my friends. I feel a particularly deep sense of obligation to William Girdner and to Joyce and Harvey Brandt, who read the entire manuscript critically. Helen Booth, Ben Botkin, Raymond Gozzi, Samuel Herman, Herbert Marcuse, Leo Rosten and Martha Wolfenstein have also given me sincerely appreciated advice and help. I also wish to express my thanks to Sylvia Clemens, who has not only waged a grim and unrewarding battle with my handwriting but found many other unobtrusive ways of being of assistance.

When *Fiction and the Unconscious* was finished and awaiting publication, I wrote Dr. Ernest Jones to ask him if he would be willing to read it, scarcely daring to hope that he would be able to find time to do so. I am not only grateful but honored that he took the time and thought well enough of the book to write the Preface for it.

Acknowledgments

Without the patience and understanding of my family, *Fiction and the Unconscious* could not have been written at all. Summer and winter, they made the adjustments which permitted me to immerse myself in the work on the book. Even while I reproached myself for my inefficiency and lack of facility, they almost never complained about the mysterious and interminable necessities which kept me from sharing many activities with them or from always being wholly present when I was about. Neither my gratitude to my wife and children for their acceptance of those truancies, on days which will not return, nor my own sense of loss about them, is within my power to express.

SIMON O. LESSER

New York—New Hampshire
1951–1956

Contents

Contents

Fiction and the Unconscious

Chapter I *The Nature of the Inquiry*

Few human activities are at once so widely enjoyed and so much taken for granted as the reading of fiction.

No one can say for how many thousands of years man has told and listened to stories. Many stories appear to have been told for a long period before they were written down. By the time man learned to read and write, much of such wisdom as he had amassed was probably already cast in story form. He had evidently created—or evolved—stories which set forth his surmises about the origin of the universe and man's relationship to the gods. The characterization of the heroes around whom these stories centered and the adventures which befell them also reveal primitive man's conceptions of what was admirable in his fellows and of the goals and dangers of human life. It must have seemed natural to man, from a very early period in his sojourn on this planet, to turn to fiction for images of his experience, his wishes and his fears. Fiction was probably among the earliest of his artifices.

In the life of the individual, too, the appetite for fiction asserts itself long before the acquisition of the ability to read and write. Children are able to enjoy stories almost as soon as they are able to talk. And not simply listening to stories. Children may make up reasonably coherent stories when they are still quite young, and there is a kind of embryonic story-telling involved in the pretense that their dolls and stuffed animals are alive and want to do this or that. One has only to observe children to see how naturally human beings take to the medium of fiction. One is also impressed—almost taken aback—by the degree of reality stories possess for children. At the start they are completely real. It is the capacity to distinguish between fiction and reality which must be acquired.

The important part the enjoyment of fiction plays in the lives of older children and adults is obscured by a tendency to think of fiction too narrowly. To some people fiction connotes only books—novels and volumes of short stories. Even

1

when fiction is thus defined, its popularity can be readily doc-
umented. Various studies of reading and the circulation of
library books indicate that in pre-adolescence and adolescence
about three-fourths of all leisure-time book reading is devoted
to fiction;[1] and in adulthood the percentage is evidently not a
great deal lower.[2] The studies of children's reading may even
understate the proportion of attention given to fiction. Some
of them do not subsume drama under fiction. A few put certain novels and plays in a separate category of "classics" and
fail to re-include them with fiction in the final tabulation of
results. Poetry is more legitimately separated from fiction;
but there is an elliptical narrative element in nearly all poetry,
and poems which have a definite narrative thread, the studies
show, are more popular than any other kind.

Even if allowance could be made for such factors, these
studies would scarcely begin to suggest the extent of the demand for fiction. They were designed to secure information
about the reading of hard-cover books. People's appetite for
fiction is satisfied through countless other channels. Today,
if not at the time many of the studies were conducted, they
consume an astronomical number of paper books—so-called
pocket books and books which for no discernible reason are
called comics though their business is to tell a story, partly by

[1] See, for example, A. J. Jenkinson, *What Do Boys and Girls Read?* (Lon-
don: Methuen, 1940); Stella S. Center and Gladys Parsons, "The Leisure
Reading of New York City High-School Students," *English Journal* XXV
(1936); "Children's Reading in England," *Wilson Bulletin for Librarians*,
VIII (1933); Louis M. Terman and Margaret Lima, *Children's Reading*
(New York: Appleton, 1925).

[2] A study conducted for the book industry in 1946 fixed the proportion of
fiction reading among adults at 58% (non-fiction, 37%; both, 2%; don't
know, 3%). However, various technical considerations make me believe
that, like many of the studies of children, this study underestimates the popularity of fiction. Its sample contained a disproportionate number of people
with some college education, a group that reads a somewhat larger proportion of non-fiction than does the less well educated. Furthermore, the figures
given are based entirely on the last book respondents had read. Considerations involving prestige may have caused some respondents to mention a
work of non-fiction, particularly if they were reading it and, let us say, a
novel at approximately the same time. See Henry C. Link and Harry Arthur
Hopf, *People and Books* (New York: Book Industry Committee, Book Man-
ufacturers Institute, 1946).

pictures, partly by words. They consume an endless stream of stories in magazines and even in newspapers. They flock by millions to the movies. If they can afford to, they go to the theater and the opera. They witness dances and participate in rituals which tell stories. In their homes they absorb an incalculable number of stories through the newer media of radio and television.

The frequency with which other forms of discourse fall into—or are deliberately given—a narrative mold also suggests the hold that mold has upon the human mind. Many biographies and histories are written, in part or from beginning to end, as though they were stories. A how-to-do-it book may take the form of an account of the way in which the author acquired the information which—apparently quite incidentally—he passes on. Similarly, an expository article on, say, conditions in mental hospitals may begin by explaining the writer's interest in the subject and then describe his quest of, and perhaps his emotional reactions to, the information which is introduced.

News stories are supposed to have a prescribed form of their own, but particularly when they are of the "human interest" variety they tend to fall into a narrative pattern. Newspaper columnists feel no constraint about telling stories or putting information in story form. Most newspaper comic strips, it is interesting to note, have long since ceased to be that: they have become episodic or continuing narratives. In the better strips the characters are clearly, if superficially, defined and inhabit the kind of consistent universe we associate with a novel or any other form of narrative art. A somewhat similar observation could be made about many of the variety shows which compete with dramatic programs for popularity honors on radio and television. They, too, employ a crude kind of characterization and try to sustain a loose kind of continuity not only among the parts of a given program but often between programs.

From gossip to those selective accounts of our own doings we give to others, much oral discourse is also cast in a loose narrative form. A great deal of humor, including that cherished portion of it we hesitate to entrust to the written word, is also conveyed by what we thoughtlessly but quite accurately call "stories." It is probably impossible to compile an exhaustive list of the ways in which man seeks to satisfy his apparently insatiable appetite for fiction.

2

Everyone is at least dimly aware of this appetite. In one way or another a large number of people are engaged in satisfying it. But surprisingly, neither the appetite nor the activity by which it is satisfied appears to arouse curiosity or attract attention. It is perhaps less a matter for wonder, though not, I think, without significance, that the activity is almost never accorded praise. The reading of fiction is seldom proscribed or strenuously opposed. Like an old dog by the fire, it has an accepted place in the scheme of things. But it appears to be suffered rather than honored.

This attitude stems in part, I believe, from certain deep, and seldom formulated, misgivings about the value of reading fiction. We tend to disparage the activity, first of all, simply because it is so effortless. In some corner of our minds exertion is associated with virtue and that which is easy with a kind of moral slackness. Thus we tend to honor the kind of reading which most nearly approximates work. Although Protestantism and the ethos of capitalism have undoubtedly fostered these attitudes, they have older and deeper roots. For centuries man has had to exert himself to subsist on earth; he has had to struggle against the temptation to relax and forget the morrow. In at least some men still another factor breeds distrust of anything which is easy: passivity is unconsciously equated with femininity and thus must be fiercely resisted.

In certain past periods the reading of fiction was often denounced as an indulgence which betrayed a weakness of will. Such direct attacks are less frequent today, but the tendency to belittle the value of fiction reading because—and to the extent that—it is easy remains very much alive. It is a factor, I believe, in the disdain most intellectuals feel for the new

mass media—motion pictures, comic books, radio and television—though I would be the first to admit that there are many
justifiable reasons for distrusting them. Its influence is more
clearly at work in the attempt to minimize the popularity of
fiction in some of the studies to which I have referred. Indeed,
in the field of library administration it is probably responsible
for policies and practices which restrict the actual circulation
of fiction to a certain extent. It is well known that many
librarians are reluctant to stock as large a proportion of fiction
as the demand would appear to warrant and the kind of fiction
in which demand bulks; in all probability they also often
"push" non-fiction more aggressively than fiction. They do
this of course from good motives. Consciously or unconsciously they probably believe that they have a responsibility
not simply to satisfy taste but to improve it; and they take it
for granted that they are improving it when they steer people
from fiction to non-fiction or from fiction which could be
easily enjoyed to fiction which is more difficult.

The tendency to assume that by and large the value of reading matter is proportionate to the amount of difficulty it offers
also manifests itself frequently in literary criticism and scholarship. To some extent, I believe, it mars so valuable and sophisticated a work as Q. D. Leavis' *Fiction and the Reading Public*.[3] Mrs. Leavis takes it for granted that the reading of non-
fiction is, in general, more valuable than the reading of fiction,
and that it is a "serious" form of reading whereas the reading
of fiction presumably is not. She appears to believe that the
search for reading matter which can be enjoyed without
strenuous effort betrays a lack of moral fiber.

To weigh the truth of the belief that the reading of non-
fiction is more valuable than the reading of fiction would take
us outside the scope of our inquiry. Perhaps the question cannot be decided: it hinges on a comparison of values of different kinds. However, we shall see that Mrs. Leavis' other
assumptions are unjustified. Although people are often able to
give impressive reasons for reading non-fiction and may be
unable to explain what prompts them to read fiction, we shall

[3] London: Chatto and Windus, 1939.

find that both the motivations for reading fiction and the activity itself are far more "serious" than is generally thought. About the degree of difficulty reading matter should present to be of optimum value, there is much to be said. I suspect that most people do tend to read too many books which are near the bottom rather than the top of their particular range of sensibility. But Chapter VIII and to an extent this entire book will suggest that, so far as fiction is concerned, we follow a sound instinct in selecting works which can be read without undue strain. Any other course would jeopardize both enjoyment and understanding.

We also tend to derogate the value of reading fiction because it represents a form of indulgence in fantasy, and on some deep level any yielding to fantasy activity is likely to be feared. Empirical studies of response to fiction, some of which we shall consider, suggest that this fear has two sources. Fantasies are feared, first of all, because of their wishful nature. The wishes may be feared on their own account and because they arouse ideas of punishment and retaliation. The second basis of fear is suggested by the ambiguity, especially in childhood, of the phrase "to tell a story": it is the fear of confusing fiction and reality, fiction and truth. Although we come to take it for granted, the ability to discriminate between fantasy and fact is one of the most significant of all psychic achievements.

The extent to which people fear fantasy evidently varies enormously. Only people whose ego organization is extremely weak—people who have a precarious hold on reality or who doubt their ability to control instinctual drives—are likely to have so deep a dread of it that any and every excursion to a world of make-believe represents a danger. But many analogies justify the assumption that everyone shares the fear to some extent. It may reveal itself, in people who feel immune from it, under exceptional conditions—for example, when they have a dream at once so terrible and so vivid that they cannot immediately shake off the impression that it is "real," or perhaps premonitory. It may betray itself also in response to fiction through the discomfort which is felt when a story comes too close to some anxiety and is not sharply enough walled off from the world of experience.

I suspect that the extent to which fantasy is feared also varies in different periods. It may have been especially pronounced, for example, in the late seventeenth and early eighteenth centuries when the *Zeitgeist* provided a kind of justification, or reinforcement, for it by exalting the importance of the tasks of the everyday world. In any case, the new middle-class reading public which was then emerging appears to have been deeply suspicious of fantasy. It was partly because of this that the fiction writers who were addressing themselves to this public larded their stories so heavily with moral sentiment and so frequently pretended that they were accounts of actual occurrences. The desire to conciliate a sensed fear of fantasy, it may be conjectured, is one of the perennial motives for "realism."

These two factors, distrust of fantasy and distrust of anything which is effortless, probably reinforce each other and exert more influence than is apparent, but I do not believe that they fully explain either the rather low evaluation we put on the activity of reading fiction or our lack of curiosity about it. Other factors probably contribute to our attitude—for example, a vague feeling of shame about the nature of the satisfactions we sometimes secure from fiction. Our lack of curiosity about what is involved in the reading experience is of a piece with a lack of curiosity about many other matters. Through the ages how much attention has been given to speech itself or to such things as man's tendency to adorn his body and tell jokes? There are so many subjects which we seem reluctant to examine closely that at first glance it might seem impossible to find any common denominator in them. However, I would hazard the guess that man is more willing to study matters connected with his physical environment and his physical activities than he is problems which closely touch his psychic and affective life. Insights about these aspects of his existence are most acceptable when they are not conceptualized but are expressed symbolically—when they are embodied in poems and stories, ceremonies and rituals. Some of the same factors responsible for "distancing" in art seem to operate upon man's curiosity, helping to determine how soon, how widely and how directly various problems will be investigated.

3

Whether or not this explanation is valid, it is certain that man's proclivity for telling and listening to stories has excited surprisingly little curiosity. Why does man take time from the tasks which are necessary for his survival for such an activity? What is the nature of the satisfactions he secures from it? What basic attributes of fiction account for its ability to provide these satisfactions? What occurs in us as we read or listen to stories? What effects does the reading of fiction have? Focussing upon tragedy rather than fiction in general, Aristotle considered such questions as these in the *Poetics*. In the context of another inquiry, Plato considered the last of them,[4] and many other philosophers, poets and critics have thrown light on one or another of them, often by their assumptions as much as by anything they have said. But among the innumerable books and essays which have been written about literature—biographies, histories, studies of genres, comparative studies, analyses of this or that aspect of poetry or fiction—I can think of no work besides the *Poetics* which has systematically addressed itself to such questions.

Of course, no work can aspire to answer them completely and definitively. No one person can hope to see, much less to say, all the true and important things which ought to be said about any single masterpiece of narrative art. It is obviously not possible to deal exhaustively with such broad and complex

[4] Though mistakenly, and, were it not for Plato's early position in the history of philosophy, it could even be said, ingenuously. Plato assumed that there is a simple one-to-one relationship between the subject matter of a literary work and its influence on readers: a poem which deals with immoral material must necessarily have injurious effects. But this is not the only possibility, as the concept of catharsis (enunciated by Plato's pupil, Aristotle) indicates.

It should be added that it was only when Plato donned the toga of a political philosopher that he was likely to make errors of this kind; when the poet in him was dominant, he was a superb critic.

subjects as fiction and the human beings who read it. All one can hope to do is to identify some of the more important factors—some of the urgent needs which cause us to read, some of the basic characteristics of fiction which enable it to satisfy those needs. Furthermore, one must be reconciled in advance to the fact that some of the things for which one is searching may elude one and that some of the things one finds may not seem important to others. These considerations would inspire a degree of humility even if one were inclined to be arrogant, but they should not discourage effort. In this book, we shall at least try to answer the kind of questions I have mentioned, and we shall try to answer them as completely, as straightforwardly, and, in a sense which will be explained, even as scientifically as possible.

The plan of the book is simple. Chapter II considers the needs which impel us to read fiction and compares and contrasts fiction with other things which satisfy somewhat similar needs. Chapters III and IV discuss some of the subject matter characteristics, Chapters V, VI, and VII some of the formal characteristics, that enable fiction to satisfy our needs. Special attention is given to the characteristics that make it possible for fiction to give us pleasure and satisfaction even when it deals with events and problems which might arouse painful reactions if treated in other forms of discourse or experienced in life itself.

Chapter VIII attempts to reconstruct the various conscious and unconscious processes involved in response to fiction. Chapter IX is devoted to a more thorough analysis of the way we grasp the meaning of fiction. Through detailed analyses of two short stories it shows the extent to which fiction may be understood unconsciously. In some instances, we shall find, the apparent meaning of a story is reversed by what we perceive unconsciously; in a great many instances the appeal of a story depends largely on things grasped below the threshold of awareness.

However, it will be apparent by this point in our analysis that our cognitive responses, conscious and unconscious, do not fully explain the powerful effect fiction sometimes has upon us. Fiction may also succeed in involving us actively in its events and it may stimulate us to spin fantasies patterned upon them, a process I call "analogizing." Chapter X discusses these participant responses to fiction. It also discusses a number of the satisfactions we secure from reading fiction, showing in each case how our spectator responses and our participant responses cooperate in their achievement. Chapter XI completes the discussion by analyzing that consummate form of satisfaction we call esthetic. It also considers some salient characteristics of the narrative genre with which esthetic satisfaction is most frequently associated—tragedy—and glances briefly at tragedy's alter ego, comedy.

The Appendix is addressed to a particular group of literary students: those who have misgivings about drawing upon bodies of knowledge not embraced in the humanities but who are willing to consider the pros and cons of the issue open-mindedly. In the Appendix, I try to persuade these students of two things which some of their colleagues already know and of the truth of which others, doubtless, could never be convinced. First, there is no basis for a ban on any kind of knowledge in exploring anything so complex as literature; the student should be free to use any concepts and data which promise to be helpful in achieving the ends of his particular study. Secondly, in discussing literature and most literary problems one can scarcely avoid the use of some kind of psychology. The only real choice open to the student, in most instances, is whether to utilize the relatively well-validated body of psychological knowledge which is now available or to depend on his own knowledge and assumptions, however inadequate and even mistaken these may be.

4

To readers used to more restricted literary studies—histories of a given period or a given genre, analyses of the work of a single author, investigations of some one resource of fiction or poetry, such as imagery or point of view—the scope of this study may seem inadvisably broad. It does, indeed, entail difficulties and disadvantages, and these should be acknowledged. However, as I shall indicate, I believe that there are decisive advantages in focussing upon fiction as broadly as I propose to.

It is difficult enough, as many critics have pointed out, to make valid statements about a form so ill-defined and variegated as the novel. Here we wish to consider every form of imaginative work basically concerned with telling a story— novels, novelettes and short stories; narrative poems; plays, whether in poetry or prose; and stories told through the various media of popular art, including magazines, motion pictures, comic books, radio and television.[5] Obviously, many observations which would be valid for the works in one of these categories—or for some of them or for works grouped on some other basis—will not hold for fiction defined thus broadly; it is necessary to reject many of the observations which suggest themselves. What is more discomforting is the difficulty of stating tenable observations so that they will not provoke dissent. Unless one wishes to clutter the text with innumerable qualifications and sooner or later weary the reader, it is necessary to speak broadly in terms of what are sometimes called "ideal constructions"—pervasive tendencies realized with widely varying degrees of success in different works. In the nature of the case these tendencies will not reveal themselves with equal clarity in all stories, and in one or another story, I have no doubt, some of them may not be in evidence at all.

Nevertheless, it seems obviously worthwhile to try to identify these enduring general characteristics, most of which are present in every story and which, in the aggregate, enable us to recognize a given work as a story. It seems reasonable to suppose that they are the qualities which will do most to ex-

[5] I believe that many of the points to be developed hold for what the University of Chicago group of critics call "didactic," as well as for "mimetic," works. In the greatest didactic works (e.g., *Pilgrim's Progress*) the story is not so far subordinated to the author's expository purpose as not to have the characteristic qualities and virtues of the story form. However, it will be apparent that I am speaking primarily of mimetic fiction, and that certain points will not apply, or will apply only in part, to some didactic works.

plain the appeal of fiction, and as soon as a number of them
have been identified and analyzed I believe it will be apparent
that, in fact, this is the case. There is another advantage in
trying to identify the characteristics, though it is one with
which we shall here be less directly concerned: many of them
are clearly desirable and thus constitute excellent natural criteria for evaluating fiction. Other things being equal, those
stories are best in which the characteristics are exemplified
most clearly and completely.

If these general characteristics are unappreciated now, it is
because many of them—for example, the concreteness and
movement characteristic of fiction of every age and every
level of complexity—are taken for granted and seldom examined. Instead of the qualities which differentiate one genre
from another, or one work from another, being considered in
the light of the underlying characteristics common to fiction,
as would seem logical, it is the qualities *peculiar* to a given
body of literature which usurp the center of attention. Literary scholarship, for example, has been preoccupied with such
problems as the relationship of the literature produced at a
given time with the sensibility of that particular period and
with the reasons for the emergence—or decline—of a given
emphasis or a given genre. Almost inevitably, too little attention has been paid to the qualities the literature of one age has
in common with the literature of the preceding age and all
other ages; almost inevitably, the characteristics common to,
say, a new and a waning fictional genre have been slighted.
I am, of course, speaking quite broadly. Scholars and critics
have investigated many other kinds of problems, and certain
individual characteristics of literature, such as diction, have
been analyzed in general terms. But it is safe to say that relatively little attention has been given to the comparatively
ubiquitous and changeless factors. So far as I know, for example, no one has attempted, as we shall here, to identify the
more or less pandemic and immutable needs which lead men
to read fiction and the more or less universal attributes of fiction which enable it to satisfy those needs.

Yet, as Maud Bodkin declares, if the images of literature

"can be considered . . . as related to the sensibility of a certain poet, and a certain age and country," they can also be considered "as a mode of expressing something potentially realiz-
able in human experience of any time or place." [6] If countless
once-enjoyed works of fiction lose their popularity, and in some
cases all but disappear from view, it is also true that other works
of fiction—*Don Quixote,* let us say, or *The Decameron, Robinson Crusoe* or *Hamlet*—enthrall successive generations of
readers in many lands, readers who differ from one another in
innumerable respects. The works produced in one age do not
supplant all those written before, as some literary histories
would almost lead us to believe. A twentieth-century reader
with a liking for Proust and Joyce may also enjoy Fielding
and Thackeray; it may not occur to him that there is any
inconsistency involved in enjoying both a heroic romance and
a rogue story, despite the much emphasized differences between these genres. The characteristics common to the fiction
of all ages, and to all of the fiction of a given age, are at least
as important as the differences. They are worth studying also
because they help to explain the differences. Once we perceive the dynamic function of such a universal formal attribute
of fiction as control, we can more readily understand why
there are variations in the degree of control in different works
and the work characteristic of different periods.

In view of the scope and difficulty of what is being attempted, it is obviously impossible to deal with these variations
explicitly—to illustrate and analyze the way control manifests
itself in many different works. Nor is it possible to do something which would be equally interesting—indicate the way
in which readers who differ from one another in personality
structure would be likely to respond to a given amount of
control. This study is not intended and should not be expected
to compete with other valuable ways of investigating literature, with historically oriented studies, for example, or intensive analyses of carefully restricted issues. We shall not be
able to deal exhaustively with our own particular subject, the
relatively universal and timeless aspects of the appeal of fic-

[6] *Archetypal Patterns in Poetry* (London: Oxford, 1948), p. 315.

tion. But the questions with which we shall be concerned are of crucial importance. Their secrets have been long and zealously guarded, and the attempt to cast light upon them will, I believe, compel us to look at both fiction and ourselves more searchingly than we ordinarily do.

5

A word must also be said about the tools to be used in our inquiry, about what is sometimes called methodology. At one point I had hoped to develop a *naturalistic* esthetic of response to fiction, a theory that could not be dismissed as simply another opinion, another of the endless and never more than partially successful attempts to pluck out the heart of art's mystery. But I soon found that much of the empirical knowledge about response which would be required for building such an esthetic does not as yet exist. Of course, even if it did exist, it might be impossible to use it with sufficient objectivity to develop a theory that could presume to call itself scientific. Perhaps because literature can be approached in so many different ways and involves our emotions so deeply, it seems to resist detached and systematic examination. The most closely reasoned discourse about it—say, such an essay as Hume's "Of the Standard of Taste"—is likely sooner or later to take a turn another student will regard as mistaken and here and there omit considerations as important as those taken into account.

But if it is not feasible to develop a truly scientific esthetic of response to fiction, I can see no objection to developing one which is as scientific as possible. This has been my endeavor. The esthetic presented here is admittedly speculative, but it is based upon and squares with all the relevant empirical knowledge I have been able to ferret out. All else being equal—an important qualification, as I am well aware—I believe that a theory of this sort enjoys a better chance of proving sound than one which is entirely conjectural.

Though the existing body of empirical knowledge which has relevance for our inquiry is neither so large nor so complete as one would like, it is far larger than is generally appreci-

ated, especially among students of literature. For reasons discussed in the Appendix, the knowledge has been largely
ignored.

The most important constituent of this body of knowledge
—the foundation of much of the rest—is psychoanalytic psychology. Though psychoanalytic findings and formulations
are difficult to apply to literature, and have often been mis-
applied, their potential value when they are used correctly
and tactfully is, I believe, inestimable. The supreme virtue
of psychoanalysis, from the point of view of its potential utility
for literary study, is that it has investigated the very aspects of
man's nature with which the greatest writers of fiction have
been preoccupied: the emotional, unconscious or only partly
comprehended bases of our behavior. Unlike other psycholo-
gies, but like Sophocles and Shakespeare, Tolstoy and Dostoevsky, Melville and Hawthorne, it has concerned itself with
the surging non-rational forces which play so large a part in
determining our destiny as well as the part of our being which
tries, often in vain, to control and direct them. It offers us
a systematic and well-validated body of knowledge about
those forces.

It ought to be apparent that the findings of such a psychology should be helpful in explicating many of the things
conveyed through fiction—and in particular the deepest levels
of meaning of the greatest fiction. I deliberately use the word
explicate. It is my assumption that as we read we unconsciously *understand* at least some of a story's secret significance; to some extent our enjoyment is a product of this
understanding. But some readers go on to try to account for
the effect a story has had upon them, and to report what they
discover. It is in connection with these later critical activities,
which must be sharply differentiated I believe from the reading experience itself, that psychoanalytic concepts are likely
to prove invaluable. They may make it possible to deal with
a portion of our response which was not hitherto accessible
to criticism—permit us to explain reactions which were intuitive, fugitive and often non-verbal, and supply the key to the
elements in the story responsible for those reactions.

Unfortunately, even this most obvious way of utilizing the knowledge psychoanalysis has put at our disposal has *not* been quickly or widely recognized. It is perhaps more understandable that the knowledge has not been utilized to help explain the significance of the formal qualities of fiction. These are difficult to analyze on the basis of any set of assumptions; we are usually content to admire and identify them. Furthermore, we assume—within certain limits, I believe, quite correctly— that these qualities satisfy certain idealistic needs, which most people do not think of as falling within the purview of psychoanalysis. In fact, analysis is as interested in these needs as it is in the forbidden libidinal and aggressive impulses with which it is more frequently associated. Matters could scarcely be otherwise if only because the psyche is an entity and because our idealistic needs are related to our "bad" impulses both genetically and dynamically; they arise in part from the felt need of controlling those impulses, and they are sometimes emphasized in order to defend oneself against forbidden impulses or to atone for yielding to them. As I shall attempt to show in a very preliminary way in Chapters V, VI and VII, analytic concepts suggest many new ways of approaching some of the problems which arise in connection with form. It will be more apparent that they are likely to be helpful in exploring the processes of response to fiction. It has long been recognized that emotional considerations play a part in response to art and that to some extent our apprehension of a work of art is immediate and intuitive rather than reasoned.

It seemed desirable to consult the work of Freud and his followers for still another reason: they have investigated a number of subjects which are closely connected with our own field of inquiry. The book Freud regarded as his masterpiece deals with dreams;[7] and dreams philosophers and poets from the time of Plato have known to have some relationship to art. Freud also discusses those waking dreams we call fantasies. A 1908 paper discusses the use of fantasies in fiction, and some of the ways in which they are transformed to be made pleas-

[7] *The Interpretation of Dreams* in *The Basic Writings of Sigmund Freud* (New York: Modern Library, 1938).

ing to the reader.[8] Still more valuable, in my opinion, is the work which has been done by Freud and some of his followers on play and wit. Wit in particular is a close analogue of fiction (and literature in general). Unlike dreams, which are autistic, wit is a social product and must be intelligible. At the same time, it must not be so readily intelligible that its full meaning is consciously noted and formulated during the instant when it is enjoyed. The attention must be diverted from some of the things being expressed. What Freud calls technique in his analysis of wit functions in somewhat the same way in which we shall find that form functions in fiction.

Freud and his followers have, of course, also devoted a great deal of attention to literature itself, and some of their studies will be referred to in the course of this book. As it happens, however, relatively few of these studies have been centrally concerned with the effect of literature upon readers or other problems connected with response. Two other interests have been dominant. Freud, and his followers after him, turned to literature first of all for clarification and confirmation of their hypotheses. Time and time again Freud paid tribute to poets and storytellers for their intuitive understanding of psychological mechanisms he was laboriously struggling to formulate. Literature was scanned as a kind of supplementary form of evidence. Secondly, it was studied, as dreams or any other psychic productions might be, for the light it shed upon its creators. By and large psychoanalytic interest in literature has run backward, from the work of art to its creator, whereas ours will flow forward, from the work of art to the reader.[9] But of course these several interests are not

[8] "The Relation of the Poet to Day-Dreaming," *Collected Papers*, Vol. IV (London: Hogarth, 1948). Also in *Delusion and Dream* (Boston: Beacon, 1956).

[9] I have deliberately included little biographical information about the authors of stories which are considered. I assume that the meaning of any story can be communicated to a receptive reader who knows nothing of its creator, not even his name. It follows that interpretations may be based on what is given in a story, and should be judged by how completely and satisfactorily they account for what is given. For our purposes, biographical or any other kind of background information would be of little more than corroborative value. On occasion, I realize, such information may also help

unrelated, and many analytic studies of literature contain material which is directly or indirectly of value in developing a theory of response. In recent years, furthermore, the subject of response has elicited greater interest.

There is still another source of scientific information about some of the questions with which we shall be concerned—the studies of response to fiction to which I have already referred. A few of these studies have been made by analysts, but the majority have been conducted by psychologists, sociologists and educators, some analytically oriented and some not. The interests and objectives of the investigators also vary widely. A number of studies have had some immediate practical aim. A great deal of work has been and is being done for commercial purposes.

As is to be expected in view of these differences, there is a wide diversity among these studies. Possibly because the field is such a new one, some of them are of little value; they have glaring methodological weaknesses or are based on doubtful assumptions about fiction, the reading experience or psychology in general. Still other studies, including most of the commercial ones I have been able to examine, are adequate in terms of their own purposes, but too superficial to throw much light on the problems we shall consider. However, the better studies give us exact and trustworthy information on various matters about which we could only speculate before and in some cases call attention to factors which a theoretical analysis might neglect.

In addition to utilizing the traditional sources for literary studies, throughout *Fiction and the Unconscious* I have drawn upon such sources of empirical knowledge as I have men-

---

a student to see things he would otherwise miss. But care must be exercised in stating *what* they help him to see. In the overwhelming majority of cases, according to my experience, the additional insights they suggest pertain not so much to anything *in* a story as to such matters as the relationship of a story to its age or to the way the creator of a story felt about things which happened to him. English is often so taught, at all educational levels, that background information actually distracts attention from literature qua literature to such predominantly non-literary considerations.

tioned. They help to illuminate the very first subject we should consider—the needs which impel us to engage in such an activity as reading about the imaginary doings of imaginary people.

Chapter II *The Reader of Fiction*

The meagre satisfaction that [man] can extract from reality leaves him starving.

FREUD[1]

In nostalgic moments we may tend to think of childhood as a time of almost unbroken happiness, free of the strivings, frustrations and complexities which make adult life so burdensome. But when we look more closely we discover that children, too, have their anxieties and discontents; they turn to reading as one way of dealing with these. The painful truth is that at each stage of our lives we are dissatisfied, unhappy and anxious a large part of the time. No matter how often we are reminded of this fact by philosophers and religious seers—or, more agonizingly, by events in our own lives—we only occasionally and momentarily accept its validity. We cannot, of course, deny that pain, dissatisfaction and disillusionment are inevitable aspects of human experience, but we can and do seek to minimize their significance. For example, we may attempt to treat painful aspects of experience as exceptional or even accidental. No matter what we have gone through, we tell ourselves with a stubbornness which has something magnificent about it that the next phase of our lives will fulfil more of our longings and give us less cause to feel wretched. Only exceptional men, or the rest of us in moments of exceptional honesty, face the possibility that there may be something about life itself which is inimical to our desire for happiness.

It is useless, and adolescent, to complain about the frustrating quality of much of our experience, and by and large man does not complain. Indeed, as we shall see in more detail when we analyze comedy and tragedy, the very works which call attention to the grimmest aspects of life pay tribute to the

[1] *A General Introduction to Psychoanalysis* (New York: Garden City, 1938), p. 325.

resiliency of the human spirit. *Candide* is at once the saddest and the gayest of books. These victories are achieved not only in literature, but in a sphere we hold more lightly despite the consolations it offers—the sphere of wit. Two old Jews were bemoaning the sadness of the world and the trials and tribulations of their own people. "Life is hard, hard," concluded one. "Better we should not have been born at all." "Yes, but who can have such luck," replied his companion. "Maybe one in a million." Many stories are like this, covertly counseling us to accept the human situation at the same time that they acknowledge its painfulness.

The joke reveals something else: the endeavor of human beings to wrest enjoyment from even the most unsatisfactory aspects of life. Man is an indefatigable seeker of pleasure. If human experience does not yield enough satisfaction—and, of course, it does not—then he will strive at least to protect himself from the pain it may give rise to and to create other worlds more in accord with his desires. With the first of these defenses, which include all the means men employ to keep the world from hurting them or to dull themselves to unavoidable suffering, we are not immediately concerned. Art, including fiction, is neither a means of avoiding pain nor of dulling oneself to it: neither a renunciation nor a narcotic. Like play, fantasy and wit, which are its close relations, it represents an attempt to augment the meager satisfactions offered by experience through the creation of a more harmonious world to which one can repair, however briefly, for refuge, solace and pleasure. .

Later in this chapter we shall discuss some of the common and distinguishing characteristics of these various attempts to create worlds less niggardly and more responsive to our needs than the aloof world of nature. But first, in a spirit of inquiry rather than complaint, we should try to understand why experience is not more satisfying. The information we obtain will help us to identify the attributes of fiction which enable it to satisfy needs frustrated by reality. And it will explain why men take time from the exigencies of living for such a curious pursuit as reading stories.

2

One will be forgiven a moment of hesitation before plunging into an attempt to deal with man's discontents. They are too numerous, too protean, too overlapping to identify satisfactorily, much less catalogue. But fortunately our purposes do not require either an exhaustive listing or a classification in accordance with some ideal scheme. If we consider first some of the more important causes of human unhappiness and then illustrate the ways in which they frustrate some of the more basic human needs, we shall probably chance upon the more important shortcomings of experience for which men seek compensation in the arts.

Some of these shortcomings are so inexorable a part of the human situation that it seems irrational to attempt to escape them. Man is a biological organism, destined to die after an uncertain span of time. Moreover, unlike other animals, he knows that he must die, so that in addition to the physical pain he may experience from the decay of his own body he cannot escape the mental anguish which comes from knowing that his joys, his achievements, his relationships are transient and that sooner or later his strivings will be cut short by death. Man must live his life in one particular epoch. Though bisexual, he cannot, like Orlando, experience life now as man, now as woman. At any given time he is more circumscribed still. He is bound to one place, one occupation, one phase of life.

While man cannot escape these limitations, he can and does seek to circumvent them. Though there are wide differences among people in the intensity with which they long for that which they have not, only rare individuals seem capable of feeling fully satisfied with their lot more than momentarily. One of the dearest desires of children, of *all* children, is to be grown-up. Adults are no less perverse: we all have regressive strivings, and no matter how firmly these are subdued in moments of health and purposive behavior, we yield to them frequently—daily, for example, in the experience of sleep, which among other things represents a return to that blissful, undisturbed peace we knew before our entrance into the clamorous world. Psychoanalysis teaches us that no infantile desires are ever entirely relinquished. They or their derivatives demand a measure of satisfaction throughout life, and if adulthood is too thwarting the paths back to them may be found, as in neurosis, and in disguised fashion they may regain their dominance of our lives.

Many of the limitations of human life are all the more galling because they are so slowly perceived. One portion of us, the id, the repository of our instinctual, unsocialized impulses, never accepts them, but in adolescence they are denied even by the rational, directing part of our personality whose duty it is to keep us in touch with reality. Thus misled, all but a minority of people who are unusually successful or mature tend to find growing up not a process of unfolding, in which their powers and horizons gradually widen, but a process of contraction, of being led to smaller and smaller enclosures. This sense of life as a series of progressive restrictions may oppress us even if the pasture in which we are finally confined is a pleasant one, if we love and are loved by our wife, have children of whom we are proud and a job which is not unrewarding. Perhaps we have dreamed and not entirely relinquished the dream that we could have these things and many others besides: fame, wealth, the love of many women, numerous jobs each more successful than the last in exhibiting our powers. It is a long time before we learn that every choice involves a renunciation—usually a whole series of them. Even when we realize this, we do not cease to mourn the potentialities which could not be utilized in our life as it has been lived. Waste is inevitable in human experience, but it is hard to accept.

We are fortunate, of course, if the lessons life has to teach us are not still more painful. Neither wife nor children, career nor social circle may measure up to either the gaudy dreams of youth or the more sober expectations of early adulthood. This may be because we expected too much; our friends may be fine people and good companions and disappoint us only because they seem unlikely representatives of that brilliant society we dreamed of captivating. More probably than not, however, fate will have really dealt harshly with us in one or more ways. Trusted friends may have forsaken us at a crisis in our life when we particularly needed their understanding and help. The wife we had loved may have failed us, or we her. We may have a child who was born with some defect or permanently crippled by early illness. We ourself may have been denied the opportunity to pursue a longed-for career by illness, economic pressure or some unforeseeable event, such as war, which disrupted our life.

Some of these examples help to identify another of the enemies of man's struggle for happiness—the nature of the world in which he lives. The world is not a relentless foe, but neither is it a dependable ally. It may smile upon man one year with bountiful harvests and wipe out the fruit of his labor the next with storm or flood. It may give us a handsome and gifted child, then steal his life in a senseless accident. The sense of being a neglected stepchild of nature is evidently intolerable to man. Her indifference makes him feel lost and insecure, a random visitor in a chaotic and purposeless world. Man solicits and bribes, even bullies, nature to be more responsive to his needs, but since she remains churlishly unconcerned, he is forced to ever greater efforts to overcome his feeling of lostness and bewilderment. He invents schemes to make the universe intelligible and he strives to order his own experience and invest it with significance. The wish to feel at home in a purposive universe is one of the factors responsible for the birth of art as well as philosophy, religion, science and the other instruments man has devised to calibrate the world in accordance with his own needs and perceptions.

At least two other causes of unhappiness seem unalterable aspects of the nature of things. Our very constitution, Freud points out in *Civilization and Its Discontents*, seems to limit our capacity for experiencing happiness. "What is called happiness in its narrowest sense comes from the satisfaction— most often instantaneous—of pent-up needs which have reached great intensity, and by its very nature can only be a transitory experience. When any condition desired by the pleasure principle is protracted, it results in a feeling only of mild comfort; we are so constituted that we can only intensely enjoy contrasts, much less intensely states in themselves." [2]

This constitutional factor explains the quick feeling of satiety which accompanies the fulfilment of physical desires and may be responsible for the distinction man draws between pleasure and happiness. In addition, it undoubtedly has something to do with the fact that the achievement of our more general objectives seldom gives us as much satisfaction as we had anticipated. Of course, disillusionment has many other sources. The very effort involved in reaching our goals seems to depreciate their value. It gives us time to estimate them more realistically; it makes us grimly aware of the heavy price we must pay for the attainment of anything we want, a factor we had almost certainly neglected to take into account in our youthful daydreams. Perhaps at bottom we resent the fact that we have to pay any price at all. What we want is unqualified love and admiration; there is something sad about having to prove our worth. Usually, too, in achieving our objectives we must make certain compromises, and even when these involve no dishonesty, as the law would define it, but rather a discreet accommodation to standards approved by society, the effect is the same: the goals become tarnished. Since, moreover, we ourselves change in pursuing them, becoming weary if not cynical, it is not so surprising that we often feel disenchanted with our goals before we have actually achieved them; even proximity may subtract from their worth. Disillusionment is such an unavoidable part of human experience that philosophers as well as coiners of epigrams have asked whether it is not even more unfortunate to be granted one's desires than to be denied them.

Once identified, the kind of obstacles to happiness which have been discussed are readily accepted as part of the human situation. For some reason, as Freud remarks, we find it difficult to regard the ill treatment we receive from our fellow

[2] Freud, *Civilization and Its Discontents* (London: Hogarth, 1939), pp. 27-28.

human beings in the same light. No matter how often and how deeply people may wound us, their cruelty and even their indifference may continue to surprise us, to seem, at each fresh encounter, exceptional and inexplicable. We can see how mistaken this view is simply by observing children at play. Sooner or later most of them are likely to receive some blow or hurt from their combative companions. As a member of a species with a primitive tendency toward aggression, every man must expect a certain amount of harsh treatment from his fellows.

3

To these sources of unhappiness we must add those which are inevitable concomitants of culture. The complex fashion in which culture—any culture—exacts a toll in human happiness for the benefits it confers has been traced with such skill by Freud in *Civilization and Its Discontents* that only a few summary statements are necessary here. Quite obviously, culture requires a great deal of instinctual renunciation: it can extend such advantages as security and justice only by strictly regulating man's sexual and aggressive impulses; it must impose some limits on sexual expression also so that energy will be available for the tasks it wants done. What is not immediately apparent is the extent to which these necessary and apparently reasonable controls interfere with the goal of personal happiness.

Society could scarcely exist without prohibiting incestuous object-choice, yet Freud characterizes this prohibition as "perhaps the most maiming wound ever inflicted . . . on the erotic life of man." [3] In general, the regulation of sexual impulses involves an unavoidable—a disproportionate—loss of pleasure. "The feeling of happiness produced by indulgence of a wild, untamed craving is incomparably more intense than is the satisfying of a curbed desire." [4] Cultural demands not only interfere with that complete erotic fulfilment which is such an important component of happiness. They—or more

[3] *Ibid.*, p. 74.
[4] *Ibid.*, pp. 32-33.

accurately the conflict between them and prohibited desires, including sexual ones—are a primary cause of anxiety and neurosis, and thus of unhappiness.

The control of aggression is also achieved, even more directly than the control of sexuality, at the price of a measure of happiness. With something we could call cunning if the process were a deliberate one, civilization utilizes aggression to control aggression. A great store of aggressive energy is internalized and put at the disposal of an institution of the mind, the superego.[5] The superego then stands guard over the ego,[6] to use Freud's comparison, like a garrison in a conquered city. It betrays the source of its energy by making demands of such severity that they are difficult if not impossible to fulfil. The tension between the despotic superego and the hard-pressed ego, desperately attempting to reconcile its behests and instinctual pressures, is what we experience as a sense of guilt.

It would be difficult to exaggerate the amount of suffering caused by the sense of guilt, which is pervasive in civilized man. In extreme cases it may be a cause of crippling neurosis; in innumerable people it leads to more or less chronic feelings of unworthiness and depression. Since the superego is an institution of the mind, it is aware of thoughts as well as deeds

[5] The superego may be regarded as a kind of deposit within the psychic structure of the influence of the parents and others who have shaped the individual—of their personalities and of the standards, ideals and prohibitions they have transmitted. It is an intrapsychic carrier of the traditions and tabus of society. Although the superego embraces what is called "conscience," it should not be confused with it, for much of the superego's functioning is unconscious; it may pass judgment not only on actions and contemplated actions but on wishes the individual may not be aware he entertains. It should be noted in passing that both the judgments of the superego and its punishments often have an irrational character; for various technical reasons connected with the formation of the superego, they are often far more severe than those of the parents. While the superego behaves like the parents in making threats and imposing various forms of actual punishment (or more accurately by compelling the ego to do so) whenever its standards are transgressed, like the parents also it may bestow approval and love when its demands have been fully met. For a further discussion, see Freud, *The Ego and the Id* (London: Hogarth, 1942); Otto Fenichel, *The Psychoanalytic Theory of Neurosis* (New York: Norton, 1945), Chap. VI and *passim*; and Ives Hendrick, *Facts and Theories of Psychoanalysis* (New York: Knopf, 1939), especially pp. 148-49.

[6] For a discussion of the ego, see pp. 306-7.

which transgress its demands, and it requires that both be punished with the same severity. The punishment may take outer as well as inner forms. Feelings of guilt may lead people not only to give themselves up for crimes they have committed but, incredibly, to commit crimes so that they will be punished or to try, unconsciously, to mess up their lives.[7] They are one of the most frequent causes of illness and accidents. They are often responsible for inhibitions and self-defeating tendencies which make success difficult even for people of superior ability. In passing, we should note that guilt feelings also have some effects which may be regarded as constructive. The desire to allay guilt plays a highly important role in both the production of art and, as we shall see, in response to it. But there is hardly any way, destructive or constructive, in which one can achieve more than a temporary peace with a severe superego. Renunciation of instinctual satisfactions does not help matters, for the prohibited wishes persist and are observed. Indeed, for a variety of reasons which we cannot here consider, it is precisely the people who struggle most valiantly against their sinful impulses who are most mercilessly tormented by conscience.

This is by no means an exhaustive list of the ways in which the course of cultural development tends to conflict with the goal of individual happiness, but we must be satisfied, in dealing with so large a subject, to suggest only the more important points. At least one other major source of discontent remains to be considered: the influence of our particular culture. We have already dealt with one aspect of this subject, for by no means all of the suffering we experience as a result of the way our instincts are curbed can be regarded as the irreducible price of civilization. At least some of it must be attributed to the unnecessary and unrealistic severity with which all the instincts, including the egoistic ones, are controlled in our culture. Enmeshed as we are in that culture, we

---

[7] Cf. Freud, "Some Character-Types Met With in Psycho-Analytic Work," especially Section III, *Collected Papers*, Vol. IV (London: Hogarth, 1948). For a more extended discussion of the effects of guilt, see Karl Menninger, *Man Against Himself* (New York: Harcourt, Brace, 1938).

have no way of knowing how much control is indispensable, how much gratuitous. The growth of anthropological knowledge has dispelled the illusion that even primitive societies give the instincts free sway. Nevertheless, so cautious and conservative an observer as Freud could not resist the conclusion that the amount of renunciation demanded by our culture represents an unwarranted extreme. Since economic factors play such an important part in psychology, determining in the last analysis, for example, whether conflicts will or will not produce neurosis and certain forms of psychosis, the unnecessary severity with which the instincts are curbed in Western society may cause a disproportionate amount of suffering. A mild relaxation of those curbs might produce a very considerable reduction in the incidence of mental disease and in the intensity of the sense of guilt and the sense of cultural privation from which so many suffer today. Apart from the contribution such a relaxation would make to the happiness of those who comprise society, it would seem desirable in terms of the interests of society itself. It would have a cohesive influence, for beyond any question the sense of deprivation which gnaws so many people is one of the factors responsible for feelings of alienation from society and antagonism toward it. More moderate standards might also reduce the hypocrisy which is so pervasive in our civilization and make possible a more intelligent approach to the rearing of children, education and many other matters.

So much has been written about other characteristics of our culture which cause unhappiness and dissatisfaction that one cannot deal with the subject without betraying subjective bias. But most observers agree that acquisitiveness and competitiveness are two of the more important barriers to happiness. It is to be conceded that they are not primary factors; they arise from certain more or less universal tendencies in human beings and are to be found, in some degree, in most cultures. Their influence is to some extent a secondary consequence of cultural failures in other areas: possessions may be prized as compensation for insufficient instinctual gratification and impulses to amass wealth heightened by feelings of insecurity. Yet even if acquisitiveness and competitiveness are no more than what philosophers call proximate causes, they deserve our attention because they are such powerful and pervasive enemies of the enjoyment of life.

Acquisitiveness and competitiveness induce us to give up many experiences which would be a source of happiness and they rob many of the activities we undertake of some or all of their pleasure-giving capacity. To take the most obvious example, they may cause men to choose the kind of work which promises to make them rich, not the kind which promises to make them happy. In consequence, a man's chosen occupation may give him no opportunity to utilize some skill which affords him pleasure and satisfaction—painting, let us say. Perhaps he has foreseen this and promised himself that he will paint in his spare time. Once committed to getting ahead, however, he may soon find that he has little or no spare time. His work or activities associated with it may steadily encroach upon his leisure. Furthermore, he may find himself too tired to paint in what free time he has, and his talent may atrophy. The very way of seeing the world on which the impulse to paint depends may ultimately be lost as a result of absorption in his work or anxiety about his progress. Simultaneously he may lose or find it prudent to abandon many other pleasurable activities, be they as innocent as dressing colorfully or startling people with heterodox opinions.

These sacrifices might not be in vain if the things for which they were bartered fulfilled their promise. But deals of this sort with life seem extremely hard to conclude. Perhaps one has deliberately made certain compromises to achieve material success in the belief that one's private life will provide compensation for uncongenial work and a refuge from relationships marred by ulterior considerations. Even when the success materializes, such arrangements seldom work out according to plan. It seems difficult to remain just a little corrupted. For one thing, any reservations about competing in all-out fashion put one at a disadvantage in comparison with one's more abandoned colleagues. If they manipulate their social life in such a way as to advance their careers, it is difficult to resist the pressure to do likewise. It may seem necessary to entertain a few of the right people from the office purely as a defensive maneuver. Sooner or later all of one's invitations may be determined on the basis of similar considerations. Friendship may be renounced as a luxury. The values of the marketplace may come to influence every decision, every judgment.

Apart from its ultimate effects upon character, such a development quickly breeds envy and forecloses various possibilities of happiness. One may become discontented with one's wife because she is not a skilled social strategist or dissatisfied with one's home because it is not sufficiently showy or is located in Long Island rather than Westchester. A plethora of possessions may not quiet one's envy of wealthier neighbors or keep one from wanting still more. Social life becomes less relaxed and less rewarding. Guests invited for ulterior reasons are less likely to prove good company than people to whom one is spontaneously drawn and may not be suitable at all for the exchange of important confidences. Though the attempt to corral famous guests may yield some gratifying victories, it is also likely to involve frustrations and even humiliations. The conversion of entertaining into a business enterprise gives rise to certain suspicions about the invitations one receives.

Many other characteristics of our culture clash with our desire for happiness. The rapidity of technological change leads to economic insecurity and fear. The extreme division of labor required by a highly industrialized society limits the number of jobs that can give a sense of accomplishment and, like urbanization and standardization, has a dehumanizing, depersonalizing influence, inimical to dignity and happiness. The list is endless. Culture in general seems indifferent if not hostile to the goal of individual happiness. In our particular society the cleavage between cultural aims and the quest for happiness seems particularly wide. The individual is under intense pressure to sacrifice many sources of enjoyment and to accept values and attitudes which deprive sanctioned activities and relationships of much of their pleasure-giving capacity.

It is because of such factors as these that man finds it so

difficult to secure sufficient satisfaction from life—arbitrarily using that term to refer to our ordinary activities and eliminating such areas of experience as are represented by art.

4

If a man could articulate his grievances about life so defined, he would perhaps complain first about the extensive deprivations to which he is subjected and secondly about the unsatisfactory nature of much of the experience permitted him. The distinction is not a perfect one: the two complaints sometimes tend to merge. Nevertheless, there can be no doubt that, quite apart from any specific dissatisfactions we may have about what befalls us, we are sometimes oppressed by the feeling that life is more limited and impoverished than it should be. Even children are not always free of this feeling. Anyone who observes them closely notices that they are sometimes overcome by feelings of emptiness and boredom. But they may feel that growing up will automatically alter this state of affairs; the boredom may even express a covert desire for adult satisfactions.

It is perhaps in adolescence that we are most nearly free of the feeling that life is cramping. There seems to be time, energy, plasticity for everything. Thus choice does not present insuperable problems; somehow or other we manage to crowd in nearly all the things we want to do. Our dreams of the future are boundless. Ignoring both the limits of our powers and the difficulties in the way of achievement, we scarcely face the possibility of failure, or we think of it as no more than a way-stop along the road to ultimate success. We may not even face the fact that success in one field may preclude a career in another. We are equally cavalier about the limitations imposed by time and our mortality. The idea of death does present itself, but usually only as a source of sweet sorrow in connection with burgeoning sexuality; it is devoid of immediacy and threat.

This Faustian interlude is brought to an abrupt and painful close as soon as we begin to face adulthood realistically. We begin to see that we must prepare ourselves for one occupation and at least temporarily abandon the idea of pursuing others. In the sexual realm the need for choice is no less inexorable. Sooner or later we must confine ourselves to one woman among all the alluring ones the world holds. Many individuals, of course, do not yield to these limitations without a struggle. They may shift from job to job or woman to woman—or perhaps play Don Juan for a time, then settle down to be a devoted paterfamilias. But such changes do no more than postpone the realization that experience does not offer one an infinite number of satisfactions. One cannot simultaneously know what it is like to have many women and be the devoted lover of one. In the occupational field and others frequent shifts may jeopardize one's chances of succeeding in anything. Sooner or later we come to see that life tends to confine each human being to a single role. We might add "at any given time," but the qualification does not really mean so very much.

The restrictions forced upon us by the fact that we can play only a single role in life are purely quantitative and may not strike some observers as being restrictions in any important sense. However much merit this view may have from the standpoint of attained maturity, the fact remains that relatively few people can accept their station in adult life without some sense of disappointment, some feeling that they are being asked to give up a great deal. One portion of our personality, the unsocialized id, never assents to the sacrifices involved in playing a single part in life and remains forever uncommitted, forever unreconciled to giving up anything. Furthermore, even a mature person must acknowledge that many desirable things are often jettisoned in growing up. For example, concentration on the practical objectives and obligations of adult life may gradually make us less generous, less idealistic, less concerned with others than we were in youth. It may dry up the springs of spontaneity. It may close our eyes to the beauty of the external world and our minds to general questions about which we should be concerned.

Obviously, adulthood does not always involve this kind of ossification. On the contrary, as people grow older they may become more honest and more idealistic, more concerned with the suffering of others and with social inequality. They may become poignantly aware of many areas of experience of which they were previously oblivious. For a fortunate minority of people adulthood is what it should be for all—a period of unfolding and ripening. We all know individuals who have attained a measure of serenity, men who are happily absorbed in their work, women who seem fully content with their roles as wives and mothers. But we know many more people, including some judged to be quite successful, who get very little out of life and who betray feelings of disappointment and unhappiness even when they try to put a good face on things. The content and attitudes—perhaps we should add, the evasions—of our mass media reveal the poverty of interests and the cowardly torpor of the vast majority.

As we grow older, our sense that human life is thinner than it should be may tend to intensify rather than diminish. Our reconciliation to certain deprivations may not keep pace with our growing realization of the limits of human life. In part this may be because certain already existing barriers become more clearly defined. We may come to see that we may never "run" the company for which we happen to work and that it may take years of effort to reach the top in our department. At the same time we may become more aware of certain of our own limitations and be compelled to notice new ones—a loss of drive, perhaps, or some evidence, impossible to overlook, that we are less flexible or imaginative than we once were.

It is perhaps the fear of death which makes us most painfully aware of how little we may expect from life. Once acquainted with this fear, we may find it still more difficult to accept the invisible bonds which restrict us. We may strive frantically to crowd as many pleasures as possible into the span of time remaining to us—only to be reminded by the meager satisfactions our activities yield, the troubles in which they involve us, or internal feelings of shame and guilt, that it is not easy to throw off a yoke worn for years. Or we may recognize the futility of such middle-aged galvanizations or resist the lure of newly awakened impulses out of fear of jeopardizing what we have patiently built up over the years. Fear may even lead us to accept the ties of respectability with what may outwardly appear to be unqualified docility. In fact, whatever we do or refrain from doing, we may be more continually gnawed by the feeling that life denies us too much.

5

The deprivations to which we are subjected are also a principal source of the feeling that the experience permitted us is much less rewarding than it should be. They may defeat their own purpose and leave people preoccupied to an unwholesome degree with the satisfaction, direct or indirect, of instinctual urges. The deprivations are a primary cause of anxiety[8] and the prohibitions responsible for some of them produce both anxiety and, as we have already seen, guilt; these in turn make life burdensome and sustained happiness impossible. Finally, because a person who feels he has little finds it difficult to give, deprivations are partly to blame for the coldness of the world, the grudging slowness with which it bestows recognition and love.

Man is dissatisfied with experience on many other counts. He must live in a world he never made; the world of phenomena is bewildering and confusing—indeed, fundamentally unfathomable. Nature is as comprehensible as it is, idealistic philosophers since Kant have taught us, only because we apprehend it through those forms of understanding possible to us. The order which we perceive is no more than a reflection of the structure of our minds. For answers to the larger and more abstract questions posed by his presence in a perplexing universe man turns to religion, philosophy or science rather than to art. But most of the time we are not concerned with such questions, but with the problems which arise as a result of our everyday experience and speculations. Why do our

[8] Cf. Freud, "The situation, then, that [the child] regards as a 'danger' and against which it wants to be safeguarded is one of non-gratification, of a growing tension due to need, against which it is helpless." *Inhibitions, Symptoms and Anxiety* (London: Hogarth, 1936), pp. 106-107. Later, with the creation of the superego and "the depersonalization of the parental institution" (*ibid.*, p. 111), anything likely to make the ego feel that the superego is displeased with it may cause anxiety, since such displeasure contains the threat of punishment or withdrawal of love.

friends act as they do? What is it like to be carrying on an extramarital love affair? Why is our son sullen toward us so much of the time and how usual is such behavior? Why are we so often irritable toward him? We are constantly seeking answers to such questions—and preferably answers with the same immediacy and concreteness with which the problems present themselves to us.

We are dissatisfied with life also because it seems so much duller than we feel it should be; the moments of excitement and exultation are much too far apart. This feeling, too, stems in part from the fact that so many areas of passionate experience are forbidden to us, but it has other sources as well. For example, the tabu against strong expression of feeling does a great deal to rob life of intensity. Its ultimate effect is to make our emotions themselves more pallid, and it is responsible for certain immediate losses, whether or not we are conscious of them. One has only to observe children to see that an experience is not complete until it is articulated and shared. We are seldom aware of how much we prize fervent expression for its capacity to heighten and relieve emotion, but our delight in the resonances of blank verse, the respect we pay to fluency however it manifests itself, show that we are not wholly oblivious of these values.

We are much more sensible of the social losses involved in the inhibitions on direct and impassioned expression. One of our deepest desires is for communion, the feeling of knowing and understanding our fellows and being understood by them. In most social intercourse this desire is thwarted and, it almost seems, parodied. Frankness and vehemence are looked on with disfavor. We are discouraged from discussing many of the subjects which most deeply interest us and are constrained to discuss a limited number of stale topics which do not. Miraculously, even from such poor gambits as are permitted intimacies sometimes ensue, but far more often social occasions bring us close to no one and, even when they are not boring, leave us mildly frustrated. To those who feel a need to discuss some pressing problem they may be a source of acute disappointment.

Innumerable other factors tend to keep life on a dull, level plane. Part of the time life may offer us too few sensations and excitements; then we may become so thickly involved in affairs that we do not have time to respond fully to anything. When we become absorbed in an emotional problem, life may display a supercilious lack of concern with sustaining our interest, much less a particular mood. Our schedule may compel us to rush from a passionate assignation to a business conference in which we must force ourself to play an active role. An attempt to resolve a serious problem may be interrupted by a trivial phone call or the arrival of the laundryman. The worst of it is that we may half welcome such interruptions because we are afraid to feel deeply and face our problems. Ill or fatigued, beset by anxieties or preoccupied with practical affairs, we are seldom on tiptoe to obtain the best that life has to offer. Much of the time many of our responses and a great deal of our behavior is mechanical and automatic: we are responding to the surface of things with the surface of our minds.

Perhaps the ultimate difficulty is that we expect too much of life. Even if our experience were far richer, less baffling and more intense than it is, we would not be without our discontents. Our demands are too various, too intricate, too shifting, too contradictory to obtain full satisfaction in the longest and most eventful life. The realm of experience is not sufficiently plastic to permit the gratification of all our needs. We live in time, and there is not sufficient time to act out all the impulses which stir within us. Consider Leopold Bloom: how many days, lives even, would have been necessary to develop to their conclusion the tendencies, evanescent and changing, which he experienced in twenty-four hours.

Our needs are not even compatible with one another. We insist unreasonably on being both Don Quixote and Sancho Panza. As George Orwell puts it:

. . . noble folly and base wisdom, exist side by side in nearly every human being. If you look into your own mind, which are you, Don Quixote or Sancho Panza? Almost certainly you are both. There is one part of you that wishes to be a hero or a saint, but another part of you is a little fat man who sees very clearly the advantages of staying alive with a whole skin. He is your unofficial self, the voice of the belly protesting against the soul. His tastes lie towards safety, soft beds, no work, pots of beer and women with 'voluptuous' figures. He it is who punctures your fine attitudes and urges you to look after Number One, to be unfaithful to your wife, to bilk your debts, and so on and so forth. Whether you allow yourself to be influenced by him is a different question. But it is simply a lie to say that he is not part of you, just as it is a lie to say that Don Quixote is not part of you either, though most of what is said and written consists of one lie or the other, usually the first.[9]

Though some people, notably compulsives, are more agonizingly torn by contradictory impulses than are others, no one is free of them. Our desires, our attitudes are never of a piece, however much they may appear so. Indeed, appearances are often deceptive. The vehemence with which a given viewpoint is expressed may be a measure of the attraction the opposed viewpoint holds. Generosity may be a defense against stinginess, mildness a reaction-formation to strong aggressive feelings. As fiction writers know intuitively, impulse and counter-impulse lie close together. *The Prisoner Who Sang,* an almost forgotten novel by Johann Bojer, shows how one man adopted many different disguises to act out the conflicting tendencies which tormented him. In Caldwell's *Trouble in July* it is the character who first senses the danger of a lynching and organizes a posse to prevent it who finally acts as the leader of the lynch mob. Stevenson's "Dr. Jekyll and Mr. Hyde," Somerset Maugham's "Rain" and innumerable other stories deal with similar themes. Newspapers remind us of how frequently people attempt to carry out contradictory impulses in real life. The June 11, 1951, *New York Times* reported the arrest, in Massapequa Park, Long Island, of three young volunteer firemen "on charges of starting a fire they later helped to extinguish."

To some extent life permits the gratification of contradic-

---

[9] *Dickens, Dali and Others* (New York: Reynal & Hitchcock, 1946), pp. 135-36.

tory tendencies. A single action—the decision to marry, let us say—may express numerous and even opposing needs. If we are fortunate, the woman we select for our wife may satisfy desires apparently impossible to reconcile; she may be at once a pure mother and an abandoned mistress. Sometimes, too, claims not satisfied by one action can be readily satisfied by others. But obviously the possibilities along these lines are limited. Most of our choices involve the renunciation of some of our desires and potentialities, and each decision we make reduces the number of possibilities still open to us. We have only time and opportunities for a limited number of actions. We are deterred from radical experimentation, too, by the fact that our actions involve consequences. We see that we will jeopardize what we most want if we do not deny certain of our tendencies. If we want to live respectable and productive lives, we must avoid dissipation though we are inclined to it and we must drive ourselves though we are lazy. Life holds us to a certain consistency.

6

It is to make good some of the deficiences of experience that people read fiction. A perfectly satisfied person, Freud declares, would not daydream. Nor would a perfectly satisfied person feel any compelling need to read stories. We read because we are beset by anxieties, guilt feelings and ungratified needs. The reading of fiction permits us, in indirect fashion, to satisfy those needs, relieve our anxieties and assuage our guilt. It transports us to a realm more comprehensible and coherent, more passionate and more plastic, and at the same time more compatible with our ideals, than the world of our daily routine, thus providing a kind of experience which is qualitatively superior to that which we can ordinarily obtain from life. In the next five chapters we shall consider some of the properties of narrative art which enable it to provide these satisfactions. But first we must take note of certain characteristics of the needs which lead us to read.

We should be aware, first of all, of their extraordinary strength. Whether we have longed for understanding and responsive friends, a passionate and perfect love relationship, power over others, or the world's acclaim, it is certain that some of the desires which have gnawed at us for years have been only partially or temporarily fulfilled, or not fulfilled at all, by the life which has been our lot. On one level we may be reconciled to the prospect that they will never be fulfilled, but on another they are not relinquished and some of them may become more intense through the years. This is true of the satisfactions we deny ourselves as well as those denied us by life. The temptations we triumph over stubbornly retain their strength; sometimes they seem to have more vigor than the regulating components of our personality which maintain a precarious supremacy over them.

Despite their strength many of the needs which press for satisfaction through reading are only dimly known to us or are entirely unknown. This characteristic is not unrelated to the fact that the needs are unrequited by life. The very fact that certain needs are denied may make us aware that they are selfish or otherwise unacceptable and so cause us to disown them. But many of the needs are never acknowledged to begin with. We have many impulses and desires which we quickly recant or entertain only in moments of exceptional honesty or, it may be, defiance. Still other impulses arouse so much aversion that they may not even be admitted to awareness or are repudiated and pushed from awareness almost instantaneously; to use the psychoanalytic term, they are repressed.

A study by Dr. Martha Wolfenstein shows that even four-year-olds may have impulses—jealous and hostile feelings toward siblings, for example—which they may feel ashamed of and want to deny.[10] Dr. Wolfenstein's study also brings out the significant fact that these impulses arouse varying amounts of anxiety and guilt in different children. The standards of the parents and the culture (and later of the ego and superego) and a whole host of additional factors which we cannot pause to consider determine whether a given tendency

[10] "The Impact of a Children's Story on Mothers and Children," *Monographs of the Society for Research in Child Development*, No. 42, XI, 1946 (Washington, D. C.: National Research Council, 1947).

will be accepted, acknowledged only occasionally or completely repressed.[11] The fact that some of our dark impulses are at least occasionally admitted to awareness may give rise to confusion. Knowing that these impulses arouse shame in others, we may have the illusion that we have no desires which we dare not face. In reality, of course, we are oblivious of still other desires—the ones which would arouse most shame and anxiety in us. Psychoanalysis invariably reveals that each individual has innumerable impulses, ideas and fears of which he has been ignorant or only fugitively aware; behind the admitted guilty wishes there always lurk others which are energetically repressed.

It is essential, for two reasons, to insist on the vastness of that almost inaccessible realm in us which our night impulses inhabit like subdued but sullen beasts. First of all, in number and intensity these are the impulses which are most important among those which seek and secure satisfaction in the reading of fiction. Secondly there is a tendency in us, against which we must be on guard, to deny the existence of this realm, or if we cannot do this, to minimize its importance. Much of the resistance to psychoanalysis arose from the stress it put on repudiated impulses of which mankind wanted to remain unaware.

Repression must not be thought of as something which went on in the dim past now cloaked by the veil of childhood amnesia. In most people certain infantile ideas, interests and impulses—most particularly those which are frowned upon and later subjected to repression—tenaciously retain their strength. Indeed, in the dark they may ramify "in more unchecked and luxuriant fashion" and take on "extreme forms of expression, which when translated and revealed to the neurotic are bound not merely to seem alien to him, but to terrify him by the way in which they reflect an extraordinary and danger-

[11] For what remains perhaps the best exposition of repression, see Freud's 1915 paper on the subject, *Collected Papers*, Vol. IV. See also the essay "The Unconscious" in the same volume; *A General Introduction to Psychoanalysis*, Chap. 19; and Otto Fenichel, *The Psychoanalytic Theory of Neurosis*, especially pp. 148-151.

ous strength of instinct." [12] Throughout life repressed early
impulses continue to strain for expression and discharge, and
the struggle against them is a fierce and continuous one, requiring a constant expenditure of energy.

Moreover, new desires, fears and suspicions so repugnant to
us that they must be repressed continue to arise throughout
life. Some of these are never admitted to consciousness; others
are momentarily admitted but quickly expelled. Anyone with
sufficient honesty and courage may be able to bring to light
some material of the latter sort, though except in analysis the
ideas which arouse most antipathy and anxiety are certain to
elude one, and the most conscientious effort may uncover, not
really repressed material, but only the relatively accessible
ideas which have won precarious lodgment in the preconscious
but are seldom openly faced. Did we ever have incestuous
sexual impulses? Or desire to hurt, even to kill, someone for
whom we assure ourselves we feel nothing but love? Did we
ever, even for a minute, hope that a friend doing better than
ourselves would suffer a setback in his career or some other
misfortune? Did we once have a flicker of fear that our beloved was betraying us with someone of her own sex or a
member of her family? Have we ever wished that a relative
would die so that we could come into an inheritance or a col-
league so that we could have his job? It is ideas of this sort
which are repudiated and repressed.

Even though we shall be anticipating points to be developed
more fully later on, we should take brief note of some of the
qualities of narrative art which enable it to satisfy needs of
which we ourselves are unaware. Repressed tendencies can
only secure expression when they are sufficiently disguised so
that their connection with a repudiated impulse is not perceived by the censorious ego and when they do not threaten to
lead to action.[13] Great fiction can easily satisfy these conditions. The kind of tendencies which would be disavowed are

[12] Freud, "Repression," *Collected Papers*, IV, 87.

[13] Cf. Freud: ". . . as soon as an idea which is fundamentally offensive
exceeds a certain degree of strength, the conflict takes on actuality, and it is
precisely activation of the idea that leads to its repression." "Repression,"
loc. cit., p. 90.

usually disguised and are invariably displaced onto others. Their consequences are dramatized with as much vividness as their attraction. Finally, by a number of devices to be considered in Chapter VII, the tendencies are "distanced" and isolated from the world of our everyday experience, so that we can adopt a spectator attitude toward them. A final condition which facilitates the communication of repressed material is that the ego should be somewhat relaxed—it is during sleep or at moments of tiredness that repressed trends most readily reveal themselves—and this condition, too, we shall find to be met whenever fiction is read with enjoyment.[14]

Of course, fiction is by no means the only thing which fulfils these conditions. Repressed tendencies seek and secure satisfaction in a wide variety of ways. Let us take a single example, deliberately selecting an idea that seems foolish and farfetched to the intellect: the idea—the wish, really—that the mother is virginal. Hans Zulliger has shown how this wish secures symbolic representation in a typical adventure story for boys, *The Red Toad*.[15] In their excellent study of the movies, Wolfenstein and Leites found that the wish helps account for the popularity of the recurring motion-picture situation in which a couple seems guilty of some sexual misbehavior but is ultimately proven innocent.[16] The wish also finds expression in some of our most widely held religious beliefs and ethical convictions. To some extent it probably influences our attitudes and conduct—to our own mothers, to mothers in general, and to the women we may be considering as the mothers of our own children. In an unusually penetrating sociological study, Robert Merton found that the wish plays an important part in the popularity of Kate Smith. It is not a matter of indifference that Miss Smith is motherly and attractive, but quite asexual.[17]

Repression is only one of the factors responsible for our

[14] Cf. Ch. VIII.
[15] "Der Abenteurer-Schundroman," *Zeitschrift für psychoanalytische Pädagogik*, VII, 1933.
[16] Martha Wolfenstein and Nathan Leites, *Movies: A Psychological Study* (Glencoe, Ill.: Free Press, 1950).
[17] *Mass Persuasion* (New York: Harper, 1946).

ignorance of the many needs which lead us to read fiction. Numerous needs which could be readily admitted to awareness remain vague and amorphous simply because we have not discovered the experiences, real or vicarious, which would satisfy them. We turn to fiction, it could almost be said, not so much to satisfy already known needs as to find out what our needs are. This statement, we shall find, is not altogether accurate, for the needs may remain unidentified even as we satisfy them, but it is certainly true that literature is prized in part because it does so much to enlarge our understanding of the satisfactions and modes of response available to us. As Joseph Wood Krutch remarks, "If every individual had to discover for himself all those awarenesses and sensitivenesses which we take for granted even in the most slightly cultivated person, it is unlikely that many would ever discover more than a very small part of what is now the ordinary experience of living." [18] Literature gives us forms for our feelings—often a variety of forms; as Krutch puts it, "a repertory of roles amongst which we have only to choose." [19]

Most of the needs which we seek to satisfy through reading fiction are not only unidentified but vague and unspecific in their very nature. They may make themselves known to us only in the form of quite indeterminate tensions, pressures or feelings of anxiety. Like physical hunger, they may be imperious and yet readily appeased by many types of nutriment. The comparison cannot be pushed too far. As we shall see more particularly in Chapter VIII, a number of requirements must be met for a given book to satisfy a given reader. In at least one respect, however, the comparison fails to do justice to the mobility of our psychical needs, and the wide range of experiences capable of satisfying them, for it ignores the capacity of the mind to analogize. Because of that capacity, a novel may possess intimate significance for a reader even when it has no readily apparent relationship to his own situation or problems.

Many of the satisfactions we seek through reading, further-

[18] *Experience and Art* (New York: Smith and Haas, 1932), pp. 92-93.
[19] *Ibid.*, p. 84.

more, cannot be adequately described in subject matter terms, however elastic. We may be seeking fiction which justifies a particular balance of forces in our own psychic economy, redresses an imbalance or provides compensation for a situation in which conflicting needs cannot be reconciled in any fashion, so that we are upset and unhappy. For example, we may search for novels which, regardless of theme, give the emotions freer sway than they enjoy in our life at the moment. Or we may seek stories in which transgressions are very strictly penalized or which in some other fashion satisfy our masochism. Or we may be looking not so much for a particular balance between id-ego-superego components as for a story which expresses a particular attitude—the urbane acceptance of human frailty to be found in *South Wind*, let us say, or the evangelical espousal of sensuality prominent in some of the later work of D. H. Lawrence. We may desire to find a particular attitude expressed to confirm some position toward which we are groping or which we have adopted but about which we feel unsure. Or we may want to replace some emotional stance with which we are dissatisfied. Finally, we may read in search of the satisfactions associated with form. Desires of this sort may exist in combination with subject-matter interests, but they may be of predominant importance or be the only factor impelling us to read at a particular time.

Thus, apart from the needs of which it is essential that we remain unaware, many of the needs which seek satisfaction through reading are no more than dimly known to us or are entirely unformulated. To those familiar with the part the unconscious plays in every aspect of man's life, this state of affairs will occasion no surprise. We are no better acquainted with the needs which prompt us to go to night clubs or participate or take interest in certain sports—or, for that matter, with most of the needs which account for our engaging in activities and making decisions which we are more accustomed to think of as purposive and rational. Most of the time we grope about quite blindly, driven by we know not what needs and in search of we know not what satisfactions. At least so far as reading is concerned the situation is not therefore hopeless. On the contrary, most people seem to experience little difficulty in finding the kind of fiction which meets their purposes. The very vagueness of some of the needs which spur us to read makes them easy to satisfy.

As we shall see more in detail in Chapter IX, even in the act of satisfying our needs we usually fail to identify them. It is essential that this be so when we are satisfying repressed needs. To identify them would automatically reawaken the conflict which caused them to be repressed to begin with. Instead of pleasure we would experience revulsion and anxiety. One is thrust from the Eden of art, too, when, abandoning detached absorption in its loveliness, one permits oneself to become involved in problems of good and evil.

7

We read fiction to secure richer fulfilment of desires no more than partly satisfied by life and to allay the anxieties and guilt feelings our experience arouses. It might seem reasonable to expect, therefore, that the more pressing the desire, anxiety or guilt feeling, the stronger would be the impulse to read. But now we come upon one of those complications which make generalizations about esthetic and psychological matters so difficult—and produce so much impatience and, it may be, distrust among students of these subjects.[20] In some respects the facts flatly contradict our expectations: if anxiety or pressure arising from instinctual needs exceeds a certain point, one is unlikely to feel an impulse to read and is incapable of receiving the kind of pleasure characteristic of the reading experience if one does read. For a time the solace and satisfaction of fiction reading are foreclosed to one.

For a number of reasons it is difficult to say at what precise point this comes about. There are wide individual differences in the capacity for tolerating anxiety and instinctual pressure. Any given individual varies in his capacity for tolerating them at different times. A great deal depends, too, upon the char-

---

[20] Needless to say, these are unenlightened responses. When examined, the complication in question serves to enhance our respect for the importance of purely quantitative factors in psychology.

acter of the fictional work which may present itself for consideration: even when one is somewhat disturbed, one may be able to become absorbed in a movie or a fast-moving thriller but not, let us say, in a typical nineteenth-century English novel. When anxiety or instinctual pressure becomes too urgent, however, no form of fiction is likely to engage or hold one's interest. *A certain degree of freedom from anxiety and instinctual pressure is necessary before one is likely to want to read or can enjoy reading.*[21]

Narrative art deserves our utmost respect, but it must be respected for what it is—what Freud calls a "substitute gratification." Fiction is not discontinuous with reality. Though it deals with shadows, by some magic which can still not be fully explained it can temporarily relieve anxieties and satisfy desires aroused by our actual experience. For a time, an absorbing story can even make us forget cold or hunger or sexual tension. But no one can confuse the satisfactions fiction offers with warmth or food or a sexual partner, and if the need for these is too imperious the benefits fiction can confer will not be desired. They are available only to those free of pre-emptive fears and pressures and possessed in consequence of a reasonable amount of patience and some capacity for sublimation.

To take what is perhaps the most obvious example, a person tense with sexual desire will probably not "feel like" settling down for a comfortable evening's reading. Circumstances permitting, he will satisfy his desire or at any rate seek to do so. Should he attempt to disregard his sexual tension and read,

[21] It would be extremely interesting to discover if the same principle does not apply to play. I would suspect that children overcome by rage or any other strong feeling would seek to relieve it directly and would have no patience for the delay, control and symbolic representation which are involved in play. With daydreams it is the other way around: the stronger the feeling of emotional deprivation, the faster the rate of fantasy formation. In this respect, it must be conceded, daydreams do not seem to belong in the series in which they have been placed. Wit presents a mixed and complicated picture. By and large wit does not demand as much of its audience as fiction does because of the speed with which it offers its gratifications. Because of their aphrodisiac value, "dirty" jokes may be especially prized when sexual excitement is felt, although even in such circumstances a joke may backfire and produce displeasure if there is no prospect, acceptable to the ego, of relieving the tension it serves to heighten.

the kind of enjoyment he ordinarily secures from reading will almost certainly elude him. If he picks up a novel which turns out to have a thin sexual content, his attention will probably wander. On the other hand, if the book he selects is rich in sexually exciting material, he is likely to pay disproportionate attention to this, and, curiously, the reading experience is then more likely to arouse displeasure than enjoyment; sexual stimulation is pleasurable only when there is a prospect of eventual gratification.[22] A final possibility is that scenes in the novel will be seized upon as a stimulus to sexual fantasies or even masturbatory activity, and the attempt to read abandoned after all. It is obvious enough that each of these possibilities precludes not only anything resembling esthetic response to fiction but even correct understanding of it.

Intense anxiety or any other overpowering emotion is likely to have equally unfortunate effects. A person frantic with anxiety would not be likely to attempt to read. Fiction might be shunned precisely because it deals with emotional material with intimate reference. If an intensely anxious person does read, his anxieties are almost certain to interfere with response. He may distort what he reads to assuage his anxieties. Or—perhaps despite efforts in this direction—his anxieties may be so quickly raised that it will prove difficult to follow a story, much less enjoy it. Similarly, a person who, let us say, is mourning the death of a loved one may read, if he reads at all, in search of a consolatory message; his grief may make it impossible for him to read with the degree of objectivity necessary for understanding. In general, people overwhelmed by strong feelings are likely either to react negatively to what they read or to use what they read for their own purposes.

Katherine M. Wolf and Marjorie Fiske have shown that children whose interest in comics is "patently violent and ex-

---

[22] Cf. Otto Fenichel. "The pleasure of sexual excitement, called forepleasure, turns immediately into displeasure if the hope of bringing about a discharge in subsequent end pleasure disappears; the pleasure character of the forepleasure is tied up with a mental anticipation of the end pleasure." *The Psychoanalytic Theory of Neurosis*, p. 15.

cessive" use comics in this fashion.[23] For example, if they are so insecure that they need the sense of an all-powerful protective figure hovering over them, they will accept Superman even if they have no illusions about the actuality of his powers. Instead of overcoming their feeling of weakness by identifying with him as they read, they tend to deify him, to regard him as a tutelary figure whom they can call on whenever they feel troubled.

An unwillingness to "let go," to relax even for a short time the control usually exercised by the scrutinizing ego, is also inimical to the reading of fiction and the enjoyment of it. The unwillingness may be sporadic, a temporary defensive measure employed by the ego at times when it fears it may be overwhelmed by instinctual pressure it does not want to see further raised. Much more usually, however, it is chronic. A surprising number of people keep themselves under close surveillance nearly all the time. As Dr. Wolfenstein says, they "oscillate between severe ego-dominance and a knocking out of the ego by means of drinking." [24] Obviously such vigilance implies a weak ego organization, a fear that if the ego relaxed even a trifle it could not maintain order in its own house.

A certain reduction of control by the ego seems essential for both the creation and the enjoyment of fiction. A strained alertness may even interfere with understanding, for in its language and its logic fiction reflects the primary processes which govern unconscious thought as much as it does the secondary processes of conscious thought.[25] So far as enjoy-

[23] "The Children Talk about Comics," *Communications Research, 1948-1949*, edited by Paul F. Lazarsfeld and Frank N. Stanton (New York: Harper, 1949).

[24] "The Impact of a Children's Story . . ." p. 51.

[25] Cf. Freud, "Formulations Regarding the Two Principles in Mental Functioning," *Collected Papers*, Vol. IV. In this exceptionally significant paper, written in 1911, Freud makes the distinction, now well established and well known, between the pleasure principle and the reality principle, and shows how these two modes of mental functioning reflect themselves in various of our psychic and cultural activities. Even after the reality principle achieves dominance, play and daydreaming remain subordinated to the pleasure-principle. . . . "Just as a nation whose wealth rests on the exploita-

ment is concerned, an over-alert attitude entails a double loss. It leaves too little energy available for the considerable amount of pleasurable unconscious activity we shall find to be involved in response. And, inefficient for understanding as the attitude is, it jeopardizes the concealment of elements which might arouse aversion and anxiety if brought to light.

As will be developed in Chapter VIII, most readers are intuitively aware of the kind of relationships which have been discussed here and seek fiction which they can enjoy without strain. Even the posture of fiction readers is typically relaxed. Nor is it accidental that fiction reading is associated with night, vacations, periods of recuperation from illness and lazy, rainy afternoons—these are all ideal occasions. In his engaging introduction to *Grimm's Fairy Tales*[26] Padraic Colum points out that, particularly before artificial light and communication were much developed, the drowsy period before bedtime was an ideal one for storytelling. At that time, "A rhythm that was compulsive, fitted to daily tasks, waned, and a rhythm that was acquiescent, fitted to wishes, took its place."

A final impediment to the enjoyment of fiction is fear of fantasy. Both Dr. Wolfenstein's study and a study by W. Lloyd Warner and William E. Henry of responses to the "Big Sister" radio program[27] reveal that some people have such a fear. To a considerable degree the fear is no more than another aspect of the factor we have just been considering: it, too, reflects the misgivings of an ego which is weak, or feels itself so, about its capacity to control roused emotions. The Warner-Henry description of the psychological structures of

---

tion of its land yet reserves certain territory to be preserved in its original state and protected from cultural alterations, e.g. Yellowstone Park." *Ibid.*, p. 17. In agreement with the point of view adopted here, Freud declares: "Art brings about a reconciliation of the two principles . . . with his special gifts [the artist] moulds his phantasies into a new kind of reality, and men concede them a justification as valuable reflections of actual life." *Ibid.*, p. 19.

[26] New York: Pantheon Books, 1944.

[27] "The Radio Day Time Serial: A Symbolic Analysis," Genetic Psychology Monographs, 1948. Reprinted in *Reader in Public Opinion and Communication*, edited by Bernard Berelson and Morris Janowitz (Glencoe, Ill.: Free Press, 1950). The quotations are from p. 20 of the Monograph.

the wives of "the Common Man level" among the listeners to the "Big Sister" program reveals this clearly. These women show "a dulled use of imaginative power and suppression of personal resources available for attacking emotional problems." They "seem to distrust even imaginative expression, to fear spontaneity and impulsivity. They want to keep this under control." These women shy away from direct references to sex. The heroine of the "Big Sister" program, whom they greatly admire, is the apotheosis of "restrained and nonimpulsive goodness."

Dr. Wolfenstein's study points to some of the other motives a weak ego may have for fearing fantasy. Some of the mothers in her sample seemed to fear that if their children took too much pleasure in the fantasy spun by Sally in "Sally and the Baby and the Rampatan" it might indicate that they had mistaken ideas about reality; interestingly, the more information mothers had given their children about "the facts of life," the more antagonistic they tended to be about the little girl's fantasy. Many of the mothers appear to have been unduly apprehensive about their children's ability to distinguish between make-believe and reality, even allowing for the actual difficulty children have in this area. Some of the mothers also revealed the closely related fear that "bad" impulses which secured expression in fantasy might be carried over into real life. Some also seemed to feel that it was a reflection upon them if their children had any fantasy life whatsoever. With a quite exaggerated faith in their own powers, they assumed that, if only they managed matters properly, every wish their children might have could be fully satisfied in actuality. This belief itself bespeaks an underlying fear of the fantasy life of their children.

One mother willing to tolerate the most extreme expression of hostility by her oldest child toward the younger children was quite unwilling to accept the indirect expression of hostility embodied in the Rampatan fantasy. "Apparently the indefinite threats of fantasy seemed more dangerous to her." [28] Using a phrase of Nina Searl's, Dr. Wolfenstein declares that

[28] Martha Wolfenstein, "The Impact of a Children's Story . . . ," p. 48.

this woman exemplified a "flight to reality." Dr. Searl's paper, "The Flight to Reality," [29] tends to confirm the impression that the insecurity of the ego is the factor primarily responsible for fear of fantasy. The basic motive of fantasy formation, Dr. Searl points out, is wish fulfilment. The wishes may be feared on their own account and because their gratification may lead to punishment. Concentration on the reality situation serves as a defense against both aspects of indulgence in fantasy.

8

In the next five chapters we shall consider some of the attributes of fiction which enable it, within the limits we have discussed, to provide compensation for the deprivations and disappointments of experience, to relieve our anxieties and allay our feelings of guilt. But it is worth pausing first to compare fiction reading with other activities which have the same general purpose. In seeing how it resembles and differs from these we shall draw closer to some of the essential characteristics of narrative art.

Following in modified form the scheme developed by Freud in *Civilization and Its Discontents*, we may say that there are three great groups of "auxiliary constructions" [30] by which man seeks to make life more supportable. First, he may seek to make himself insensitive to disagreeable aspects of reality by the use of drugs or intoxicants. Secondly, he may seek to minimize the danger of painful rebuffs by confining himself to certain areas of experience or deliberately limiting his demands on life. While this particular group is an amorphous one which embraces a wide variety of approaches to life, asceticism may perhaps be taken as its archetype. In essence, asceticism involves the renunciation of instinctual gratification in order to escape the torment the pursuit of it involves. All the other approaches in the group seek to avoid pain by some form of renunciation, more or less explicit. For example, some

[29] *International Journal of Psychoanalysis*, Vol. X, 1929.
[30] The phrase is Theodore Fontane's. It is quoted by Freud in *Civilization and Its Discontents*, p. 25.

people seek happiness in loving rather than being loved, hoping thereby to save themselves from the suffering caused by unrequited love. Others concentrate all their energies on their work, avoiding competitive struggle with their fellows and the turbulent world of sensuous experience so far as they are able. Still others compete fiercely for the material satisfactions life has to offer but fear and shun introspection and close personal relationships.

In addition to seeking, like these other auxiliary constructions, to make life more tolerable, art, including fiction, has one other important characteristic in common with them. It, too, seeks to further man's independence of the outer world. But there the resemblance ends. The first two groups of constructions represent capitulations of various kinds and degrees before the painfulness and difficulty of the human situation. Intoxication, for example, represents a more or less complete withdrawal from the world—from either seeing it or attempting to wrest any satisfaction from it other than the satisfaction provided by the state of intoxication itself. It might be said to represent a temporary withdrawal, but the use of intoxicants tends to become habitual and may itself weaken whatever inclination one may have had to contend with the world. Asceticism represents a more or less permanent renunciation of any endeavor to secure certain types of satisfaction from life. Indeed, it implies an attempt—not, of course, always successful—to close one's eyes to certain possibilities, certain areas of experience. Perhaps because we sense how much loss they entail, we despise certain approaches to life embraced in these two groups of auxiliary constructions and cannot bring ourselves to feel more than mixed admiration for asceticism. Precisely because we all sometimes feel an impulse to abandon the unequal struggle against life, we feel some contempt for those who yield to the impulse and esteem those who grapple with life against the odds.

At first glance, recourse to art, including fiction, might also seem a kind of retreat. Like the use of intoxicants, reading represents a temporary withdrawal from the harsh real world. The withdrawal, furthermore, is to a symbolic world, a world of shadows, whose gratifications cannot, in any real sense, ease our hunger or warm our bodies. The impression of retreat may be heightened by the very willingness of fiction to grant our desires and concern itself with our problems. The world of fiction is palpably different from the world of experience, however much fiction itself may strive to efface the difference, flattering life and pretending that only minor alterations might be necessary to make the real world splendid and responsive and reasonable.

Whatever appearances may suggest, in fact the reading of fiction implies no reluctance to face or struggle with the real world. While fiction alters the facts of experience, a fundamental purpose of those alterations, as the first and greatest esthetician, Aristotle, realized, is the achievement of an imaginary world more lifelike than life itself, more directly and honestly concerned with essential problems, more supple in its expression of every aspect of man's nature, less burdened by distracting irrelevancies. Undoubtedly many of the alterations are made at the behest of the pleasure principle: the world of fiction is more gratifying and less fearful than the world of experience. But even children are dissatisfied when these effects are attained at the expense of the reality principle. They put definite limits on the departures from reality they regard as permissible, and indignantly repudiate stories, no matter how much they were once loved, when their lack of realism becomes apparent. Adults are even more insistent that fiction should not disregard reality,[31] and, of course, have far stricter standards of what respect for truth entails.

There is undoubtedly a great deal of fiction which sidesteps, minimizes or sugar-coats the disagreeable. But so far are such evasions from the essential purpose of narrative art that we intuitively assign a low value to work of this character

---

[31] An empirical study conducted by Dr. Martha Wolfenstein indicates that most normal and neurotic, as opposed to psychotic, adults prefer realistic story endings to "happy" endings which are implausible and unrealistic. See "The Reality Principle in Story Preferences of Neurotics and Psychotics," *Character and Personality*, Vol. XII, 1944. Dr. Wolfenstein's study also indicates that, as we would expect, a preference for veracious art is positively correlated with age, with intelligence and with education.

or try to find some basis for excommunicating it from the realm of art. Among stories whose artistic authenticity cannot be questioned we give the highest place precisely to those works which ignore no aspect of man's nature, which confront the most disagreeable aspects of life deliberately and unflinchingly—to Greek and Shakespearean tragedy, for example, and to such serious comedies as *Candide, Don Quixote* and *Gulliver's Travels.* It is all the more significant that such judgments are natural ones, not, like many criteria proposed by critics, disguised exhortations to believe this or that.

Though fiction, like anything else, can be misused, reading does not ordinarily represent a flight from life or an attempt to blind oneself to its horrors. Some people are under the illusion that they read to "escape" themselves and their problems, but we have already begun to see how inadequate this concept is. Reading is a means of dealing with our most urgent problems, even those we ordinarily shun. The greatest fiction poses these problems in their most essential terms. It gives form to our most fleeting impulses and fully discloses their consequences and ramifications. When we read fiction, moreover, we are ordinarily relaxed and secure, so that we can see things that might elude us at other times. In imagination we can experiment, try out various approaches to our problems, alter this or that circumstance to discover what results ensue. It would be a serious error to suppose that psychic activity of this sort is without value because it is largely unconscious.

Since fiction strives to resolve the tensions it arouses, reading fiction ordinarily leaves us feeling refreshed and restored, in a good frame of mind for coping with any task which lies before us. About the longer-range effects of reading we cannot speak with as much certainty, but there is no reason for believing that reading would discourage the average person from participation in the world of affairs. Though the reading of fiction may make us aware of the limits we must put on some of our expectations and even dispose us to give up certain experiences, such effects are more than counterbalanced by what it does to make us aware of the satisfactions the world affords and to whet our appetite for our share of them. It may also influence us to seek finer kinds of satisfaction than we might otherwise search for.

The superiority of fiction and, it might be added, art in general over the first two groups of auxiliary constructions derives largely from its honesty, its refusal to disregard any aspect of human experience. Its pre-eminence in its own group, which includes play, fantasy and wit, also derives in part from its commitment to the reality principle. Fiction, play, fantasy and wit are alike in that they all represent substitute gratifications. They are alike, too, in that they all rearrange the facts of reality to mold phantom worlds more harmonious, more gratifying and less fearful than the world of experience. They differ fundamentally in the extent to which they are willing to depart from reality to achieve their effects. Neither wit nor fiction is willing to violate reality, but wit will not go to the lengths fiction does to pay homage to the reality principle in any positive sense. Play and fantasy do not disregard reality, but their primary allegiance is clearly to the pleasure principle.

Play is in a sense the father of fiction[32] and has parallels with it which deserve our attention. Like fiction, play is at once linked with reality and distinguishable from it. Like fiction too, it is taken with great seriousness.

Pre-analytic students of play had observed, correctly, that it provides functional pleasure: joy in the activities and functions involved in the child's development. But the fact that a given form of play receives preference at a given time suggests that play has still other determinants. A child who has just been taken to the dentist is likely to play "dentist." Both this fact and the form the game takes indicate that the child is discharging affects and seeking to assimilate the experience he has undergone; above all, in this particular case, he may be seeking to relieve the anxiety the visit to the dentist aroused. Play may also be utilized to master instinctual tensions and to fulfil wishes. The little girl playing with a doll is gratifying her fondest wish: to be grown-up and have a child of her own.

Some of the means play utilizes to achieve its objectives are

[32] Cf. Freud, "The Relation of the Poet to Day-Dreaming."

also worth observing. The child who plays "dentist" after visiting one will almost certainly play the part of the dentist himself and assign his partner in the game the role of patient. By adopting the active role he gains control of a situation he has had to suffer passively. Play also reproduces the original or imaginary situation which is its prototype in miniature scale. For example, the anxiety and pain which may have been involved in the visit to the dentist would be much diluted in the game. Finally, play may alter various individual aspects of the situation on which it is based—above all, its final outcome. Fenichel has summed up much of this: "The psychological function of play is to get rid of . . . tensions by the active repetition or anticipation of them in a self-chosen dosage and at a self-chosen time." [33]

Fantasy, the successor to play, in some ways represents a step backward. The child ordinarily feels no need to conceal his play, and while play may be solitary, it is just as frequently social. In contrast, adults tend to hide their fantasies from others. They know, or believe, that they have no business daydreaming; they are supposed to be concerning themselves with the important things of life, such as earning a living. They are ashamed also of the subject matter of their fantasies, which nearly always revolve around the fulfilment of egoistic or erotic wishes. Either intuitively or as a result of experience they know that their fantasies will please no one but themselves.

The same kind of fantasies provide the raw material of a great deal of fiction. But fiction disguises the egotism and forbidden impulses which underlie fantasy, subjects them to the controlling influence of form. Providing pleasure without arousing aversion, fiction comes to be generally accepted, and when we read we can "enjoy our own day-dreams without reproach or shame" [34] because they have been made more palatable and because we know that others share them. Of the

---

[33] Otto Fenichel, *The Psychoanalytic Theory of Neurosis*, p. 373. For an excellent longer discussion of play, see Robert Waelder's article, "The Psychoanalytic Theory of Play," *Psychoanalytic Quarterly*, II, 1933.

[34] Freud, "The Relation of the Poet to Day-Dreaming," p. 183.

numerous advantages fiction possesses over fantasy, not the least important is its capacity for relieving guilt, whereas day-dreaming tends to intensify it.

Wit shares many of the advantages of fiction and deserves more respect, it seems to me, than it is customarily accorded. It too utilizes form and disguise. It too is a social product. It too confronts unsavory aspects of human life and human nature and, without sacrifice of honesty, attempts to salvage some satisfaction or some basis for continued self-respect from the encounter. The principal limitation of wit arises from a basic characteristic on which its effect depends—its economy. Wit looks at life no less candidly than fiction, but its glance is a quick, almost a nervous one. Thus wit cannot offer us the pleasure we obtain from following the slow, inexorable development of a complex emotional situation. It cannot provide us opportunities for the gradual assimilation and mastery of feelings of instinctual excitation, anxiety and guilt. Even its success in quickly evoking and then relieving such feelings is achieved at a certain cost. For example, in securing the acquiescence of the ego and superego for the expression of the aggressive or erotic impulses with which it is so frequently concerned, wit depends upon surprise attack: it utilizes only so much concealment as is necessary to induce these censorious components of the psyche to relax their vigilance momentarily. The laughter at the individual joke cannot be taken back, but, as though in requital for being deceived, the ego withholds a certain amount of trust and approval from wit itself.

Chapter III *The Materials of Fiction*

> As for what concerns me in particular I have only in my
> life carried to an extreme what you have not dared to carry
> halfway, and what's more, you have taken your cowardice for
> good sense, and have found comfort in deceiving yourselves.
> So that perhaps, after all, there is more life in me than in you.
> Look into it more carefully!
>
> DOSTOEVSKY, *Notes from Underground*

We turn now to a question which seems to present insuperable difficulties: What are the essential characteristics of
fiction that enable it to satisfy the needs which impel people
to read? The question is difficult most obviously because the
realm of fiction is so vast and so diverse. What generalizations
can one make that will hold without too many qualifications
for *Anna Karenina* and *Madame Bovary*, all of Shakespeare's
plays and Chaucer's *Troilus and Cressida*, *The Red and the
Black* and *Moby Dick*, short stories such as Maupassant's
"A Piece of String," Joyce's "The Dead" and Chekov's
"Grief"—and, as well as these, the movies showing in town,
current magazine fiction and rental library favorites? But this
is perhaps an easy, almost a cowardly, way of stating the difficulty. The truth is that any single narrative work which
causes us to feel deeply seems to contain inexhaustible riches.
What can one say about *Hamlet* that will do justice to its
vitality and complexity, its beauty and its power? The greatest narrative works seem not only infinitely rich, but inviol-
able, determined to safeguard their ultimate secrets. No matter how many ways we approach them, and how much we
discover which is valid and revealing, we may conclude our
study with the feeling that many of the sources of their appeal
and authority have eluded us. Thus certain works continue
to tantalize generation after generation of critics.

Fiction— the novel, in particular—seems the most inclusive,

the most "impure," [1] of all art forms. It seems inadequate to say that the world of fiction is coterminous with the entire realm of experience, unless one defines that term very broadly, for one accepts many stories—*The Trial* is as good an example as any, but the same thing applies to *The Rime of the Ancient Mariner* and many of the stories of such writers as Hawthorne and Poe—not so much because one believes, more than provisionally, that they depict some happening which occurred or would be likely to occur in the world of our daily affairs as because they give shape and substance to the most incorporeal and fleeting fancies of our infinitely fecund minds. [2] As though it were not enough to explore the entire world of experience, to capture the precise quality of any event, however subtle and delicate or massive and complex, fiction also lays claim to the vaster and less accessible realm of our fantasies and dreams. What is perhaps equally remarkable is its willingness to incorporate matter which would be rejected as indigestible by any more fastidious form of art. In fiction one may find information about winning ladies or battles; exact descriptions of the planning and commission of crimes and the operation of law courts; philosophical speculations and accounts of historical and contemporary events; letters, essays, diary entries and sermons; bills of lading and informal balance sheets; literary criticism and scientific theories; cryptograms, puzzles, sketches and blanks. Omnivorous, fiction seems confident of its ability to assimilate any kind of material and utilize it for its own purposes.

We are encouraged to believe that we can find order in this diversity by the fact that so many storytellers, living and

[1] I use the word in the sense Robert Penn Warren employs it in his brilliant essay, "Pure and Impure Poetry," *Kenyon Review,* V, 1943. Reprinted in *Criticism, The Foundations of Modern Literary Judgment,* edited by Mark Schorer, Josephine Miles and Gordon McKenzie (New York: Harcourt, Brace, 1948).

[2] Cf. Coleridge: " . . . it was agreed, that my endeavours should be directed to persons and characters supernatural, or at least romantic; yet so as to transfer from our inward nature a human interest and a semblance of truth sufficient to procure for these shadows of imagination that willing suspension of disbelief for the moment, which constitutes poetic faith." *Biographia Literaria,* Ch. XIV.

dead, have seemed to share a common idea of what those purposes are. It would, of course, be an illusion to suppose that their ideas coincided exactly. Furthermore, they did not face the difficult task of formulating what they knew; only a handful of fiction writers have been literary theorists as well. In a sense, however, this makes it all the more remarkable that fiction writers, laboring separately, have been guided by such similar objectives and have turned out products so readily identifiable for what they are. We are seldom in much doubt about whether a given work should be called a story.

In this and the next chapters let us confine ourselves to the attributes of fiction which are connected with subject matter. It is not too difficult to define the subject matter of fiction in a rough, preliminary way. Whatever else fiction may be said to deal with, it is surely safe to say that it deals, either manifestly or covertly, with our emotional problems. One kind of fiction, of which *The Trial* will serve as a typical example, revolves around our inner feelings and conflicts—often around desires and fears of which we are only dimly aware and whose effect upon our lives we might find it impossible to trace. A second kind of fiction, of which *Robinson Crusoe* may be taken as typical, deals with our real-life problems—for example, the problem of wresting a living from an indifferent or hostile environment. Even in such fiction, it should be added at once, everything may be so altered that the reference to our own predicament may not be apparent. For example, Crusoe is placed in a situation in which not simply his success but his very life depends upon his willingness to exert himself, his ability and his resourcefulness.

In at least a general way we also know how fiction states these problems. We know, for example, that it objectifies and externalizes them. We know also that it poses them concretely, in terms of an ordered sequence of happenings and, usually, in terms of individualized human beings. Even when the protagonists are animals or institutions—the whale in *Moby Dick* or the court in *The Trial*—the situation is not so very different, for the non-human protagonists are invested with some measure of personal significance; often, for example, they are projections of some aspect of the hero's psyche.

Fiction, then, provides us with images of our emotional problems expressed in an idiom of characters and events. It may be noted in passing that in one sense these images are perfectly intelligible, while in another their significance and relevance to our own interests may be said to be hidden from view. These characteristics are important—we shall appreciate their importance more fully as we proceed—but it is apparent that our description is not yet complete. Some of the factors which explain the appeal of what fiction has to tell us have not yet been identified.

2

If we have not made much headway, we believe that we are at least on the right path. But the view that our emotional problems constitute the basic subject matter of fiction is in competition with many others. Sooner or later we shall have to consider some of these alternative viewpoints. It will probably be better to indicate at once what seem to me their limitations. I shall try to do so briefly, even at the risk of seeming arbitrary.

Many critics maintain that fiction is primarily concerned with intellectual, social or moral issues. That many works are concerned to some degree with one or another of these is hardly disputable. But as soon as we begin to consider concrete cases we find that relatively few are centrally concerned with such issues. Take *Anna Karenina*—a good "touchstone" for weighing any theory about fiction and a particularly suitable example in the present instance, since at first glance it might strike us as being engaged with some sort of "issue." We know that Tolstoy was an original thinker of some consequence, and social and moral issues were among the things he reflected upon most deeply. Many of his ideas on these and other matters appear in *Anna Karenina*. We cannot read the novel without learning a great deal about nineteenth-century Russian society and the operation of moral codes; Tolstoy insists, for example, that it was the seriousness with which

Anna and Vronsky took their love which led society to excommunicate her. The novel is certainly concerned with
intellectual, social and moral issues, but if we are asked to
name a particular issue around which it may be said to revolve
we cannot, I believe, offer a satisfactory answer. Anna's conflict is between her love for Vronsky and her love for her son.
Her tragedy arises from the fact—here society assuredly
enters in—that she cannot contrive to have them both. It
could be argued that the dilemma which confronts her would
never arise in another kind of society. But Tolstoy does not
make a point of this, nor does he state Anna's conflict in moral
terms.

A second example leads to another consideration. Chekov's
"Grief," a story about which I shall have more to say later on,
might at first glance appear to be suggesting some sort of
statement about society or about mankind. Chekov's humble
protagonist, unable to find any human being who will sympa-
thize with him in his sorrow, ends by unburdening himself to
his horse. But is the final scene of the story intended to stimulate certain reflections or to bring to a pitch the emotions
Chekov is seeking to convey? This raises a more general question: When a story *is* concerned with some social, intellectual
or moral issue, does that concern explain the profoundest
effects of the work upon us?

Perhaps somewhat different answers are required for the
three types of issues mentioned. It is impossible to deny that
the novel of social protest often owes its appeal to the issue
with which it deals. Indeed, it may enjoy great initial success
precisely because it exploits some already existing interest or
calls attention to a problem in which people feel they ought
to be interested. But the quick oblivion which overtakes most
works of social protest suggests that the interests to which
they appeal are shallow as well as ephemeral. It is only when
such works simultaneously refer to other problems more intimate and more enduring that, as literature, they are likely to
survive the social problem with which they deal. *Uncle
Tom's Cabin* is read today only as a historical document or a
curiosity. Of course, some protest novels have deeper refer-

ence or—there is the classic example of *Don Quixote*—depart from and even reverse the social intention which gave them birth. But *Don Quixote* is an exception. The history of literature suggests that the imagination of writers is much less likely to be quickened by "issues" than by themes which obsess them for reasons they cannot readily explain.

The jibe made unjustly of a certain fiction writer, that his mind was never violated by an idea, can certainly not be directed against fiction in general. To some extent at least all fiction, like all poetry, is, in Santayana's phrase, "a theoretic vision of things" or, in Arnold's, "an interpretation of life." Ideas interpenetrate all fiction and they form the scaffolding of a number of distinguished narrative works, from *The Divine Comedy* to *Brave New World*. But such works are relatively rare, and it is readily demonstrable that they do not owe their appeal to the ideas they contain per se: the ideas have been assimilated to the narrative and invested with emotional fervor. The symbolism of *The Divine Comedy* stirs such deep reverberations that the poem has continued to appeal to generations of readers who do not share either Dante's religion or his *Weltanschauung*. Though Aldous Huxley is not to be despised as a thinker, the ideas he advances in *Brave New World* would not seem very exciting if they were not both dramatized and projected with satiric bite.

The claim that moral issues constitute the basic subject matter of fiction is, I believe, seriously inflated. In our culture "moral" is such an honorific term that many writers about literature employ it freely without any clear reference whatsoever. Allusions to a novel's "large moral implications" or "sense of moral commitment" are often made, it appears, in the belief that they cannot possibly do any harm and may resuscitate a flagging literary paper. Perhaps, too, they give those who employ them the comfortable assurance that they belong among the righteous elect. These reflections are ungenerous, but I can think of no other satisfactory explanation for the frequency with which such phrases are trotted forth, no matter how slight the provocation. One encounters them, for example, in discussions of such a novel as Fitzgerald's *Tender*

Is the Night. This remarkable novel chronicles the dissolution of a marriage and the disintegration of a promising man. Its subject, unmistakably, is fear of failure; it gives form to its author's deep and profoundly moving fears that he was a failure, or might become one. At no point is the novel centrally concerned with moral problems.

Indeed, it is glaringly apparent that most great contemporary fiction writers are preoccupied with other kinds of issues.[3] It would be too glib to attribute this entirely to the notorious secular tendencies of our age. We must reckon with the fact that relatively little of the great narrative art of the past has posed issues in moral terms—surprisingly little if we consider the hold morality has had for centuries on the minds of men. One explanation is that there are things in us older, as well as younger, than morality. After pointing out that *Oedipus the King* and *Lear* are as lacking in explicit moral meaning as the myth of Osiris or the images of springing corn or the serpent, one of the most perceptive of modern critics, Maud Bodkin, declares: "The glory that may be felt in any of these images, when to an individual it becomes a symbol of the life that is both within and beyond himself, is something older and more profound than morality as we understand it."[4] There are other explanations as well, some of which will suggest themselves as we gain a clearer understanding of the essential nature of narrative art.

There is, however, a very considerable body of fiction, some of it of the very first order, which is explicitly concerned with moral issues or readily lends itself to moral interpretation. In my analysis of "I Want to Know Why," in Chapter IX, I have made the point which I believe holds for most such fiction: moral meaning is present, but lies relatively close to the surface; in work of any importance, intensive analysis almost invariably uncovers other meanings and other

[3] I have in mind such writers as Proust, Joyce, Virginia Woolf, the earlier D. H. Lawrence, the Thomas Mann of the stories if not always of the novels, Hemingway and Faulkner—the latter despite the statement he made at the time he received the Nobel Prize. Such occasions seem to inspire such statements.

[4] *Archetypal Patterns in Poetry* (London: Oxford, 1934), p. 286.

sources of vitality more directly connected with the central intention of the story and its impact upon us.[5] In some fiction obtrusive discussion of moral issues seems to be employed quite clearly as a façade, designed—how "deliberately" we cannot say—to distract our conscious attention from the work's latent meaning. This seems conspicuously true, for example, of Melville's *Billy Budd*,[6] a story on which I shall comment at greater length later on.

There remain a certain number of works concerned at a very deep if not the deepest level with moral problems. One such work—I do not need to pay tribute to its greatness—is *Macbeth*. Macbeth is aware of many of the things which are impelling him to murder Duncan. He sees the horror of the deed and admits the absence of any consideration which would extenuate it. And he foresees the consequences of the murder with clairvoyant accuracy. The central issue of the play could hardly be put in more explicitly moral terms.[7]

[5] In a paper on *Pamela* (*College English*, 14, 1952) I have tried to get at the same point in indirect fashion. On every page *Pamela* makes us aware of moral considerations—and, as Joseph Wood Krutch among others has pointed out, its morality, to our modern taste at least, is incredibly offensive. Very well, then, *Pamela* is a bad novel and should no longer possess any appeal. But in fact it still seems to give enjoyment to many readers who cannot be dismissed as insensitive. In my paper I have tried to identify the sources of its appeal. But my more general purpose was to suggest the limited extent to which our response to any narrative work is determined, positively or negatively, by its moral values.

[6] I had almost mentioned *The Scarlet Letter* as another example. But perhaps in that novel the surface morality is intended to distract our attention not so much from the action of the story as from another way of judging the action and the characters, one which Hawthorne did not wish to make too explicit; *The Scarlet Letter* is perhaps a moral novel whose morality is usually misunderstood. See Régis Michaud's illuminating interpretation in *The American Novel Today* (Boston: Little, Brown, 1928). Cf. also D. H. Lawrence's discussion of the novel in *Studies in Classic American Literature* (New York: Seltzer, 1923) and Lloyd Morris' in *Rebellious Puritan: Portrait of Mr. Hawthorne* (New York: Harcourt, Brace, 1927).

[7] There are, of course, many subsidiary problems in the play which cannot be described as moral, and can be illuminated only by psychological analysis. Among these may be mentioned the theme of childlessness, which so interested Freud, and the relationship, tantalizing in its complexity, between Macbeth and Lady Macbeth. I must confess to having a feeling that even the central issue of the play is more complicated than, in my desire to seem reasonable, I have made it appear. What a curiously opaque work *Macbeth* is, for all its apparent simplicity and candor.

But of how many other works can one say the same thing? Certainly of no more than a very few. Much more frequently a character makes a foolish misstep, like Lear; or is blind to some of the forces playing upon him, like Hamlet; or acts in a state of frenzy during which he misapprehends everything, like Othello; or drifts into a situation the consequences of which he does not foresee, like Antony. The fact remains that there are some works centrally concerned with moral issues, just as there are some which are concerned with social and intellectual problems. And there are numerous border-line cases; the issues in *The Ambassadors*, for example, can be analyzed to advantage in either moral or psychological terms. There are no hard and fast divisions between "moral" and "psychological," "social" and "personal," "intellectual" and "emotional." Indeed, concepts of what constitutes a moral issue vary more widely than I have perhaps suggested. If most efforts to state the issues of fiction in moral terms seem inadequate or even misleading, and some strike one as unwitting attempts to call attention to the author's, or critic's, virtue, or to cajole the reader, it must be admitted that one occasionally encounters a conception of morality sufficiently enlightened, noble and complex to do justice to the material with which it deals. Only two points are worth insisting upon. Any kind of problem must be invested with a great deal of feeling before it becomes a suitable subject for fiction. And in reading any great work of fiction—*Macbeth* as well as *Hamlet*, *The Divine Comedy* as well as *The Canterbury Tales*—consciously and unconsciously we satisfy emotional needs.

3

Two other views about the subject matter of fiction remain to be considered. Perhaps no one would claim paternity to the first of these in precisely the form in which I shall state it. However, some critics appear to believe that the essential business of fiction is to give us a picture of man in society, of "manners," of man in his more or less public pursuits, in interaction with people from his own and other social classes. Quite as much as the belief that narrative art is primarily concerned with intellectual, social or moral issues, such a view tends to rivet our attention upon the surface of fiction. It puts a great deal of importance upon setting and fails to do justice to factors which have demonstrably more to do with our interest in fiction.

To assess this position it is essential that we understand the way that setting functions in fiction, and perhaps no one has discussed this subject more brilliantly than Edwin Muir. He is too perspicacious a critic to maintain that the social setting of the novel, the genre to which he confines himself, is always of central interest to us or that all novels have a setting which could be described as social. In one type of novel, which Muir calls the dramatic novel, he asserts that the setting is no more than a background for the human drama. Because the scene of such novels may be "coloured and dyed by the passions of the chief figures, because we always see them against it, and closed in by it," [8] it may be realized with a greater intensity than in the contrasting type of novel—the novel of character. In the dramatic novel, of which *The Return of the Native* and *Wuthering Heights* may be taken as examples, the scene is never prized for its own sake; it "is not an ordinary and particular scene at all, like the Sedley's drawing-room, or Sir Pitt Crawley's country estate, but rather an image of humanity's temporal environment. The Yorkshire moors and Wessex . . . are universal scenes where the drama of mankind is played out." [9] According to Muir, the scene of dramatic novels is likely to be primitive; such novels are seldom concerned with "manners, costumes, . . . and all the other properties of changing civilisation. . . . The articulation of space is vague and arbitrary. London might be a thousand miles away from Wuthering Heights or Casterbridge. But from the London of *Vanity Fair* and *Tom Jones*, . . . every place has its just geographical distance, and no part of England . . . is inaccessible. . . . We are conscious of England in *Tom Jones* and *Vanity Fair*; we are only aware of the Yorkshire

[8] *The Structure of the Novel* (New York: Harcourt, Brace, 1929), pp. 65-66.
[9] *Ibid.*, p. 66.

moors and Egdon Heath in *Wuthering Heights* and *The Return of the Native*." [10]

Perhaps Muir here pushes the antithesis too far: there is a sense in which Budmouth and Paris are very much present in *The Return of the Native*. But in general the distinction he makes is a valid and illuminating one. There are undeniable differences in the way scene is treated by Thackeray and Hardy. We assent to the fact that the former is interested in showing us that "the human scene, that world in itself, is infinitely various and interesting; that Queens Crawley is a very different place from Russell Square. . . ." [11]

But Muir may be implying more than this; he may mean that Thackeray is more interested in his settings than in his characters. Elsewhere Muir declares, "When we think of Thackeray's characters we think of them in the costume and against the background of their time; their clothes, the houses they live in, and the fashions they observe, are part of their reality; they exist in their period as in a suddenly fixed world." [12] Much as I admire Muir's literary acumen, here I feel I must part company with him. We find it quite natural, I should say, to re-costume Miss Sharp in this year's fashions and transplant her to New York—and, despite Thackeray's lamented reticence, which he knew so well how to circumvent, we tend to see her at times with no clothes at all. We are far too fascinated by the young lady to let her remain an inert and purely decorative part of a period montage. By the end of Chapter II of *Vanity Fair* we are at least as interested in Becky Sharp as we are ever interested in Eustacia Vye. It is a somewhat different kind of interest and it is satisfied, in Muir's terms, in space rather than in time. This consideration alone makes it necessary that setting be treated differently in the two novels. Different kinds of backgrounds are needed to make us see the ways in which Eustacia Vye and Becky Sharp will fulfil their destinies. While the differences should not be effaced, they should not be permitted to obscure the fact that

[10] *Ibid.*, p. 66 and pp. 64-65.
[11] *Ibid.*, p. 68.
[12] *Ibid.*, p. 66.

in both novels setting is subordinated to the larger interests of story and character; in neither novel does the setting distract our attention from the action. This is not to say that, in either novel, setting functions solely as "means." In good fiction no element ever does: each aspect of storytelling is prized for its own sake, as well as for the contribution it makes to the whole. But when setting usurps the center of the stage, when a writer has more to tell us about milieu and manners than about action or character, we may be sure that we are in the presence of a second-rate talent.

All the empirical evidence on response to fiction which I have been able to secure indicates that readers are much more interested in what setting helps to reveal, in the story it helps to set forth, than they are in setting per se. Studies of the reactions of younger readers indicate that they invariably focus upon the action and the emotional configuration of the principal characters. Setting may facilitate the acceptance of a story—for example, an exotic setting may serve the purposes of disguise, or conformity to known facts may contribute to the illusion of realism—but among the deeper reverberations stirred up by reading, setting seldom appears to play an important part. The action is readily transposed to some ground physically or psychically more familiar to the reader.

Information given me by psychoanalysts about the response of their patients to fiction indicates that adults treat setting in very much the same fashion. For example, when they "analogize" [13] it is nearly always on the basis of the action—the predicaments and relationships of the characters. Even when the setting is one with which readers are familiar, it may be replaced by a different one, more appropriate for the personal drama they wish to enact.

What Tolstoy said of the Biblical story of Joseph, that it "may be transferred to any surroundings, and it will be just as comprehensible and just at touching," [14] appears to hold for many stories and not, as he supposed, for just a few.

---

[13] See Chapters VIII and X.

[14] "What is Art?" *Resurrection, What is Art? The Christian Teaching* (New York: Willey Book Co., n.d.), p. 301.

Whereas Muir believes that in a certain type of novel our interest shifts to the social background against which the human drama unfolds, Tolstoy feared that "the exclusiveness of the sensations conveyed" and "special details of time and place" would keep even such writers as Cervantes, Molière and Dickens from being sufficiently universal. Both Muir's belief and Tolstoy's fear appear unfounded.

We cannot overlook one final viewpoint about the subject matter of fiction, though it does not seem to me entitled to much respect: this is the view that the value of a story is not related to any aspect of subject matter but derives solely from form. At bottom, I believe, this view rests on a fear of what fiction tries to express and an impulse to discuss it in terms which are devoid of threat and so easy to manipulate that they confer a sense of power. Perhaps, too, it rests on a desire to divorce literature sharply from life. The view has a specious plausibility, for no one can think about fiction very long without realizing that its appeal never depends entirely upon its content. But it is equally false to suppose that it depends entirely upon form.

And for the best of reasons: in reality there is no such thing as "content" and no such thing as "form." All we have is the story itself, an entity in which whatever is being communicated is already structured and expressed in a certain way; it is this entity, the work as a whole, as given, which moves us or fails to do so. To get at particular attributes of the work which appear to account for certain of its effects upon us, to facilitate analysis, and also to facilitate exposition—we cannot blurt out at once all that we feel about a complex work—we may feel driven to invent or employ certain terms. "Content" and "form" are potentially among the more useful of such terms, for some of the observations a story may suggest appear to relate primarily to its expressive content and still others to matters of style and technique.

There are innumerable borderline cases, however, and there is no case where *either* what is being said *or* the manner of saying it—in so far as these can even be separated—is a matter of complete indifference. Potentially powerful material will not only fail to stir us if it is not presented dexterously; for reasons which will become clearer as we proceed, such material must be handled with particular skill or it will seem offensive and arouse anxiety and painful impressions. But the converse is also true: material with no real reference to the human predicament can be presented with the utmost skill and it will still seem vacuous and inconsequential.

It is entirely possible that the terms "form" and "content" should be entirely avoided. But if they are used, it is obvious that they should be used with tact and discrimination; otherwise they will only cause confusion. Two cautions appear particularly important. Those who use the terms have to remember that content and form are no more than hypostatized constructions, and that there is a certain arbitrariness in assigning any given attributes to one or the other; it is impossible to say categorically where one ends and the other begins. Secondly, it is necessary to respect *both* content and form. If one is going to attribute the effect of fiction entirely to one or the other, it is hardly worth employing the terms in the first place; one would do better to discuss a work as an entity.

These cautions have been disregarded by certain self-styled "formalist" or "Aristotelian" critics, who write as though content and form had definite and existent reference and exalt form at the expense of content. These critics have obscured the fashion in which the expressive content of fiction contributes to its total impact. And, ironically, they have done formal analysis itself—potentially a valuable approach to fiction—a grave disservice.

Upon the latter of these consequences we cannot spend much time. We know that "content" and "form" are abstracted from a common matrix. It seems only reasonable to suppose that, to the extent that discretely formal problems arise during the creation of literature, a—and perhaps *the*—basic consideration determining their solution is how best to present the material struggling for expression. So close are the connections between form and content that one cannot proceed far in the analysis of either if one takes them as autonomous. The critic who tries to ignore the substance of litera-

ture and to discuss it in rigidly formal terms has fatally ham-
strung himself. The ultimate rationale of the formal effects he
takes note of will elude him: he may observe their inner consistency, but will not be able to account for their appropriateness His work will suffer not only because it disregards the
light that substance casts upon form but also because it blinds
itself to the light form can cast upon substance, refusing to
move—as for example the criticism of G. Wilson Knight
sometimes does—from perceptions about imagery to deeper
insights into character and motivation. By his very definition
of the task of criticism the rigidly formal critic limits himself
largely to cataloguing and comparing—operations which may
reveal his ingenuity and scholarship, but seldom deepen our
understanding of literature. His work is inevitably exhibition-
istic and arid.

The means formal critics employ to disparage content are
worth scrutinizing, for our analysis may help us to understand the way in which the expressive substance of a work
may be said to contribute to its power. Sometimes they write
as though content refers not to anything *in* a story but to the
underlying raw material out of which it was fashioned. It is
easy enough to demonstrate that this material does not account
for the power of the work. At other times they identify content with a summary which they expect to be altogether inadequate. "Clearly," write Messrs. Wellek and Warren, "the
aesthetic effect of a work of art does not reside in what is
commonly called its content. There are few works of art
which are not ridiculous or meaningless in synopsis." [15] But
why should content be equated with some synopsis of it?
Content is gutted of much of its meaning when it is identified
either with the underlying raw material for a story or the
kind of synopsis Messrs. Wellek and Warren have in mind.

Perhaps this can be best illustrated by reference to that
perennial subject of literary discussion, *Hamlet*. In *The Interpretation of Dreams* Freud advanced the theory that Hamlet is inhibited in avenging his father by unconscious guilt
arising from his own Oedipal desires. "Hamlet is able to do

[15] *Theory of Literature* (New York: Harcourt, Brace, 1949), p. 140.

anything but take vengeance upon the man who did away
with his father and has taken his father's place with his mother
—the man who shows him in realization the repressed desires
of his own childhood. The loathing which should have driven
him to revenge is thus replaced by conscientious scruples,
which tell him that he himself is no better than the murderer
whom he is required to punish." [16] "So *Hamlet* is about the
Oedipus conflict"—thus runs the argument—"But———"—
and here some work of accepted lightweight quality is named
—"is also about the Oedipus conflict. Obviously the fact that
Hamlet deals with the Oedipus conflict has nothing to do with
its appeal."

Most readers will recognize the conclusion as a *non sequi-
tur*. In the first place, no one could claim that the Oedipal
theme is more than one component of the subject matter of
Hamlet. But the essential point is that the contribution this
one theme makes to the appeal of the play has been obscured
by a particularly savage form of reduction: the theme has been
contracted, not to a synopsis, but beyond that to what is
meant to be an opprobrious label.

To show the part the theme does play in our response to
Hamlet, we would have to proceed in precisely the opposite
fashion: we would have to do justice to the theme *in its ful-
ness*. We would have to suggest the infinite cunning with
which it is orchestrated in nearly all the play's key relationships and in innumerable actions and speeches. As one ex-

[16] *The Basic Writings of Sigmund Freud* (New York: Modern Library,
1938), p. 310. Everything said about *Hamlet*, here and later on, assumes
the validity of Freud's interpretation. It has been ably elaborated and
defended by Ernest Jones in "A Psycho-Analytic Study of Hamlet," *Essays
in Applied Psycho-Analysis* (London: The International Psycho-Analytical
Library, 1923). For a revised and expanded version of this essay, see *Hamlet
and Oedipus* (Garden City, New York: Doubleday Anchor Books, 1955).
See also my paper, "Freud and *Hamlet* Again," *American Imago*, 12, 1955.
As Jones maintains, all the alternative explanations which have been advanced to account for Hamlet's delay are unsatisfactory. They are either
inconsistent with certain elements in the play, as, for example, the theory
that Hamlet is in general indecisive disregards the speed with which he acts
on a number of occasions; or, like the theory advanced by J. M. Robertson
and popularized by T. S. Eliot, they ask us to believe that the play is an
inexplicable hodgepodge inexpertly assembled from various sources—a suggestion which our response belies.

ample, we would have to mention the contrast between the way Hamlet and Laertes go about avenging their fathers; if one accepts the form-content dichotomy, one may surely regard the Laertes strand of the plot as part of the "matter" of the play. We would have to mention Hamlet's relationship to the Ghost, Claudius and Polonius;[17] Laertes' relation to his father; and Fortinbras' relation to his uncle, the King of Norway. We would have to mention the play within the play, Hamlet's relationship with Ophelia, his melancholy and innumerable other things.

Moreover, we would have to suggest not only the richness but the subtlety of the elements in the play which carry the Oedipal theme: we would have to describe them *in their particularity*. In the next chapter we shall see the extent to which the appeal of the play depends on the fact that Hamlet's guilt, envy of Claudius, ambivalence toward his father and desire for his mother are all internalized. Oedipal notes are struck often in *Hamlet*, but they are always muffled. To suggest the specific quality and effects of these notes I should have to write many pages and anticipate points better made in other connections.

Fortunately, what I mean by particularization can be illustrated by reference to another genre, the expressive content of which can be dealt with more pithily. Those who believe that Freud would have accepted the phrase "Oedipus conflict" as a complete explanation of the subject-matter appeal of *Hamlet* may suppose that he was content to regard the Moses of Michelangelo as the rendition in stone of a powerful patriarchal figure. In fact, Freud probed endlessly to account for the effect this deeply admired statue had upon him, to ascertain precisely what it represented. "The giant frame with its tremendous physical power," he ultimately concluded, ". . . [is] a concrete expression of the highest mental achievement that is possible in a man, that of struggling successfully against an inward passion for the sake of a cause to which he has devoted himself." [18] It is when particularized in this fashion that

[17] Cf. pp. 102-3 and 108.
[18] "The Moses of Michelangelo," *Collected Papers*, IV, 283.

subject matter may be said to participate in the effect of a work of art.

4

So complex are most problems connected with fiction that one cannot discuss them, even in provisional fashion, as briefly as one would like. I return, after what I am aware has been a long detour, to my own attempt to discover the essential subject matter of narrative art.

I have stressed the fact that it is primarily concerned with our emotional problems. Is it possible and advantageous to specify the problems? It is not without significance that so many great narrative works deal with the Oedipus conflict. One thinks at once of the drama after which the conflict was named, of *Hamlet, The Brothers Karamazov, Rosmersholm* and that remarkable Oedipal comedy, *The Playboy of the Western World*. But these are only some of the more obvious examples. If we try to think of works which deal not with the entire Oedipal constellation but with some one of its aspects or legacies—the silver cord theme, let us say, or the search for a good father—more titles suggest themselves than it would be profitable to list. Still more occur to us when we think of the various phases of the Oedipus conflict. In a model literary paper, free of any forcing, Dr. Mark Kanzer has shown how exactly *Oedipus at Colonus* recapitulates the events connected with its dissolution.[19]

Similarly, if we consider in its broadest terms another of the emotional constellations identified by Freud, the "family romance," we see that it constitutes the subject matter of a great deal of adult as well as children's fiction. Basically, the family romance refers to the effort of young people to emancipate themselves from their parents and surpass them. How many new novels appear each year which treat this theme! We should also take account of the many stories which deal with

[19] "The 'Passing of the Oedipus Complex' in Greek Drama," *International Journal of Psychoanalysis*, XXIX, 1948. Reprinted in *The Yearbook of Psychoanalysis*, V, 1949 (New York: International Universities Press, 1950).

some combination of the Oedipus conflict and the family romance; the line between the two is by no means sharp.

Many other themes might be mentioned, each of which will immediately suggest certain titles to any reader: the conflict between the individual and society or between the individual and the nature of life itself; conflicts between lovers or between love and desire, or between love and some other attachment; competition between two people for the love of a third person; conflicts between violent and prohibited impulses of all kinds and the forces which restrain them; conflicts between the desire to remain honest or pure or generous and the temptations and pressures which beset one. To some extent, of course, these are overlapping categories. Furthermore, they do not exhaust the subjects with which fiction deals. We must seek categories which are discrete and more general.

We are struck by the frequency with which the word "conflict" occurs in our list of themes. Many writers—Brooks and Warren among others[20]—have emphasized that some conflict lies at the center of every story; Coleridge, of course, emphasized the importance of this factor in literature generally. And, fortunately, one or two critics have tried to describe in the broadest possible terms the conflict around which fiction, or a particular genre, may be said to revolve. Limiting herself to tragedy, Maud Bodkin declares that it mirrors the struggle between two conflicting attitudes toward the self; it shows the anarchistic, omnipotent self, the self that will tolerate no hindrance or denial, the selfish, ambitious power-seeking aspect of the self, in conflict with the chastened, social self—the self which corresponds with a more realistic sense of what we may ask of life for ourself after due allowance is made for the rights of others. "The archetypal pattern corresponding to tragedy may be said to be a certain organization of the tendencies of self-assertion and submission." [21] Ad-

---

[20] In their Introduction to *Understanding Fiction* (New York: Appleton, 1943).

[21] *Archetypal Patterns in Poetry*, p. 23.

mirable as this statement is—it has elements to which I cannot
pause to do justice—it seems to me too specific to cover all
tragedy; it seems more applicable to *Macbeth* than to *Hamlet*,
for example, and more applicable to *Lear* than to *Othello*.

Hanns Sachs offers a definition which is more serviceable.
The basic subject matter of fiction, he suggests, is the struggle
between impulse and inhibition. If we define "impulse" very
broadly, so that it covers, let us say, the desire to communicate
one's grief, as well as instinctual urges, and if on the obstacle
side of the ledger we take cognizance of external impediments
as well as internal inhibitions, this formula will cover if not all
then at any rate a large portion of the world's fiction.

5

Our description of the subject matter of fiction may be
reasonably comprehensive and accurate, but now misgivings
of a more fundamental character demand consideration. Are
we ourselves on a false trail? Have we made any headway
toward a definition of fiction by observing that it is centrally
concerned with conflict? While we secure satisfaction from
overcoming obstacles, conflict itself—real conflict—is not a
source of pleasure to us, but rather of pain. Why should the
fictional presentation of our conflicts give us pleasure or satisfaction?

The answer immediately suggests itself: there are decisive
differences between the way conflicts are dealt with in fiction
and the way they make themselves felt in life. Detailed consideration of some of those differences will have to be post-
poned until later, for they pertain primarily to form. Formal
characteristics deserve most of the credit for the fact that in
reading fiction we can consider our most troublesome conflicts in detached security—indeed, most of the time without
being aware that the conflicts are our own.

There are also two crucial interlocking differences in terms
of what is said, in terms of content, in the way conflicts are
dealt with in fiction and in life. In the first place, fiction gives
our conflicts a much more thorough airing. Directly or indirectly it tries to represent every consideration which might

be advanced to justify or oppose the satisfaction of a given impulse—to give the impulse its full measure of attraction and yet remind us of everything which whispers that we should not yield to it. There are many ways of stating this important characteristic. Using terms in which Edward Glover describes art in general, we may say that fiction gives us compromise formations whereby repressed and repressing forces obtain expression in one and the same product.[22] Or we may say that fiction heeds the demands of both the reality principle and the pleasure principle, or that it provides a forum in which the positions of the id, the ego and the superego all receive a hearing.

We esteem fiction not a little on the basis of this one characteristic. We have all had the experience of feeling the continued pull of some desire though we have marshaled impressive arguments against gratifying it and perhaps reached a decision we thought of as final. Almost as common is a persistent feeling of uneasiness about some course of action which every logical consideration appears to recommend. Evidently we find it very difficult to dredge forth all the factors we should consider in resolving our conflicts and to give each its just due.

We appreciate fiction, secondly, because it seeks to reconcile the various claims it brings forward. Moreover, in keeping with its willingness to hear all sides, it strives for resolutions based upon maximum fulfilment, rather than the illusory kind achieved by denying or slighting certain claims; it seeks resolutions which, to use a happy word of Robert Penn Warren's, are "earned" rather than forced. Obviously such resolutions are more richly satisfying and more stable than the provisional solutions of our problems with which we must so often be content in life.

Of course, even in fiction such resolutions are only occasionally achieved. None but the greatest narrative works give us the impression of having overlooked nothing, no relevant consideration, no possibility of harmonizing apparently incompatible elements. Here, as elsewhere, I am describing a

[22] *Freud or Jung* (New York: Norton, 1950).

tendency rather than an invariable accomplishment. It should be noted, too, that in life itself we may experience moments of illumination in which we see ourselves and our dilemmas with sudden clarity, and perhaps even find solutions to problems which, until then, appeared to admit of none. But such moments of revelation, and usually of more complete self-acceptance, are rare in life; some people never experience them. Narrative art much more frequently gives us a sense of having dealt equitably with all the forces which stir within us; it characteristically achieves a broad view. We must try to understand why this is so.

6

We are already acquainted with the factor primarily responsible for our tendency to disregard certain considerations and falsify matters when we weigh our own problems: it is repression, or, more basically, the underlying anxiety which stirs this mechanism into activity. In a general way we also know the kind of things we prefer not to take into account: they are things which would make us anxious, for example, ideas which would arouse feelings of self-reproach or jeopardize an adjustment to life which we fear to upset even though it leaves us unhappy.

What may surprise us is the range of the ideas which can arouse anxiety. Of course we do not wish to be reminded of impulses we find it difficult to cope with or of selfish and malicious motives. But we may be no more willing to face anything which will remind us of relatively trivial shortcomings, of peevishness, let us say, or stinginess. Even ideas which it might be expected we would welcome, or at any rate regard with indifference, may be rejected because in some roundabout way they mobilize anxiety. For example, we may try to discount some generous and idealistic action because, to excuse our own corruption, we are trying to convince ourselves that no one acts unselfishly. Or we may try to disavow feelings of revulsion toward life because they call for a more searching examination of our own situation or our society than we feel prepared to make.

Under the most favorable conditions there are many facets of human experience, many kinds of situations, many surmises about why people act and feel as they do, which we are unable to consider objectively. When we are involved in a conflict which could disrupt our life, the situation is still worse. A certain degree of blindness and a certain amount of distortion are almost inevitable. It is worth illustrating this, although any example, presented in expository terms, must seem sketchy and crude.

Let us take a case which arises frequently enough in life and will also suggest parallel instances in fiction—the case of a man involved in a serious extramarital relationship. How likely is he to see either the relationship or any of the people involved in it with any clarity? He may not even admit that a problem exists, however unhappy everyone may be, for any resolution of the situation involves danger and possible loss. What is more certain is that, to justify his own conduct or to escape the full force of the conflict, he will alter the facts this way or that. He may try to disparage his mistress and his feeling for her, acknowledging only those qualities in her about which he is ambivalent, such as her physical beauty, and denying that he is drawn to her by anything but sexual attraction. In keeping with this he may pretend that his marriage is better than it is and stifle complaints against his wife he would be justified in making. Alternatively, he may endow his mistress with qualities which she does not possess and deny his wife her own virtues.

It is our fears, obviously, which lead us to evade and falsify our problems. *But in reading fiction we do not have to be afraid;* there honesty is possible and welcome. We turn to fiction because we know that there we will find our problems imaged in their full intensity and complexity, everything faithfully shown, the desires and fears we have slighted drawn as distinctly as anything else. Unconsciously we want to see justice done to those neglected considerations—they are a part of us too.

We value fiction in part because it redresses balances. It tries to annihilate the unctuous lies we live by—the lies which other forms of communication, incidentally, from newspaper editorials to political oratory, tire us by trying to sustain. It exposes, sometimes, of course, too indecorously, the backside of life.[23] In the words in which the hero of Dostoevsky's *Notes from Underground* seeks to justify himself, it carries to an extreme what we have not dared to carry halfway, and it does not mistake cowardice for good sense or tolerate self-deception. A phrase Edward Bullough uses to describe art in general seems particularly applicable to fiction: it gives us a "sudden view of things from their reverse, usually unnoticed side." [24]

In terms of content this means most obviously that fiction makes restitution to us for some of our instinctual deprivations. It emphasizes "sex" to augment the meager satisfactions available through sanctioned channels and to allay our guilt feelings about our frequent transgressions of those sanctions, either in deed or in desire. It gives expression and outlet to aggressive tendencies which we are expected to hold in strict leash though they are covertly encouraged by our competitive culture. The present vogue of detective stories and melodramas has here its explanation. It is equally important to realize that fiction provides an outlet for idealistic and contemplative tendencies thwarted in our daily experience; in a phrase of Kenneth Burke's, it is a "corrective of the practical."

---

[23] This is most obviously true of the novel, which, as D. H. Lawrence pungently maintains, is the most difficult of all media to fool. "Somehow, you sweep the ground a bit too clear in the poem or the drama, and you let the human Word fly a bit too freely. Now in a novel there's always a tom-cat, a black tom-cat that pounces on the white dove of the Word, if the dove doesn't watch it; and there is a banana-skin to trip on; and you know there is a water-closet on the premises. All these things help to keep the balance." "The Novel," *The Later D. H. Lawrence* (New York: Knopf, 1952), p. 191.

[24] " 'Psychical Distance' as a Factor in Art and an Esthetic Principle," *A Modern Book of Esthetics*, edited by Melvin M. Rader (New York: Holt, 1935), p. 318. Cf. Havelock Ellis: ". . . when we think of a book proper, in the sense that a Bible means a book, we mean . . . a revelation of something that had remained latent, unconscious, perhaps even more or less intentionally repressed, within the writer's own soul, which is, ultimately, the soul of mankind." Preface to *The Dance of Life*.

"A great work of art," writes Louise Rosenblatt, "may provide us the opportunity to feel more profoundly and more generously, to perceive more fully the implications of experience, than the hurried and fragmentary conditions of life permit." [25] This is certainly the case, though as Chapter II reminded us, generosity and contemplation have even more formidable enemies than the ones Miss Rosenblatt names, notably the pressures upon us to live prudently and even selfishly.

Fiction, then, makes good certain omissions in our lives. It serves as a devil's advocate for tendencies in ourselves we may be afraid to defend; it depicts precisely those aspects of experience our fears cause us to scant. Out of the vast body of fiction available to us, from the past and the present, we choose those works which we believe will best perform this service for us, and our search is no less purposive because in large part it is pursued unconsciously. [26]

In its zeal to do justice to our repressed tendencies fiction is in constant danger of overstating the case for them. Particularly if it does this too directly, with a minimum of disguise and control—we think at once of such a writer as Henry Miller—it is likely to arouse aversion rather than pleasure. But it is not always easy to say whether a work of fiction or a reader is responsible for a failure of this sort. A work which in the perspective of time may seem well balanced may cause us to recoil because it insists on telling us more of the truth, above all more of the truth about ourselves, than we are prepared to accept. As Havelock Ellis declares in the passage of *The Dance of Life* from which I have already quoted, certain books "may have to knock again and again at the closed door of our hearts. 'Who is there?' we carelessly cry, and we cannot open the door; we bid the importunate stranger, whatever he may be, to go away; until, as in the apologue of the Persian mystic, at last we seem to hear the voice outside saying: 'It is thyself.' "

---

[25] *Literature as Exploration* (New York: Appleton, 1948), p. 45.
[26] Of course the choice of books is governed by other considerations also. Cf. Ch. VIII.

7

In emphasizing the tendency of fiction to plead the cause
of impulses we ourselves might hesitate to defend, we have
perhaps done it a disservice. For admirable as that tendency is,
it is no more than one aspect of a more general—but far more
elusive—characteristic. This is the tendency to see a problem
from every possible point of view, to balance demands, to harmonize claims and counter-claims. It is this characteristic
which we must now examine more closely. It lies close to the
very heart of fiction. More than any trait connected with content rather than form, it explains fiction's capacity to deal with
our problem in a manner which leaves us satisfied. We have
not yet analyzed the trait sufficiently to disclose its underlying roots or to illustrate the way in which it manifests itself.
We have not even given it a name.

Nor can we do so yet. We can, however, make a more determined effort to describe the characteristic, utilizing the help
of various critics who have been aware of it and sought to
define its essence. It is a product of what Keats meant by
Shakespeare's "negative capacity"—his willingness to tolerate
uncertainty and doubt, to take cognizance of viewpoints directly at variance with ones being proclaimed. In John
Dewey's terms, it is an outlook which "accepts life and experience in all its uncertainties, mystery, doubt and half-knowl-
edge and turns that experience upon itself to deepen and intensify its own qualities." It is what F. Scott Fitzgerald had in
mind when he declared that "The test of a first-rate intelligence is the ability to hold two opposed ideas in the mind at
the same time, and still maintain the ability to function." Lionel Trilling, who recognizes the importance of the tendency
in fiction generally, has explained why it is invaluable in the
novel of social purpose: the novelist who takes sides, who
shows for example that an excluded group has a different and
better ethic than the excluding group, may not be able "to
muster the satirical ambivalence toward both groups which
marks the good novel even when it has a social *parti pris*." [27]

[27] *The Liberal Imagination* (New York: Viking, 1950), p. 261.

The tendency we are seeking to understand has perhaps been most beautifully described by Yeats in "Per Amica Silentia Lunae." The search of the poet, Yeats maintains, must be not so much for the self as for the anti-self, the antithetical self, for poetry arises out of a kind of a quarrel with ourselves. "We must not make a false faith by hiding from our thoughts the causes of doubt. . . . Neither must we create, by hiding ugliness, a false beauty as our offering to the world."

In the essay, "Pure and Impure Poetry," to which reference has already been made, Robert Penn Warren has explained why a false beauty achieved by concealing ugliness cannot satisfy a mature intelligence. Exponents of pure poetry assume that poetry inheres in some particular essence from which a long (but varying) list of elements—meaning, complicated images, narrative, irony, subjective elements—must be excluded; it seeks to "over-spiritualize nature." Impure poetry, in order to be faithful to the complexities of any subject with which it deals, admits anything in human experience which is relevant. Indeed, it deliberately takes cognizance of a variety of attitudes—including, perhaps, even cynical ones —toward whatever experience it celebrates, so that the finished poem will not be vulnerable to attack from some disregarded point of view; as Warren puts it, it tries to "come to terms with Mercutio." The impure poem "arises from a recalcitrant and contradictory context." It invites resistances and achieves its goodness by overcoming them; its goodness is "earned." We can see at once why a resolution achieved in this manner would be more likely to satisfy us than one achieved by ignoring the perverse voice in us which so often objects, "No! It's just the other way around." We prefer impure to pure poetry for the same reason that we feel that no virtue can be regarded as trustworthy and no conviction as durable until they have been tested.

Fiction is perhaps more "impure" than poetry. Lionel Trilling's statement about the novel, that it is "the literary form to which the virtues of understanding and forgiveness [are] indigenous," [28] can perhaps be applied to fiction in general.

[28] *Ibid.*, p. 222.

The virtues Mr. Trilling names make themselves felt, often despite the conscious attention of writers, in some of the great verse narratives which antedate the flowering of the novel form. The classical example is Milton's treatment of Satan in *Paradise Lost*. But Milton vacillates also, Maud Bodkin points out, in his treatment of Eve, picturing her now as an innocent victim, now as a culpable agent. Indeed, "the whole course of . . . *Paradise Lost*," Miss Bodkin writes, ". . . seems to indicate a profoundly felt division and tension of the soul between loyalty and revolt—loyalty to an ideal, thought of as the will of God expressed both in conscience and in the history of the world, and on the other hand, a revolt of passion and sensibility against this ideal." [29] Throughout *Archetypal Patterns in Poetry* Miss Bodkin reminds us of many similar examples—of Virgil's justice to Dido, despite his loyalty to the patriarchal ideal, of Dante's sympathy with Paolo and Francesca.

Many additional examples of the same general character will immediately occur to any reader of fiction—Cervantes' treatment of Don Quixote, Richardson's incapacity to deny Lovelace and his most persuasive heroine, Clarissa, their vitality and appeal. "That complicated balance of elements which is necessary for good fiction," writes Joseph Wood Krutch, "seems usually to have been achieved by the imagination of a writer whose mind was to some extent divided against itself." [30] All the examples given so far would tend to suggest that the balance stems from a conflict between the conscious intention of the writer and his unconscious sympathies. But we do not know, nor does it matter, whether the balance always arises in this fashion. Probably a great deal of conscious vacillation helped determine Shakespeare's attitude toward his tragic heroes, Tolstoy's toward Anna Karenina, James's toward Isabel Archer, Joyce's toward Gabriel Conroy. What is certain is that these characters are presented to us from many different, and opposed, points of view. When a single view-

---

[29] *Archetypal Patterns in Poetry*, pp. 261-62.
[30] *Five Masters* (New York: Jonathan Cape & Harrison Smith, 1930), p. 165.

point predominates, particularly if it is a conscious and narrowly moralistic one, the fiction writer is likely, in Krutch's phrase, to win "a lugubrious triumph over his own art." [31]

The most passionate affirmations of literature, it appears, show an awareness of all the considerations which can be urged against them. The awareness may be implicit rather than explicit, sketched in rather than developed—in Shakespeare's Sonnet 116 it is crowded into a single cry, "O, no!"; but unless the awareness is there a work will lack tension and excitement and its affirmations will carry little conviction. The characterizations, the value systems of great literature, certainly of great narrative art, are all pervaded by what I like to think of as *a sense of the opposite*. The underlying attitude is one of poised and sustained ambivalence.

8

Let us see how this attitude manifests itself in a particular story, using for purposes of illustration "The Birthmark" by Nathaniel Hawthorne. This is not a simple story, for Hawthorne was not a simple man, yet Brooks and Warren seem justified in calling it a parable—a kind of story, according to their definition, "which makes an obvious point or has a rather obvious symbolic meaning." [32] Hawthorne himself says that the tale has "a deeply impressive moral."

"The Birthmark" is the story of a brilliant scientist, Aylmer, who became obsessed with the idea of removing a birthmark, which rather resembles a tiny crimson hand, from the cheek of his beautiful young wife, Georgiana. Aware of her husband's abhorrence of this flaw, of his desire to have her perfect, Georgiana agrees to let him attempt to remove the birthmark, an attempt which he feels is certain to succeed. But it develops that the crimson stain, superficial as it seems, has clutched its grasp into Georgiana's being with a strength of which Aylmer had no conception. Nevertheless, he persists, and develops a draught which to his "irrepressible ecstasy" removes the birthmark from his wife's cheek. But

[31] *Ibid.*, p. 166.
[32] *Understanding Fiction*, p. 607.

his ecstasy lasts but for a second, for "as the last crimson tint of the birthmark—that sole token of human imperfection" fades from Georgiana's cheek, she dies. "The fatal hand had grappled with the mystery of life, and was the bond by which an angelic spirit kept itself in union with a mortal frame."

The most obvious meaning of "The Birthmark," the "deeply impressive moral," is implicit in the story, but so that we cannot possibly fail to see it, is heavily underscored. We cannot have perfection. Georgiana's birthmark represents "the fatal flaw of humanity which Nature, in one shape or another, stamps ineffaceably on all her productions, either to imply that they are temporary and finite, or that their perfection must be wrought by toil and pain." By refusing to resign himself to "the limitations and imperfections of nature" [33] Aylmer rejects, in the words of his dying wife, "the best the earth could offer."

The story has a second meaning, which is also so heavily emphasized that it is hard to believe that it was not consciously intended.[34] What can be the specific symbolic significance of this crimson mark, which sometimes called to mind a tiny bloody hand—a mark which some of Georgiana's lovers had found attractive and which Aylmer, more spiritual than they, only became aware of after his marriage? Hawthorne does not leave us in much doubt. "The crimson hand expressed the ineludible gripe in which mortality clutches the highest and purest of earthly mould, degrading them into kindred with the lowest, and even with the very brutes, like whom their visible frames return to dust." The crimson mark symbolizes sexuality,[35] and Aylmer is one of those men, described by Freud,[36] who sharply disassociate heavenly and earthly love, the tender and the sensual. Such men strive "to keep their sensuality out of contact with the objects they love." [37] Just so, Aylmer

[33] *Ibid.*, p. 104.

[34] Needless to say, however, so long as the meaning is demonstrably present, it does not matter whether Hawthorne was conscious of putting it there.

[35] More specifically still, it may represent female sexuality—that is, be a castration symbol. I am indebted to Dr. Charles Fisher for this suggestion.

[36] "The Most Prevalent Form of Degradation in Erotic Life," *Collected Papers*, Vol. IV.

[37] *Ibid.*, p. 207.

rejects his wife's sexuality, ultimately with physical revulsion; and she regards his attitude as an affront.

What sort of man is this, who in his pride insists on perfection and in his refinement recoils from his wife's femininity? In reaching a judgment it might seem helpful to get outside the frame of the story for a minute and, accepting the story as a true account, try to imagine in what terms Aylmer's character and conduct would have been described by the gossips of the town. But we do not have to do this; the adverse judgments appear in the story itself. Aylmer's laboratory assistant, Aminadab, who, "with his vast strength, his shaggy hair . . . and the indescribable earthiness that incrusted him . . . seemed to represent man's physical nature" declares that if Georgiana were his wife he would "never part with that birthmark." And Georgiana herself, though docile and unembittered, bitingly indicts her husband's restless spirit. She could not, she says, hope to satisfy him for "longer than one moment . . . for his spirit was ever on the march, ever ascending, and each instant required something that was beyond the scope of the instant before."

These viewpoints are present in the story, *but they are not the only viewpoints and they are not Hawthorne's.* They are kept in poised tension with other viewpoints which show, as Brooks and Warren put it, that "The author is sympathetic to [Aylmer], and obviously sees in his ruinous experiment a certain nobility." [38] The very speech of Georgiana's from which I have already quoted contains other statements that, though not without a tinge of irony, predominantly express understanding and admiration of her idealistic husband. "Her heart exulted, while it trembled, at his honorable love—so pure and lofty that it would accept nothing less than perfection nor miserably make itself contented with an earthlier nature than he had dreamed of." It is clear, furthermore, as Brooks and Warren also point out, that if Aminadab provides a sort of measuring stick for Aylmer's folly he provides one also for his nobility. Despite his shortcomings, Aylmer, the intellectual and spiritual man, is the hero of the tale. It is difficult

[38] *Understanding Fiction*, p. 105.

to resist the surmise that he represents certain aspects of his creator. Perhaps Hawthorne, too, found it hard to accept sensuality in woman. We may be sure in any case that he knew what it meant to strive for perfection and find himself miserably thwarted. There are unmistakable autobiographical allusions in the story. "Perhaps every man of genius in whatever sphere might recognize the image of his own experience in Aylmer's journal."

But Hawthorne does not attempt to excuse the folly of Aylmer's course either; on the contrary, he mercilessly exposes it and shows its disastrous consequences. His attitude is not a condemnatory one, but neither is it indulgent. If it were, we may be sure, we would not be pleased: we would regard the story as a form of special pleading, perhaps for some weakness of Hawthorne's, acknowledged or unacknowledged.

9

It is clear enough that Hawthorne was both attracted and repelled by Aylmer; his attitude reflects a delicate balance. But why we should place a high value upon such an attitude is not immediately clear. There is still something a little puzzling about the attitude itself.

In life itself, it immediately occurs to us, the kind of interested impartiality which is indigenous to fiction is extremely rare. By a very indirect route the greatest religious and moral leaders—Hosea, for example, and Jesus—achieve judgments which are no less perfectly balanced. Aware of tendencies in themselves over which they have triumphed, they refuse, even when those tendencies have spent their force, to condemn those who succumb to them. But the attitude of fiction is not a judging attitude at all. It has so little in common with the kind of moral evaluations one commonly encounters that, in trying to describe it, one is tempted to search for some antonym of the word "moral." But then the attitude is uncommon in every area of our experience. It represents a balance of forces which is evidently extremely hard to achieve or maintain. When there is a narcissistic investment in another person, we tend to overestimate his virtues and capacities and deny or minimize his faults. When we are antagonistic, we do just the opposite—overlook good qualities and exaggerate weaknesses. We are correct in assuming that the kind of exposure of a person's failings which is characteristic of fiction is usually in the service of aggression.

In trying to clarify my understanding of the balanced attitude of fiction, I kept returning again and again, at first without perceiving why, to what is perhaps the most beautiful of all Freud's papers, the six-page note on "Humour." [39] In that special form of the comic called humor, which Freud distinguishes sharply from wit, the humorist, he suggests, "[adopts] toward the other the attitude of an adult toward a child, recognizing and smiling at the triviality of the interests and sufferings which seem to the child so big." [40] The humorist identifies himself to some extent with the father. In that very important form of humor "in which a man adopts a humorous attitude towards himself in order to ward off possible suffering," [41] the situation is not so very different: the superego, the internal representative of the parental function, strives to comfort the ego. " 'Look here!' " it says in effect, " 'This is all that this seemingly dangerous world amounts to. Child's play—the very thing to jest about!' " [42]

In fiction no such comforting takes place, nor is there usually any attempt to minimize the issues, but all the same we sense some sort of parallel. It is evident, in the first place, that the same two institutions of the mind are concerned: the ego and superego share an interest in the remorseless facing of truth which fiction insists upon, and it is, of course, the superego which requires that transgressions be punished. We suspect, too, that some sort of communication is taking place between the superego and the ego. Only one thing prevents us from divining its nature immediately: our tendency to think of the superego as stern and punitive. But the example

[39] *Collected Papers,* Vol. V.
[40] *Ibid.,* p. 218.
[41] *Ibid.,* p. 218.
[42] *Ibid.,* p. 220.

of humor reminds us that the superego inherits the kindly as well as the harsh aspects of the parents.[43] Once we realize this, we can readily reconstruct the nature of the intrapsychic interchange which the attitude of fiction stimulates: it is a kind of confession based upon acceptance and love. The ego withholds nothing and it asks for nothing, neither for extenuation of punishment nor even for forgiveness. The superego voluntarily gives the ego something it evidently values even more than these, understanding and the assurance of continued love. It notes the strivings of the ego which have gotten it into difficulty, but without revulsion or censure. Like a fond parent, the superego assures the ego: "I see your faults very clearly. But I do not condemn you. And I love you still."

Literature itself suggests how much such an attitude means to us. With his dying breath Othello beseeches precisely the kind of justice fiction tries to render:

> I pray you, in your letters,
> When you shall these unlucky deeds relate,
> Speak of me as I am. Nothing extenuate,
> Nor set down aught in malice.

We want the truth about ourselves to be known by those who love us. We long to be accepted as we are, *to tell the bad and still be loved*. Perhaps because it carries overtones of experiences in which, after estrangement, we were embraced by a beloved parent, such an attitude produces in us a rapturous tranquillity, in which there is a faint erotic element. This response, like the attitude which engenders it, has been precisely described in fiction itself. It is incarnated in Melville's *Billy Budd*. Although the relationship between Billy and Captain Vere and the sentence passed upon the young sailor have definite sexual significance, at the deepest level *Billy Budd* is a legend of reconciliation between an erring son and a stern but loving father-figure. No less instinctively than he had recoiled from Claggart's hostile assault, Billy submits to his sentence because he feels that Captain Vere has decreed it in

---

[43] Freud's paper predicts that other ways in which these kindly aspects assert themselves would be discovered.

love. Billy's expression as he sleeps before his execution makes the Chaplain who has gone to comfort him realize that he "had no consolation to proffer which could result in a peace transcending that which he beheld"; and Billy goes to his death saying, "God bless Captain Vere!"

Our own reaction to the "punishment," physical or verbal, the world inflicts upon us is seldom like Billy Budd's, but that is because we sense the hostility which ordinarily underlies it; it is against this that we recoil. We can accept censure, even punishment, from those of whose love we feel assured, and the attainment of accord with them brings us a rich kind of peace. *And this entire process can be recapitulated within the self.*

In trying to understand a single attribute of fiction we have almost inadvertently stumbled upon one of the most important kinds of gratifications it is capable of giving. In addition to satisfying various component parts of the personality, as punishment, for example, satisfies the superego, fiction can heal intrapsychic tension. The characteristic of fiction we are considering is integrative. The facets of experience and variety of viewpoints fiction strives to take into account can be conceived as representing the conflicting claims of the several parts of the psyche. In trying to balance those claims fiction is engaging in one of the activities which occupies the ego itself. And fiction works under ideal conditions. In consequence, it may take account of factors and perceive possibilities of achieving harmony which the ego might overlook. Through reading, these additional possibilities become available to us. In view of the mind's capacity for analogizing, it is reasonable to suppose that they will frequently have relevance for our own emotional problems. The reading of fiction may be of very considerable help to the ego in its own integrative activity.

Chapter IV *The Appeals to the Parts of the Psyche*

Narrative art, then, deals with and attempts to resolve our emotional conflicts in a way which does full justice to all the factors which are relevant. In trying to understand why we place such a high value on this characteristic, we have perhaps described those factors too exclusively in one set of terms. Fiction mirrors, we have said, the struggle between the kind of considerations to which we give obeisance in our daily living and the kind we tend to disregard and even repress. But it also mirrors the struggle between id, ego and superego, and between the pleasure principle and the reality principle—between our wishes and the forces, internal and external, opposed to their fulfilment. To some extent these are overlapping categories, but each of them may contribute something a little different to our understanding of fiction. Sometimes it is advantageous to approach the same story from more than one point of view.

For example, the aspect of "The Birthmark" on which we have focussed our attention thus far, the skill with which Hawthorne has presented Aylmer and his experiment in a balanced light, functions as "means" rather than as "end": it is a device to insure our neutrality while a portentous drama is played out. This drama centers around the clash between two deep-seated wishes and our defenses against them. Without identifying the forces on each side, we could not fully account for our response to "The Birthmark."

The more buried of the wishes is a variant of the desire, discussed in Chapter II, that the mother be virginal; here the wish is that the wife, who we may suspect is to some extent a mother-surrogate, should be free of the "stain" of sexuality. The wish which emerges more clearly may seem quite foreign to us in the form in which it is expressed. Do we have any desire to achieve perfection or to make those around us perfect? Perhaps not; perhaps few of us have impulses as unreasonable as this. On the other hand, it is a commonplace that we may be unduly sensitive about the faults—perhaps we are not always even justified in calling them that—of members of our family and others close to us. Cannot this sensitivity be readily equated with the desire to have them different in this or that respect? Frequently enough we even express our dissatisfaction, in effect goading them to change. Aylmer's desire to make his wife perfect represents no more than an extension of a tendency present to some degree in nearly everyone. The extension facilitates our understanding of the tendency. It is justified, too, perhaps, because the tendency is particularly likely to assert itself without check toward those whose relation to us may involve some degree of subordination—toward women and children. Every parent and teacher has probably experienced the impulse to mold a child this way or that—an impulse not easy to subdue even when one senses that the changes desired are not in accord with the child's natural bent. We are, of course, more cautious about trying to influence adults, but, particularly if we have a wife as tractable as Georgiana, we may find ways of letting her know which of her personality traits endear her to us and which ones we would like her to efface.

However, our defenses against the wishes dealt with in "The Birthmark" are as powerful as the wishes themselves. The wishes arouse anxiety—so much anxiety that, instead of being approached from the point of view of the impulses it seeks to satisfy, the story could be regarded as an attempt to examine and reinforce certain dim but intense fears. The impulse to overspiritualize love or woman is opposed to our knowledge of reality, which tells us that any such attempt is foredoomed to failure. Fears that are more indistinct, but no less strong, warn us against tampering with the personality of others. We have some premonition—perhaps we know from experience—that good and bad are intermingled and that efforts to change a person, even when successful, may have calamitous consequences we had not foreseen; we may chasten a child only to find that at the same time we have made him less joyous, less enterprising and less creative. We know, too, that attempts to change people can lead to a kind of death—death of their love for us. We may be deterred by still vaguer dreads—feelings that in seeking to change another we are arrogating to ourselves a God-like function, which we have neither the right nor the wisdom to assume. The human personality and the human body are ringed by a sacred sheath, which we fear to violate.

So powerful are these fears that our dominant reaction in life to the kind of experiment Aylmer undertakes would probably be one of abhorrence. The ultimate purpose of Hawthorne's attempt to present Aylmer in balanced perspective is to quiet our fears so that the wishes which motivate his experiment, which are also urgent, can be given their opportunity. Aylmer's sincerity and idealism give us a sense of kinship with him. We see that the plan takes shape gradually in his mind, almost against his conscious intention. We are reassured by the fact that he loves Georgiana and feels confident that his attempt to remove the birthmark will succeed. Thus at the same time that we recoil we can identify with Aylmer and through him act out some of our secret desires.

Those desires are frustrated—or we should say, to be faithful to the story, fulfilled only momentarily and at a tragic cost. Behind this resolution we can discern narrative art's respect for the reality principle. Regularly in fiction—perhaps more regularly than in life—mistakes and transgressions are punished. The punishments satisfy not only the superego but the ego; they assure it that fiction is not tempted to disregard the dearly bought knowledge that sooner or later we are likely to be called to account for our misdeeds and our mistakes.

In many other ways fiction shows its regard for the reality principle. Even when wishes are fulfilled, the obstacles to their fulfilment are given full weight. Indeed, great fiction may be more resolute than the facts warrant in its rejection of easy successes. Coincidences sometimes occur in life, and fate and accidents sometimes smile upon our purposes. As D. W. Harding writes: "Everyone has a bit of luck from time to time: the three miraculous wishes provide a dramatic compression of that possibility. . . . Anyone might be downtrodden and finally be given a helping hand and succeed in turning the tables; a fairy godmother is a vivid way of saying how delightful that would be." [1] It is to be noted, however, that the examples are chosen from fairy stories. It is surprising how infrequently great fiction utilizes instances of unexpected good fortune, except perhaps for its own ironic or bittersweet purposes.[2] Unexpected bequests, opportune introductions, accidents which throw together a young man and the woman he desires seldom occur in the fiction to which we accord our respect. It is only meretricious fiction which gratifies wishes readily.

If fiction is as grudging as this, how, it may be asked, does it represent an improvement upon life. It may appear that the claims of the pleasure principle are being scanted. But closer examination reveals that even such a story as "The Birthmark" affords us more gratification than may at first be apparent. The story not only gives expression to impulses which are ordinarily repressed; it gives them a sympathetic hearing— an opportunity to show whether they can be gratified without causing trouble or pain. There are obvious gains in being able to conduct tests of this kind with no more danger and no greater expenditure of effort than is involved in reading a story. Furthermore, even though the resolution of "The Birthmark" is negative, it affords us satisfaction. It confirms the wisdom of the ego in keeping a rein on the impulses to which Aylmer succumbed; this, perhaps, must be scored as a victory for the reality principle. But in another way the outcome of the story satisfies the pleasure principle as well,

---

[1] "The Role of the Onlooker," *Scrutiny*, VI, 1937.

[2] By eliminating the extraneous factor of economic pressure, the bequest made to Isabel Archer sets the stage for a more rigorous test of her judgment and sensibility. Of course, by making her attractive to such a man as Osmond, it also exposes her to a kind of test to which she would not otherwise have been subjected. To take another kind of example, the discovery, by the little clerk of Maupassant's wonderful story, "The Jewels," that the jewelry in his possession is genuine and fabulously valuable is a prelude to the realization that his dead wife, to whom he is still devoted, had been unfaithful.

or perhaps we should say the entire personality. Hawthorne has carefully prepared us for the probability that Aylmer's experiment will fail. The ending of the story satisfies certain emotional expectations, like a note for which our ears are waiting.

The example reminds us that narrative art has, as it were, certain internal resources it can exploit for our pleasure even when, in terms of external reference, the satisfactions it can offer are limited. How rich those resources are we shall perhaps better appreciate after we have completed our consideration of form. But in terms of content, also, fiction strives to give us as much pleasure as it can without resorting to falsehoods: the satisfaction of our desires is the propelling impulse, the reality principle is the restraining one. Fiction endeavors to gratify as many of our longings as possible, but the very effort to teach us how they can be reconciled with one another and with reality compels it to take cognizance of the ineluctable limits of the human situation.[3]

We fail to realize how much wish fulfilment occurs in narrative art because the wishes underlying many stories escape conscious notice. We are, of course, aware of the extent to which popular fiction satisfies erotic or ambitious desires. But, as the example of "The Birthmark" may suggest, in the greatest fiction wishes are ordinarily disguised with subtle

[3] I am aware that this formulation somewhat resembles I. A. Richards'; e.g., "The experiences of the artist, those at least which give value to his work, represent conciliations of impulses which in most minds are still confused, intertrammelled and conflicting. His work is the ordering of what in most minds is disordered. . . ." There can be no more important service than this, Richards believes, for "the conduct of life is throughout an attempt to organise impulses so that success is obtained for the greatest number or mass of them, for the most important and the weightiest set. . . ." While some sacrifices may be necessary in the interest of stability, a systematization must be judged "by the extent of the loss, the range of impulses thwarted or starved. . . . That organisation which is least wasteful of human possibilities is . . . the best." *Principles of Literary Criticism* (New York: Harcourt, Brace, 1934), p. 61 and *passim*. I believe that these insights, which underlie Richards' entire theory, are valid and extremely valuable. Unfortunately, Richards lacked a psychology which would enable him to specify in sufficient detail how they apply to literature. His language sometimes suggests, too, that the achievement of a better systematization is a more rational and conscious endeavor than I conceive it to be.

care. Certain wishes, furthermore, are inherently difficult to identify.

We seldom pause to consider, for example, how many of our wishes are essentially negative in character. Dr. Lawrence S. Kubie has called attention to the tendency of some relatively complicated temperaments to "react to disappointment with bitterness and irony, which expresses itself in an effort to belittle that which is unobtainable. Much of the so-called 'classical' erotic literature satisfied the needs of such readers."[4] This sort of "sour grapes" psychology may be a factor in our response to many narrative works which emphasize disillusioning aspects of experience or the need for contenting oneself with a very modest sort of happiness. It may lurk, for example, behind the response of some readers to the subdued expectations of Jane Austen's heroines. As Geoffrey Gorer has pointed out, in Jane Austen's novels the brilliant young man is bound *not* to succeed; the heroine always marries a reliable but much less exciting man.[5] It seems reasonable to assume that at times Miss Austen must have longed for a husband her equal in intelligence and sensibility; if so, one unconscious determinant of her writing may have been the need to assure herself that, if she *had* married, she would have probably been disappointed in her husband. Whether or not the biographical surmise is correct, readers whose situation and sensibility resemble Jane Austen's might extract some such consolation from her novels. For other readers, of course, her heroes will seem quite splendid and desirable enough.

"The Poor Fiddler," a story by the Austrian writer Grillparzer, which Hanns Sachs has analyzed,[6] suggests that even the theme of failure may conceal wishful elements and perverse satisfactions. The hero of the story is a young man who fails to pass a crucial examination in which he has to recite some Latin verses. Though he knows them well, he stumbles over a single word, then becomes confused and panicky. The

---

[4] "God's Little Acre: An Analysis," *Saturday Review of Literature*, XI, No. 19 (Nov. 24, 1934).

[5] "The Myth in Jane Austen," *American Imago*, 2, 1941. Reprinted in *Art and Psychoanalysis*, edited by William Phillips (New York: Criterion, 1957).

[6] "What Would Have Happened If . . ." *American Imago*, 3, 1946.

boy's father, an important, ambitious man, feels so humiliated that he stops his son's studies. The boy becomes a humble copying clerk, then sinks deeper and deeper in the world, finally becoming a common street fiddler. However, he never loses his integrity.

Now, as a boy Grillparzer himself stumbled over a word in a public examination—but without any of the unfortunate consequences which befell his hero. His father sent the professor a present; young Grillparzer was passed and thus made eligible to enter the University. He went on to become director of the State Library and a famous man of letters. To some extent, perhaps, "The Poor Fiddler" expresses feelings of guilt and anxiety—Grillparzer's doubts about whether he was worthy of the honors he had received. But a wish lies concealed behind the anxiety: the man who fails does not have to compete; he does not constantly have to prove himself and exert himself. Sachs cites biographical evidence to show how deeply Grillparzer hated the petty conflicts, frustrations and trivialities of middle-class life. Many readers share his hatred. Like Grillparzer, in actuality they may be unwilling to surrender status to achieve a more honest and less arduous life, but like him also they may have persistent impulses to make just such an exchange.

2

We have saved until last the most useful and inclusive means of describing the subject-matter satisfactions offered by fiction—the way in which it strives to please the component parts of the personality and harmonize their demands. Not until much later in this book can we hope to do this subject full justice. Subject-matter appeals to id, ego and superego are dynamically interrelated with those offered by form, and we shall not become acquainted with one of the most important appeals narrative art makes to the ego until we discuss tragedy and shall not perceive how directly it sometimes represents the psychic institutions until we discuss overdetermination. However, we can begin to make good our claim that at its best fiction (and, we may say, art in general) offers us a kind of satisfaction seldom obtainable either in life itself or through other forms of "auxiliary constructions"—a satisfaction based on the richest possible fulfilment of all our emotional needs.

We have already considered some of the more important ways in which fiction satisfies the ego. We have seen that it is no less strict than the ego itself in considering the demands of reality and no less intent than the ego upon striving for integration. Even when fiction gratifies wishes, it does not neglect reality considerations. These secure representation, even in fairy stories, as the dangers and difficulties which stand in the way of wish fulfilment; in more mature art they are represented by various internal impediments as well, by doubts and inhibitions. The complex harmonizing activity of narrative art is a kind of subtle tribute to the ego's concern with integration. At times at least, it has been suggested, the reading of fiction may help the ego in dealing with its own problems, calling attention to considerations and ways of resolving conflicts the ego may have overlooked. It is possible that to some degree the reading of great fiction increases the ego's capacity to deal with any problem, just as exercise strengthens the body for any physical endeavor.

Many stories also appeal to the ego by presenting ideas and perceptions which are meant to be consciously apprehended. Often these stories appeal to us primarily as observers. In any case they bring us some knowledge of value. Even this knowledge is seldom devoid of emotional repercussions, however, and these stories may also appeal to us as participants, at least up to a point. Hemingway's "The Killers" may be taken as an example of such a story. Originally, like most fiction, it attempts to involve us emotionally. Some of the power of the story derives from our identifying with Nick Adams and feeling evil and terror through him, as though for the first time. Even Ole Anderson's acceptance of the horror awaiting him is first experienced through Nick's consciousness. But by the end of the story we are outside of Nick, observing the contrast between his reaction, that of youth, and Ole Anderson's, that of age. We feel this contrast as much as we perceive it. We may not put our perception into words. But conscious awareness of the "meaning" of "The Killers" would not jeopardize its effect upon us and might enhance it, if only by disclosing the story's underlying unity.[7]

Besides offering the ego as much satisfaction as possible, fiction must adopt certain measures to neutralize the objections the ego or superego might raise to the gratification of repudiated impulses. The ego and superego are simultaneously appeased when the gratification is somehow justified. Both disguise, which must be regarded as a function of form, and the nature of the subject matter itself may contribute to this end. In children's stories it is often quite easy to see how the two factors cooperate. For example, in *The Red Toad* (mentioned in Chapter II) the real object of hostility, the "bad," fearful, sadistic father, is carefully concealed from view. Then we are given a villain whose evil nature and nefarious purposes are so heavily emphasized that neither the hatred the good characters feel for him nor his ultimate dispatch by the heroine arouses the slightest discomfort. Similarly, in "The Birthmark," the underlying significance of Aylmer's desire to remove the crimson mark is concealed and, as a further precaution, the experiment is made to appear reasonable by the prospect of its success. *Oedipus the King* dispenses with disguise, but it is made clear that Oedipus' crimes were committed without his knowledge and against his conscious intention, at the dictate of Fate. *Hamlet*, which may be regarded as a later treatment of the same thematic material, employs a particularly subtle blending of concealment and justification. The hostile and jealous feelings toward the father are not so much disguised as explicitly denied: Hamlet expresses nothing but love and veneration for his real father. The negative feelings receive passionate expression, but they are displaced onto two paternal figures Hamlet is given ample warrant for despising, Claudius, the murderer of

---

[7] As Brooks and Warren have pointed out, it is an easy story to misinterpret. See their analysis in *Understanding Fiction*, pp. 316-324.

his father, and Polonius, who as the King's counselor and
Ophelia's father has interfered in Hamlet's affairs.[8]

3

While it is primarily through form that narrative art seeks to
conciliate and satisfy the superego,[9] content, too, makes an important contribution. It has already been mentioned that fiction
is more rigorous than life itself in insisting that misdeeds and
mistakes be punished. In this and other respects fiction behaves much more like the superego itself than it does the
external apparatus man has developed to apprehend and punish wrongdoing. Unlike the police, for example, it insists that
even psychic offenses be punished. Some of the greatest narrative works, from *Hamlet* to *The Trial*, are predominantly
concerned with psychic offenses; the prohibited instinctual
satisfaction Hamlet and K. secure during that portion of their
lives which Shakespeare and Kafka chronicle does not fully
justify their punishment; but in each case the nature of the
satisfaction enables us to reconstruct the original source of
the character's guilt, which is psychic in origin. *The Brothers
Karamazov* is another narrative work in which illicit impulses
are treated with as much severity as their execution, and here
this course is inferentially defended; from one point of view
the novel can be regarded as a kind of exposition of the close
connections, the imperceptible gradations, between wish and
act. Dreiser's *An American Tragedy* exploits the same theme.

Fiction also takes the same attitude as conscience to acts of
whose guilty nature the perpetrator was unaware. It does not
matter that Oedipus did not realize that the man he killed was
Laius, his father, and the woman he married was Jocasta, his
mother; he must be punished all the same. Nor does the fact
that Aylmer's experiment had a specious reasonableness extenuate his guilt. The vast majority of the offenses with which
fiction deals are variants of Oedipus' or Aylmer's; the deliberate Macbeth-like transgression is comparatively rare. In passing it should be remarked that the regularity with which

[8] Cf. the longer discussion of the play, p. 107 ff.
[9] See Chapter V.

offenses of the first type are punished reveals something highly significant about the nature of response to fiction. The punishment must satisfy some emotional craving, and if we want even misdeeds committed in error, or apparently warranted, to be penalized, it can only mean that one portion of our minds perceives that the deeds are less innocent than they seem. Evidently the vindication offered satisfies only our conscious intelligence; our unconscious, like the unconscious of the protagonist, discerns the unsanctioned satisfaction which is secured through the apparently blameless acts. We have here a kind of internal confirmation of the existence of unconscious response.

Fiction tries to satisfy the superego not simply by refusing to let any offense go unpunished but by trying to impose the "right" punishment—one commensurate with the offense in severity and appropriate with it in nature. We unhesitatingly discredit fiction in which punishment seems perfunctory or tacked on, a mere gesture of appeasement for the instinctual gratification which is present. In the greatest fiction the punishment seems organically related to the offense it penalizes. Othello's murder of Desdemona is his crime and, perceived in a new light when he becomes aware of her innocence, his punishment. Since he has killed, however, his suicide is necessary also, to balance the scales exactly. By murdering a sovereign who has demonstrated his goodness and his love for him, Macbeth has disturbed nature; and unnatural events—sleeplessness, madness, the suicide of his lady, as well as the circumstances connected with his own death—mark his undoing. Hamlet's death seems rather loosely connected with the previous action of the play, but because he has gone about his assignment in a vacillating fashion it is appropriate that the events by which he is destroyed should be a mixture of the necessary and the apparently fortuitous.

In our culture the superego is peculiarly subject to a morbidity, a tendency to abuse its authority and deny absolution to the self no matter what renunciations it agrees to and what lacerations it accepts for its misdeeds. It is not surprising, therefore, that there is a great deal of fiction which appeals primarily, and in unbalanced fashion, to the superego, just as there is some which is not really concerned with anything but tickling the id. Sometimes the latter type of fiction masquerades as the former. Under cover of appeasing the superego it admits by the back door a great deal of instinctual gratification of a sadistic-masochistic nature. For example, in many stories, as in a lynching or for that matter a licit abuse of justice, the punishment is no more than an excuse for the release of hatred and vindictiveness. Still other stories heap calamities upon a hero or heroine for whom our sympathies are aroused, who is guilty perhaps of no more than one small misstep, and invite us to participate in an orgy of self-pity.

The meretriciousness of work which makes such covert appeals to the instincts is in most cases readily apparent. It is otherwise, I believe, with works which really cater to our sense of guilt. In our culture defenses against impulses enjoy so much respect that we are likely to stifle the suspicion that a work is unduly severe. Out of fear that we are too lenient we may instead acclaim its rigor. Yet I would maintain that some of the work of writers as highly regarded as Kafka, Joyce and Flaubert is marred by a tendency to judge human weaknesses too pitilessly.

When, identifying with the hero of a story, we have committed some transgression, we want to be punished; the punishment permits us to expiate our guilt. This is a legitimate satisfaction, of which the attempt to arouse excessive feelings of shame and guilt represents an abuse. The abuse is all the more regrettable because it interferes with what is perhaps the most important subject-matter satisfaction narrative art can offer the superego, the knowledge that other human beings are stirred by the same lusts and hatreds, the same vanity and pettiness, of which we are ashamed in ourselves. As Hanns Sachs has emphasized, the reading of fiction permits us to share and thus relieve our guilt. Without being soft, it serves as a counterpoise to the tendency, to which we are all too prone, to judge ourselves with undue severity; it helps us to see our weaknesses in perspective.

Two other ways in which narrative art makes obeisance

to the superego should be briefly noted. Fiction may invest potentially offensive material with a second level of significance designed to placate the superego. On some deep level the execution of K. in *The Trial* is a passive homosexual capitulation to the feared but longed-for father, but it is at the same time a merciless punishment. The sentencing and execution of Billy Budd represents the same kind of blending of acceptable and inacceptable elements.[10]

Finally, just as there are some stories whose predominant appeal to us, as spectators rather than participants, is to the ego, so there are some, such as Chekov's "Grief," whose predominant appeal is to the superego. Insofar as we identify with the cab-driver, Iona Potapov, we experience his despair and his frustration as if it were our own. On this level the story gives us a rather "schmaltzy" kind of masochistic gratification; it permits us to feel sorry for ourselves. But insofar as "Grief" appeals to us as spectators, it arouses our sympathy for Iona Potapov and leads us to compare ourselves with the people he encounters. We would not, we tell ourselves, treat him with the selfish indifference they display; the story gives us an opportunity to assert our goodness and largeness of heart.

4

The fact that fiction seeks to gratify our emotions leaves some people vaguely uneasy. They cannot, of course, deny that *some* fiction does this: dust jackets and magazine covers disclose the connections between fiction and our aggressive tendencies and lusts. But a great deal of literary comment suggests that only fiction of the more vulgar sort concerns itself with such subject matter. Not only is the emotional content of great narrative works ignored; it is sometimes implied that great works have little to do with our desires and fears, that

---

[10] Cf. also Maud Bodkin's observation on "Sohrab and Rustum": "Seeing in the image of the river the vision of man's life and death as the whole poem has communicated it, we experience a death-craving akin to that of infant or neurotic for the mother, but in synthesis with the sentiment of a man's endurance. It is through such synthesis that crude instincts realize themselves anew in poetic vision." *Archetypal Patterns in Poetry*, p. 67.

they are great because they are preoccupied with other and higher things, with moral issues, let us say, or problems of form.

Once such a view secures formulation, its falsity is quickly apparent. The truth is that we regard as great only that fiction which provides us a lavish amount of emotional gratification, which satisfies our deepest and most primitive longings. The greatest narrative works deal with what might be called sacred crimes, transgressions of the tabus on which human society is founded; they deal with incest and parricide, cruelty of parents to children and children to parents, ruthless ambition and murder, betrayals and lust. This is, of course, only one of the factors which lead us to call certain works great. Precisely because they deal with such themes as these, it is essential that the works also possess excellence of form. We know, too, that fiction must contrive to satisfy our desires without slighting their "mighty opposites," the defenses we have erected against them. It not only depicts the punishment the satisfaction of our prohibited impulses entails but represents the obstacles they must surmount to secure satisfaction and, it may be, even expression. If the obstacles were slighted, a work would lack tension and, another quality on which we set great store, complexity. We shall see the extent to which complexity arises from the subterfuges and indirection to which impulses must sometimes resort to secure satisfaction.

But no matter what the difficulties, no matter what happens afterwards, the greatest narrative works give our leashed impulses their opportunity. On reflection it is obvious enough that various of our impulses secure satisfaction in *Madame Bovary* and *Anna Karenina*, *Romeo and Juliet* and *Antony and Cleopatra*, *Othello* and *Macbeth*, *Crime and Punishment* and *The Iliad*. They secure satisfaction, too, of a very rich sort, in works whose heroes are as apparently free of lust and averse to violence as Hamlet and Prince Myshkin.

In actuality Hamlet and Myshkin are tormented by impulses so violent and so repugnant to their idealistic nature that they are never acknowledged. How, then, do they make themselves known to us and secure vicarious gratification? The answer is a curious one: we never become consciously aware of them either, at any rate not before we have put down *Hamlet* and *The Idiot* and begun to dissect them as critics; the repudiated impulses are communicated to our unconscious minds while their existence is safeguarded from awareness; the illicit satisfaction is procured secretly and subterraneously, without the participation of consciousness.

We have already noted one of the devices by which this is accomplished in *Hamlet*, namely, displacement. Feelings are divorced from their real source and associated with something else in connection with which their avowal becomes permissible. As a result of the disassociation, feelings which, properly identified, would arouse abhorrence secure open and passionate expression. Another mechanism of "primary process" thinking,[11] "splitting," contributes to this result. The original father is decomposed into three principal figures, the Ghost, Claudius and Polonius. The rage and jealousy and fear felt for the father can be legitimately directed against Claudius, who has murdered Hamlet's father, who though unworthy possesses his mother, who has injured Hamlet and has power and motive for injuring him further. Polonius is a depreciated father figure, against whom Hamlet enacts his rivalrous feelings toward the father and the impulse to disparage him. It should be remarked in passing that the displacement of Hamlet's hostility onto Claudius and Polonius also facilitates the eloquent expression of his sanctioned filial feelings. The respect, admiration and love which during his father's life were admixed with other elements can now be asseverated without qualification.

Displacement also makes possible the unabashed expression of Hamlet's jealous anger that another man should enjoy his mother. Here, however, the margin of success is perilously narrow. Even though we accept the legitimacy of his desire to separate his mother from such a man as Claudius, we may be fleetingly disturbed by its intensity. The coarseness of the sexual allusions, the unseemly directness with which this gen-

[11] See Freud, *The Interpretation of Dreams*, especially Chap. VI and Section E of Chap. VII.

tle prince, "the glass of fashion and the mould of form," re-proaches his mother, almost exposes his incestuous feelings; it may fugitively cross our minds that he speaks more like a rejected suitor than a son.[12] The appearance of the Ghost in the Queen's chamber, clad in his nightgown, almost compels us to observe that it was the father who was the original sexual rival. Still another displacement spares us this disclosure. Hamlet assumes, and we permit him to assume, that the Ghost has come to chide him solely for his delay in executing his mission and not, as well, for his questionable behavior toward his mother.

Also as a result of displacement Hamlet's feelings of guilt, unworthiness and melancholy receive repeated expression throughout the play, without ever being associated with their ultimate source, his parricidal and incestuous impulses. Hamlet confesses that he has more offenses at his beck than he has "thoughts to put them in, imagination to give them shape, or time to act them in." He lashes himself unmercifully; he talks and acts like a man who would find death a relief. But his feelings are blamed, with sufficient plausibility, upon things which do no more than provide an excuse for their expression —his father's death and his mother's overhasty marriage, his incapacity to perform his commission, even that most convenient of all butts, the corruption of the world.

Many other things, more than we can do justice to in a brief discussion, help us to divine unconsciously what is really going on, unknown to himself, in Hamlet's mind. The play-within-the-play is a warning to Claudius, but it is at the same time a confession that Hamlet himself—here in the guise of Lucianus, the play-King's nephew—could murder to secure a throne and a Queen. The Laertes episode shows us how a truly pious son proceeds when he wishes to avenge his father. The discrepancy between Hamlet's protestations and his failure to act arouses our suspicions. Unconsciously we come to understand very well why Hamlet cannot execute the task

[12] In the Laurence Olivier movie of *Hamlet*, as a result of what seems to me to have been ill-considered casting, the Queen and Hamlet seemed contemporaries, and his sexual feeling was embarrassingly palpable.

laid upon him by the Ghost of his father: he himself is full of guilt because he harbors the same dark desires on which Claudius has acted. And through our identification with Hamlet we ourselves, in reading or viewing the play, vicariously re-experience the same desires and guilt and purge ourselves of them.

Precisely the same sort of thing occurs in reading another narrative work which at first glance might not appear to admit of instinctual gratification, Dostoevsky's superb novel, *The Idiot*. In many respects Myshkin resembles Hamlet: he is idealistic, generous in spirit, and though physically frail, unfailingly courageous. But he is less worldly and more ascetic than Shakespeare's Renaissance Prince. Dostoevsky conceived him as a Christ-like character; it is strongly suggested that as a result of the disease from which he suffers, epilepsy, he may be sexually impotent. His closest literary analogue is not Hamlet but Don Quixote. Like him he suffers from the most endearing of all possible weaknesses: an excess of goodness. He has an overdeveloped and tyrannical superego. How can a novel with such a hero give us instinctual gratification?

It manages to do so on a lavish scale, like *Hamlet* both openly and covertly. It employs different means, however, to achieve the open expression of the particular emotional gratifications it offers—principally, intense sadistic-masochistic feelings. In *Hamlet* we identify mainly with one character, the hero, and, as we have seen, his most secret impulses can be admitted to awareness only when they are disassociated from their real source and connected with something which makes their expression legitimate. In reading *The Idiot* we identify not only with the hero, but, as he himself does, with two other characters with whom he is locked in a neurotic triangular relationship, Rogozhin and Nastasya Filippovna. Rogozhin and Nastasya are alter egos of Myshkin—passionate opposites who act out the impulses, above all the lust and aggression, the Prince so sternly represses. We in turn act out our impulses through them—with impunity because we assure ourselves that we are not like them and do not admire them. *We secure gratification by repudiating it simultaneously.*

This is what Myshkin does also. Rogozhin and Nastasya, the former in particular, can be regarded as rejected aspects of Myshkin's personality. Through Rogozhin, for example, he acts out his sadistic desires toward Nastasya. As the stupendous final scene of the novel suggests, he is a kind of passive accomplice of her murder by Rogozhin, a murder he consciously foresees as early as Chapter 3. Through Nastasya, the Prince acts out certain passive and feminine tendencies. Through our identification with Myshkin we secure, as it were at two removes, the emotional gratifications he obtains through his relationship with Rogozhin and Nastasya. In addition we share the gratifications he obtains from the relationship, no less covertly, in his own person. These are largely of a masochistic character. Both Rogozhin and Nastasya are only too glad to deliver the psychic blows the Prince unconsciously invites, and the relationship with Rogozhin satisfies pronounced passive homosexual tendencies. In its entirety the triangular relationship in which Myshkin is enmeshed represents the claims of the instincts. The novel pivots around his struggle to escape this relationship, marry Aglaia, and achieve a comparatively healthy adjustment to Russian society—the goal to which his ego aspires but for the achievement of which it lacks sufficient strength.

Dostoevsky in writing *The Idiot*, like Shakespeare in writing *Hamlet*, faced the apparently insoluble problem of at once concealing and divulging his hero's lust and murderous hates. They must be concealed both because they are sternly repressed—it would be unrealistic therefore for them to declare themselves too openly—and because if avowed they would arouse aversion. At the same time they must be communicated so that they can be understood and vicariously shared. Shakespeare solved the problem largely by means of displacement which only our unconscious would be likely to decipher. Dostoevsky presents evidence which our unwary minds are likely to glide over, but the significance of which our unconscious is unlikely to mistake.

Myshkin's involvement with Rogozhin and Nastasya is the most obvious example of such evidence. At a decisive point in the novel, the Prince's murderous impulses toward Rogozhin and desire for Nastasya are also divulged to us, but entirely by means of unconscious manifestations. In Chapter 3, Part 2, the Prince seeks out Rogozhin in his gloomy home to tell him that if it is true, as he has heard, that Rogozhin and Nastasya have been reconciled and are to be married, despite his feeling that the marriage will be ruinous for her, he will not interfere. But in the course of the agitated conversation between the two men Myshkin—not his ostensibly more violent friend—twice absent-mindedly picks up a knife which is lying on Rogozhin's desk. Later that afternoon the Prince realizes that for some hours before "he had at intervals begun suddenly looking for something." The "something" proves to be an item he had seen in a hardware store window—a knife with a staghorn handle! The very evening of his talk with Rogozhin, Myshkin finds himself irresistibly drawn to the house where he believes Nastasya to be staying. While walking there he keeps assuring himself of the purity of his intentions. He tells himself that he wishes he could see Rogozhin so that he could visit Nastasya in his company. In fact, he does see him a few minutes later—Nastasya, it turns out, is not home —and is so guilt-ridden he cannot bring himself to speak to him.

I am aware of what an injustice I have done *Hamlet* and *The Idiot* by the hurried and too-schematic discussion that my purposes and space considerations have made necessary. What is even more regrettable is the possibility that, in trying to show clearly how the subject matter of fiction can provide satisfaction to id, ego and superego, I may have inadvertently slighted the crucial point—the way in which any great narrative work simultaneously satisfies all three. However, no discerning reader is likely to overlook the emotional content of some of the works we glanced at earlier or the teeming satisfactions such works as *Hamlet* and *The Idiot* offer the higher parts of the personality. Again and again in later chapters we shall return to the fact that we reserve our highest praise for those works of fiction which satisfy and balance the needs of the entire personality.

5

There has been so much to say to define the manner in which narrative art deals with any one of our problems that we have paid only passing attention to another of its important characteristics, the fact that it may simultaneously deal with several. Even apparently simple novels such as *Robinson Crusoe*, even very short fictional works, and, it can be added, even segments of works, may admit of many different interpretations. This means that a story may mean different things to different readers, but it also means that any given reader may sense that a story has many different meanings, layer upon layer of significance. To use a term adopted from dream psychology, fiction may be overdetermined; the fiction we regard as great invariably is.

It is obvious enough that an overdetermined story is more likely than a single-faceted one to win a large audience: it may appeal to different readers for different reasons, overcoming barriers of time and space. What is perhaps more important is the fact that it is likely to make a particularly intense appeal to all readers. We sense the presence of many meanings even when, as is usually the case, we do not pause to tease any one of them out.

Other things being equal,[13] the more overdetermined the story, the richer, the "thicker" our response. Many readers appear to have definite physical reactions to stories which, they sense, have reference to many of their problems, and our intellectual evaluation of highly overdetermined fiction is also likely to be high. It is easy to surmise at least some of the reasons. Overdetermination is highly congenial to our minds; it satisfies tendencies conspicuous in both conscious and unconscious thought.[14] We are grateful for the economy

[13] See Ch. VIII for a discussion of the principal factors which influence response.

[14] The concern of the ego with integration is well known. And, Freud points out, "If the day has brought us two or more experiences which are worthy to evoke a dream, the dream will blend the allusion of both into a single whole: it obeys *a compulsion to make them into a single whole.*" (Freud's italics.) *The Interpretation of Dreams*, p. 248.

of psychic expenditure overdetermination makes possible; this would be so even if the various problems an overdetermined work referred to were on the same level of depth. In fact, topographically one would have to picture the various meanings of which an overdetermined work admits as extending not outward in space, but downward or inward. Our response is partly due to the realization that some of our deepest, our most basic conflicts are being objectified and ventilated. In a surprising number of cases, we shall find, overdetermined works refer simultaneously to external problems and intrapsychic conflicts. When this sort of fusion occurs, the way is paved for a return to primitive animistic thinking in which, in the words of Dr. Gustav Bychowski, "no abyss [separated] the Ego from Nature . . . [and] it was only natural that the weeping willow would represent the sadness of a mourning human being." [15]

The ways in which overdetermined works sometimes give form to endopsychic problems and processes deserve illustration. As we have seen, there is a sense in which all the happenings in fiction represent the claims of the different parts of the psyche and mirror their ceaseless conflict. *Robinson Crusoe*, for example, dramatizes the capacity of the ego to triumph over instinctual urges and make the individual's full energies available for productive tasks; it is a paean of praise to an image of man which was being fostered by both economic and religious forces. However, perhaps because the claims of the instincts are under-represented—they are not so much conquered as disregarded—the book does not give us the impression of dealing with an internal struggle. *The Trial* does convey just such an impression. Although it admits of many interpretations and bodies forth the problems we face in com-

---

[15] "The Rebirth of a Woman: A Psychoanalytic Study of Artistic Expression and Sublimation," *Psychoanalytic Review*, 34, 1947. Cf. Maud Bodkin, "The thought of the storm image . . . takes us back to that order of conception . . . wherein the two aspects we now distinguish, of outer sense impression and inly felt process, appear undifferentiated." *Archetypal Patterns in Poetry*, p. 47. Earlier Miss Bodkin has shown that in Ezekiel's entreaty, "Come from the four winds, O breath, and breathe upon these slain, that they may live," physical wind, the breath in man's nostrils and the power of the Divine Spirit are hardly separable.

ing to terms with many of the forces and institutions which surround us, at some deep level it also depicts a cruel struggle, with sanity and life the stakes, between the ego and the super-ego. Among other works which give us this sense of imaging internal processes and conflicts we may consider three, *Oedipus the King*, *Othello* and *Moby Dick*.

Oedipus the King is assuredly what many critics have called it—a drama of fate. More powerfully and poignantly than any of the countless narrative works written after it, it reminds us of the vicissitudes to which our lives are subject and the forces which war upon our conscious purposes. Seeing the fate that overcame Oedipus, "who knew the famed riddle, and was a man most mighty," on whose fortune all citizens gazed with envy, we realize that the supreme human failing is *Hubris*. "If any man walks haughtily in deed or word, with no fear of Justice . . . may an evil doom seize him for his ill-starred pride." Freud added depth to this interpretation by pointing out that the curse Oedipus tried vainly to escape is laid upon us all: "We [are] all destined to direct our first sexual impulses toward our mothers, and our first impulses of hatred and violence toward our fathers." [16] Oedipus acts out our most deeply buried impulses, but by showing the horror that attends their fulfilment the play purges us of those desires, strengthens our defenses against them.

Yet *Oedipus the King* revolves around another problem, too, the question of whether Oedipus' transgressions shall be permitted to come to light. Though the drama derives much of its power from the nature of the material struggling for expression, it mirrors with extraordinary fidelity the conflict which always attends "the return of the repressed": it is a drama about seeing, or, more accurately, as we would say today, a drama about what should be admitted to consciousness. The plague and the citizens invoking the aid of Oedipus represent the forces playing upon him to bring his guilt to light, so that it will no longer fester and can be purged. At various points Teiresias, Jocasta and the Herdsman represent the resistances, the fears which urge Oedipus to leave well enough

[16] *The Interpretation of Dreams*, p. 308.

alone. It is to be noted that from the beginning he is aware of the danger of his course. In a very early speech, made before the introduction of any evidence implicating him, he declares his determination to seek out the guilty person in surprising words: "let some other summon hither the folk of Cadmus, warned that I mean to leave nought untried; for our health (with the god's help) shall be made certain—*or our ruin*" (my italics). As the truth comes closer and closer to being divulged, the countervailing pressures become steadily more intense, until finally Jocasta implores Oedipus, "For the gods' sake, if thou hast any care for thine own life, forbear this search!" Oedipus is punished, in this way of viewing the play, not only for what he has done, his incest and parricide, but for his *Hubris* in seeing. His gouging-out of his eyes is an appropriate penalty on the manifest level, as well as a symbolic castration.

Maud Bodkin has shown that *Othello* mirrors another endopsychic drama: the struggle between dominant and repressed values. Her interpretation is based on a brilliant study of the play by G. Wilson Knight,[17] which itself seems always on the verge of arriving at the insight which occurred to Miss Bodkin. Othello, Wilson Knight points out, romanticizes and idealizes everything:[18] Desdemona, love, even soldiering and war. "His very life is dependent on a fundamental belief in the validity and nobility of human action."[19] Iago, "cynicism incarnate,"[20] hates Othello's romantic values and the beauty he finds in his wife and she in him. Without belief in love or fidelity he genuinely doubts the permanence of their love. It

---

[17] "The *Othello* Music," *The Wheel of Fire* (London: Methuen, 1949). F. R. Leavis' essay, "Diabolic Intellect and the Noble Hero: a Note on *Othello*" (*Scrutiny*, VI, 1937), also deserves mention. In insisting on the rapidity with which Othello becomes convinced of Desdemona's guilt, Leavis suggests his readiness, even his desire, to become convinced of it.

[18] This tendency reflects itself in Othello's language; indeed, it was through a study of this that Wilson Knight evidently became aware of it —an illustration of one of the valuable but seldom realized potentialities of formal analysis.

[19] *The Wheel of Fire*, p. 107.

[20] *Ibid.*, p. 114.

is to the destruction of something he expects to crumble that he dedicates himself.

But why does he succeed? Miss Bodkin has supplied the answer: because the doubts he whispers in Othello's ear are Othello's own. The doubts are the harder to shake off because they are not built so much on falsehoods as on

> partial truths of human nature that the romantic vision ignores. It is such a truth that a woman, "a super-subtle Venetian," suddenly wedding one in whom she sees the image of her ideal warrior, is liable to experience moments of revulsion from the strange passionate creature she as yet knows so little, movements of nature toward those more nearly akin to her in "years, manners and beauties." There is an element of apt truth in Iago's thought that a woman's love may be won, but not held, by "bragging and telling her fantastical lies." There is terrible truth in the reflection that if a man is wedded to his fantasy of woman as the steadfast hiding-place of his heart, . . . so that he grows frantic and blind with passion at the thought of the actual woman he has married as a creature of natural varying impulses—then he lies at the mercy of life's chances, and of his own secret fears and suspicions.[21]

Except as we may infer the possibility of it from what Othello feels and does, there is no evidence in the play that Desdemona ever experienced even momentary revulsion toward her warrior-husband. But any husband, not only one like Othello who is older than his wife and of a different race and background, must recognize the possibility of such ambivalence. If brought into the open, the kind of fears Miss Bodkin mentions can be coped with, though they may be a source of pain. But Othello refuses to bring them into the open; they are incompatible with the romantic values he lives by. Iago is the spokesman for the ideas, fears and suspicions Othello tries to disregard and repress; there is a sense in which the Ancient is indeed more "honest" than his General. Perhaps, as Miss Bodkin suggests, Iago should be regarded as sim-

ply a "projected image of forces present in Othello." [22] Many
critics have found him lacking in substantiality and convincing
motivation. Wilson Knight describes him as "undefined, de-
visualized, inhuman." [23] What seems certain is that Iago's
function is to voice Othello's unacknowledged doubts. It is
these, and not external machinations, which destroy the Moor.
They destroy him rapidly because he has tried to close his
eyes to dark possibilities with which it is necessary to come to
terms.

Against a setting which is curiously apposite, vast and turbulent, charged with energy and yet dream-like, *Moby Dick*
images forth the struggle of those immortal adversaries, the id
and the superego. Though many beautiful and illuminating
things have been said about Melville's inexhaustible masterpiece, I shall base my discussion largely on a single paper by
Henry A. Murray,[24] which seems to me to encompass, at the
same time that it extends, most of the more valuable insights of
earlier exegeses.[25] Besides showing how an intrapsychic conflict may be projected in fiction, Dr. Murray's paper suggests
the fashion in which cultural attitudes secure emotional expression; it teaches us a great deal about the whole concept of
overdetermination.

Seen externally, Captain Ahab, in Dr. Murray's view, is the
Devil, "Milton's hero, but portrayed with deeper and subtler
psychological insight, and placed where he belongs, in the
heart of an enraged man." [26] Seen inwardly, "Ahab is captain
of the culturally repressed dispositions of human nature, that
part of personality which psychoanalysts have termed the
'Id.' " [27] ". . . he and his followers, Starbuck excepted, represent the horde of primitive drives, values, beliefs and practices
which the Hebraic-Christian religionists rejected and ex-

[22] *Ibid.*, p. 221.
[23] *The Wheel of Fire*, p. 119.
[24] "In Nomine Diabole," *New England Quarterly*, XXIV, 1951.
[25] Dr. Murray acknowledges his indebtedness to other critics, especially
Newton Arvin. For Arvin's beautifully rounded discussion of *Moby Dick*,
see *Herman Melville* (New York: Sloane, 1950), Chapter V, "The Whale."
[26] "In Nomine Diabole," p. 442.
[27] *Ibid.*, pp. 443-44.

cluded, and by threats, punishments, and inquisitions forced into the unconscious mind of Western man." [28] "Starbuck, the First Mate, stands for the rational realistic Ego which is over-powered by the fanatical compulsiveness of the Id and dis-possessed of its normally regulating functions." [29]

The enemy, Moby Dick, upon whose white hump Ahab piles "the sum of all the general rage and hate felt by his whole race from Adam down" is the superego. This means, first of all, that he is the parents—Melville's parents, we may be sure, as well as his hero's—"the zealous parents whose righteous sermonizings and corrections drove the prohibitions in so hard that a serious young man could hardly reach outside the bar-rier, except possibly far away among some tolerant, gracious Polynesian peoples." [30] Melville, no less than Ahab, suffered a symbolic castration, and frequently enough we sense the writer's anguish behind his hero's. "How can the prisoner reach outside except by thrusting through the wall? To me, the White Whale is that wall, shoved near to me. . . . I see in him outrageous strength, with an inscrutable malice sinew-ing it."

But as a creation of a writer of large comprehension, Moby Dick is not solely the parents; the superego never had so limited a significance, despite the misrepresentations of a few so-called "revisionist" psychoanalysts. In *Pierre* Melville showed his explicit awareness "that not his mother had made his mother; but the Infinite Haughtiness had first fashioned her; and then the haughty world had further molded her; nor had a haughty Ritual omitted to finish her." Moby Dick, then, the incarnation of the superego, is also the world, the public, the upper-middle-class culture of Melville's time. He is a sym-bol of the cultural and ideological values responsible for Mel-ville's artistic and sexual frustrations, the "derivative puritan ethic of nineteenth-century America." [31] He is the other dom-inant values of the time as well: materialism and commercial-

[28] *Ibid.*, p. 443.
[29] *Ibid.*, p. 446.
[30] *Ibid.*, p. 444.
[31] *Ibid.*, p. 444.

ism and, in the intellectual sphere, rationalism and shallow optimism, the impulse to deny the dark forces in man's nature and in the world. Finally, Moby Dick symbolizes a specific conception of God Himself: he is the intimidating Calvinistic God of prohibitions and threats. Murray's interpretation helps us to understand the whiteness of the whale, as Wilson Knight's and Maud Bodkin's interpretations of *Othello* help us to understand the honesty of Iago.

In his death struggle with this maiming superego Ahab dedicates himself to implacable hostility; in Lewis Mumford's words, he becomes "the image of the thing he hates." Ahab, in one sense, is not even the whole id. Just as an enraged child may injure himself, he has completed the white whale's work and uprooted Eros from his soul. From one point of view Ahab is aggression run wild, a cancerous growth. But, though in the wrong way, Ahab is attacking the most deadly enemies of happiness and creative fulfilment, and he is seeking to avenge a real and horrible injury. In Newton Arvin's words, "He is our hatred ennobled, as we would wish to have it, up to heroism." [32] In the characterization of this "ungodly, god-like man," the sublime ambivalence of great narrative art is perfectly achieved.

[32] *Herman Melville*, p. 171.

Chapter V *The Functions of Form*

The subject of form must be approached with a curious combination of humility and boldness: humility because of the difficulties, even in the most exhaustive studies of particular works, of specifying the more important effects of form and because of the wide margin of error likely to attend one's observations; boldness because without it many important aspects of form are sure to escape attention and one will not see the ultimate significance of the formal effects which are descried.

The dangers last mentioned, far from being theoretical, have left an imprint upon every formal study of fiction with which I am acquainted. There are no studies even of individual stories which do not leave out much more than they cover. Few studies pretend to be exhaustive. The vast majority confine themselves to some single aspect of form—to metaphor, to symbolism, to point of view. In itself this is far from being undesirable. Perceptive studies of particular points can do a great deal to build up our knowledge of form. One must face the fact, too, that exhaustive studies are seldom feasible; when their objects are novels of stature, such studies, for reasons which will become apparent as we proceed, would themselves usually have to be of book length.[1] The particularized studies do, however, involve a danger. Unless they are carefully oriented in terms of the larger purposes of form, the devices they describe may gradually come to be taken for the whole of an aspect of fiction of which in the aggregate they constitute no more than a small part—just as in the social sciences the measurable phases of a problem may be temporarily mistaken for the problem in its entirety.

[1] The best formal study of narration with which I am acquainted is Percy Lubbock's *The Craft of Fiction* (New York: Cape and Smith, 1929), in style as well as acuteness of observation a model for all further work in the field. However, Lubbock found it necessary to devote some two hundred and seventy pages to an analysis of the way point of view is handled in a score of novels, and only begins to suggest the psychological effects of the one device he considers.

Weighing the risks, therefore, I prefer to consider form in the broadest possible terms. The disadvantages are obvious. It will be difficult to avoid error. Even the most carefully surveyed aspects of form can seldom be dealt with briefly. Many of the points with which we shall be concerned are usually neglected. Ideally they should be developed in the most complete detail and, to the greatest extent possible, illustrated. To deal with even one or two points in this fashion, however, would leave no room for what seems to me most needed: a survey of the problem of form in functional terms—an attempt to apprehend the purposes of form and the way in which various formal devices contribute to their achievement.

The distrust of psychology may have something to do with the failure of conventional literary criticism to approach form in this fashion, although the difficulties of formal analysis also encourage a cautious, piecemeal approach. Speaking broadly, what readers and critics alike mean by form is the whole group of devices used to structure and communicate expressive content;[2] it is upon the latter—more accurately, upon the more superficial layers of the content—that the attention of readers is focused. Thus we usually have only the vaguest awareness of formal factors. Even when a story strikes us as being well told or beautifully written—and this is about as close as we ordinarily come to paying tribute to its form—we seldom attempt to account for its effect upon us.

The most determined attempt, furthermore, may not be successful. The particular effect we wish to explain may be difficult to formulate in words; in its formal aspects to a greater degree than in its subject-matter aspects fiction approaches the non-verbal character of the other arts. Even

[2] This does not imply, it is worth stating explicitly, that form is any less important than content: the successful communication of the content depends, of course, upon the way it is expressed. Nor is the footnoted statement meant to be exhaustive. Form also reveals how the fiction writer apprehends reality and views the world. In theory at least it may tell us even more about this than does a writer's material and obsessive themes, but, whatever the situation may be in the non-literary arts, I can think of no major writer of fiction, with the possible exception of Sterne, of whom this is actually so.

when the effect is specified, we may have difficulty in tracking down the factor responsible for it. As we shall see more clearly in the next two chapters, some of the important formal means employed in fiction ordinarily escape our notice or are regarded as generic attributes of the story form. Furthermore, we soon discover that it is not usually easy to establish a one-to-one relationship between a particular formal effect and a particular cause. Many effects are achieved by the subtle interweaving of numerous devices or by the Gestalt of the form. Percy Lubbock has commented upon the rapidity with which the form of a book may be forgotten, but perhaps "forgotten" is not the accurate word, any more than it is for our frequent inability to summon the names of people to whom we have been introduced. Neither the names nor the formal imprint of the book may have registered on our minds to begin with.

This particular reference to form by Lubbock suggests still another difficulty: a tendency, to which even the forewarned critic may not be immune, to think of the word "form" in a literal and physical sense. Although Lubbock himself remarks that the word is a metaphor drawn from the material arts, he sometimes appears to believe—he clearly desires—that novels should have a physical shape, which can be apprehended and fixed in the mind. Very few do. Occasionally, to be sure, a story can be felicitously described in terms of a spatial metaphor. For example, E. M. Forster has observed that *Thais* has the form of an hourglass.[3] This is an accurate as well as a striking description, but it is worth noting that it would convey very little to a person not already familiar with the novel. It would probably not even indicate that in *Thais* the two principal protagonists change positions; and it suggests nothing whatever about the nature of the interplay responsible for the turnabout. And how many novels lend themselves as well as *Thais* to description in physical terms?

The kind of cult-like glorification of form characteristic of latter-day esthetics has also inhibited resolute attempts to uncover form's secrets. Curiously, not only esthetes, worshipers

[3] *Aspects of the Novel* (New York: Harcourt, Brace, 1927), p. 214.

at the shrine of what Clive Bell calls "significant form," but, as Dr. Harry B. Lee has observed,[4] even psychoanalysts—including some, like Freud, who have not hesitated to dissect mankind's religious beliefs—have tended to regard artistic form and beauty as unanalyzable absolutes. This tendency is evident in Freud's first paper on literature, "The Relation of the Poet to Day-Dreaming" (1908).[5] Though in this paper Freud identifies one resource of form, disguise, and suggests one of the ways in which the fiction writer makes his fantasies palatable and pleasurable—by softening their egotism—Freud proceeds to characterize the process of transformation, which he has already begun to penetrate, as the writer's "innermost secret." Furthermore, he refers to "purely formal, that is, aesthetic, pleasure" as though it had nothing to do with just such things as disguise, as though it were some mysterious and autonomous factor. The same tendency persists in psychoanalytic writing to this day;[6] and it is significant that, though there are a number of analytic papers on formal problems—including one by Joseph Weiss which we shall consider later—neither Freud himself, who so brilliantly expounded the technique of wit, nor any of his disciples has ever attempted a full-scale study of form in art. Since the arts will not begin to yield their ultimate secrets except to those who consider both content and form—the object which moves us in its entirety—this timidity is as unfortunate in its way as the tendency in some other quarters to study form as though it were unrelated to expressive content, and the esthetic experience as though it were entirely isolated from our everyday lives.

The analysis of form in any of the arts obviously presents the most formidable difficulties. It would be impudent to sup-

---

[4] "The Creative Imagination," *Psychoanalytic Quarterly*, XVIII, 1949.

[5] *Collected Papers*, Volume IV (London: Hogarth, 1948). Also in *Delusion and Dream* (Boston: Beacon, 1956).

[6] A characteristic recent statement: "But there are men with a mysterious gift who can clothe these daydreams and fictive instinctual gratifications in forms which allow others, also, to dream their dreams with them. How this is done, and what is the nature of the pleasure-premium of form and beauty which draws their fellows, is an aesthetic problem still unsolved." Marie Bonaparte, *The Life and Works of Edgar Allan Poe* (London: Imago, 1949), p. 664.

pose that any one worker, or the combined efforts of many, could ever fully explain the way form functions in a given art or in a complex individual work; the latter task, indeed, may be the more difficult. But some of the broad purposes served by form in narrative art can be discerned; and some of the means used for achieving them can be identified.

2

The aspects of narrative art we assign to form have three essential functions: to give pleasure; to avoid or relieve guilt and anxiety; and to facilitate perception—to silhouette the material with the desired degree of clarity. Perhaps it would be more accurate to say that form has but a single objective: the communication of the expressive content in a way which provides a maximum amount of pleasure and minimizes guilt and anxiety. It is certain, in any case, that the several functions which can be distinguished are closely and harmoniously inter-related. The relief of guilt and anxiety, for example, is itself one of the most important sources of the pleasure we secure from form. Some reduction of guilt and anxiety is also an indispensable condition of the rounded and compassionate kind of seeing toward which narrative art strives; our anxieties blind us to innumerable things and cause us to distort much that we believe we see. Anxiety-free perception, in its turn, is a rich source of pleasure. The achievement of any of the ends of form contributes to the achievement of the others.

Numerous esthetic theories assume that form seeks to facilitate perception. Usually, however, it is assumed that form tries to bring the object before us as clearly as possible. At least so far as narrative art is concerned, we shall find that this is not the case. Here form has a much more complex task—to convey things to us in such a way that certain meanings, those most likely to produce anxiety, will *not* emerge too clearly. In Chapters VI and VII we shall consider some of the resources of form which enable it to accomplish this delicate and difficult task.

In one fashion or another—in Plato with some apprehension,

in Horace without misgivings—pleasure, too, is usually assumed or proclaimed to be one of the objectives of artistic
form. To some extent the search for pleasure underlies all
man's activities. Even "harmless" as opposed to tendentious
wit, declares Freud, "has for its aim the evocation of pleasure
in the hearer. I doubt whether we are able to undertake anything which has no object in view. When we do not use our
psychic apparatus for the fulfillment of one of our indispensable gratifications, we let it work for pleasure, and we seek to
derive pleasure from its own activity." [7]

Man's desire to extract pleasure from the operation of
his own psychic apparatus leaves a deep imprint upon artistic
form. It expresses itself in the storyteller's search for *immediate* sources of pleasure in the handling of his material—sources
which have no necessary connection with the solution of functional problems. It is an obvious determinant of such qualities
as richness and exuberance. Its influence may be discerned in
the tendency of fiction to organize its material in patterned,
symmetrical form and to arouse and then satisfy expectations.
However, it is apparent that these characteristics simultaneously satisfy other needs. The patterned presentation of material aids perception and, because a patterned world is more
comprehensible and less threatening than a chaotic one, has a
reassuring influence. The satisfaction of an aroused expectation liquidates the anxiety which has been generated about how
a given event will turn out. When one looks at such qualities
as richness and exuberance more closely, one finds that they
too, tend, in quite indirect fashion, to relieve anxiety. They
contribute to perception, too, expressing themselves, for example, in the loving care with which even relatively unimportant aspects of a story may be developed. It is maintained
that the best way to achieve happiness in life is to concentrate
on other objectives. It seems certain that something similar
holds for our delight in artistic form: most of the pleasure we
secure arises as a by-product of the pursuit of other objectives.
The same point holds, *mutatis mutandis*, for the pleasure we

[7] *Wit and Its Relation to the Unconscious* in *The Basic Writings of Sigmund Freud* (New York: Modern Library, 1938), p. 692.

secure from the content of fiction. Though we may say we read "for fun," it is probably more accurate to say that we read driven *a tergo* by the impulse to satisfy various needs. The satisfaction of those needs is the real source of the pleasure.

If we had to assign quantitative weights to the two sources of our pleasure in reading, that which we secure from content and that which we secure from form, the first would undoubtedly bulk the heavier—just as in response to tendency-wit we secure a certain amount of pleasure, which Freud designated fore-pleasure, from the technique and a still larger amount from the release of inhibited erotic or aggressive strivings. It would be a mistake, however, to regard the two sources of pleasure as disputants for our favor; they are, rather, partners. Were it not for technique in wit and form in fiction, we could not accept the enjoyment potentially available in the content. Furthermore, the total pleasure we secure from reading should not be conceived as a mere arithmetical sum of the pleasure obtained from the two separate sources: in the case of both fiction and wit it is far, far greater. As G. Th. Fechner, whom Freud quotes, declares: "From the unopposed concurrence of pleasurable states which individually accomplish little, there results a greater, often much greater resultant pleasure than corresponds to the sum of the pleasure values of the separate states . . . ; in fact, the mere concurrence of this kind can result in a positive pleasure product, which overflows the threshold of pleasure where the individual factors are too weak to accomplish this. . . ." [8]

The reasons why form should devote itself to combatting anxiety may not be immediately apparent. Even the reading situation, however—the very act of reading—is likely to generate anxiety. More or less consciously, the reading of fiction is undertaken to gratify curiosity. An important, often an acknowledged, component of that curiosity is interest in those aspects of other people's feelings and behavior which are ordinarily concealed from view, including, of course, sexual experiences and reactions to them. Unconsciously, reading may

[8] *Wit and Its Relation* . . . , p. 724.

be associated with the infantile sexual investigations of childhood. When we sit in a darkened theater to view a play or
movie, the parallel is especially clear.[9]

Ironically—for form serves fundamentally to relieve anxiety
and guilt—even the pleasurable tone of the reading experience,
to which form, of course, contributes, may arouse anxiety in
some people in whom pleasure is generically associated with
forbidden satisfactions. Indeed, specifically formal elements,
such as rhythmical and sensuous language, may be the immediate source of feelings of uneasiness.[10]

It is, however, the subject matter of fiction which is most
likely to give rise to guilt and anxiety. Desires so repugnant
to us that they cannot be acknowledged, and our anxieties
themselves, constitute perennial themes of fiction. Even to
deal with such material in fantasy entails a certain amount of
risk. If there is not everywhere the suggestion of order and
control, if the potentially offensive material is not softened and
disguised, and if—especially in the absence of such disguise—
its connections with our own impulses and fears is not carefully concealed from view, we will experience so much uneasiness that we will be unable to enjoy what we read and in
all probability will feel repelled by it.[11] A driving purpose of
form is to transform that which might inspire terror into
something which can be contemplated and experienced without fear.

Form has a larger and still more arduous task: to transport
us to a world committed to life, to love, to order, to all the
values the superego holds dear, and thus to allay that pervasive
anxiety which is always with us, and nearly always more con-

---

[9] There are, however, two reassuring differences. The sort of "looking"
we do in reading and in the theater is sanctioned; and we are not likely to
be spied on in turn and punished for our curiosity.

[10] However, such reactions are probably too infrequent to constitute an
exception to the principle that the relations among the several objectives
of form are harmonious. Only people who have a very severe superego or
some other psychological problem—e.g., a tendency to regard lovely language as somehow effeminate—are likely to react in the manner described.

[11] Narrative art shares this double-edged character with the comic. See
Ernst Kris, *Psychoanalytic Explorations in Art* (New York: International
Universities Press, 1952), Ch. 8, "Ego Development and the Comic."

siderable in amount than the anxiety mobilized by a particular story.[12] As we have seen, the forces which impel us to read are not always specific. A person often picks up a novel in search of he knows not what particular satisfaction, oppressed by the poverty and chaos of his life, "sick with desire," eager for any fulfilment, for experiences more gratifying, companions more responsive than those he knows. The anxiety and guilt which dog one because of these desires are as indeterminate as the desires themselves, as mobile, as unrelated to any particular action or impulse as the guilt felt by Kafka's Joseph K.

Upon form falls the burden of relieving this free-floating anxiety and guilt. The highest achievements of form, it may be conjectured, are due to the double requirement of having to subdue the quotient of anxiety which is always with us as well as the anxiety which may be aroused by the subject matter of a particular story. There is a certain amount of clinical evidence suggesting that art is often if not invariably created as a defense against prohibited impulses, above all against aggressive impulses—impulses to injure and destroy.[13] Even in the absence of such evidence, however, one would have to assume that the desire to deny and atone for such impulses plays a

[12] There must, however, be a minimal degree of freedom from anxiety before narrative art can minister to us in this fashion. Cf. Ch. II.

[13] See, for example, Melanie Klein, *Contributions to Psycho-Analysis, 1921-1945* (London: Hogarth, 1948), especially the papers, "Infantile Anxiety-Situations Reflected in a Work of Art and in the Creative Impulse" and "The Importance of Symbol-Formation in the Development of the Ego." Ella Sharpe, *Collected Papers on Psycho-Analysis* (London: Hogarth, 1950). John Rickman, "On the Nature of Ugliness and the Creative Impulse," *International Journal of Psychoanalysis*, XIX, 1940. Harry B. Lee (Levey), "Poetry Production as a Supplemental Emergency Defense Against Anxiety," *Psychoanalytic Quarterly*, VII, 1938; "A Theory Concerning Free Creation in the Inventive Arts," *Psychiatry*, III, 1940; "On the Aesthetic States of the Mind," *ibid.*, X, 1947; and "The Creative Imagination."

Though the clinical examples given happen to refer to humor, not art, see also Sidney Tarachow, "Remarks on the Comic Process and Beauty," *Psychoanalytic Quarterly*, XVIII, 1949.

For excellent theoretical formulations, see W. R. D. Fairbairn, "Prolegomena to a Psychology of Art," *British Journal of Psychology*, XXVIII, 1937-38; and "The Ultimate Basis of Esthetic Experience," *ibid.*, *XXIX*, 1938-39.

part in our insistence that narrative art possess the quality of form. Our admiration of form is an indirect way of protesting our innocence of destructive impulses, our commitment to life and love. In all of its aspects form affirms its abhorrence of destruction. In W. R. D. Fairbairn's phrase, form seeks to safeguard "the integrity of the object," presenting everything in a way which emphasizes its wholeness and intactness. By lavishing love and care upon the material, it seeks to protect from death itself both the material and the object it commemorates.

Behind the concern of form for making us see the object "whole," for rendering it with such perfection that it will live forever, an apotropaic intention may also be dimly discerned. In our unconscious, dismemberment and death are the punishments that we fear will be visited upon us because of our aggressive impulses. At the very deepest level form may be an attempt to deal with these fears. It may be a magic gesture and a covert supplication—a plea to be treated with the love and almost maternal protectiveness which have been bestowed upon the artistic object. Through our response to form, it is certain, we are paying homage to the superego, not simply attempting to deceive or conciliate it, but asseverating our devotion and our unqualified acceptance of its demands.[14] And our suit is seldom refused. Immersion in artistic form has the curious consequence of quieting anxiety and relieving feelings of guilt.

It has already been suggested that, like dreams, neurotic symptoms, and wit, art, including fiction, is a compromise formation which in more or less distorted fashion expresses both our desires and our defenses against them. It seems prob-

---

[14] Cf. W. R. D. Fairbairn: "On the one hand, art-work modifies repressed tendencies in such a way as to enable them to elude the vigilance of the super-ego . . . by this means affording the repressed impulses an opportunity for expression and relieving the *tension between the repressed impulses and the ego.* On the other hand, art-work enables the ego to convert phantasies unacceptable to the super-ego into positive tributes to its authority and so relieves the *tension existing between the ego and the super-ego.*" "Prolegomena to a Psychology of Art."

able that our desires are chiefly—not, of course, exclusively—satisfied by subject matter, our defenses by form.

The conceptualization of form as endeavoring to satisfy the superego sheds light on many attributes of form and the very terms used to describe them in esthetic theory. From a fresh point of view, for example, we perceive why we prize perfection, symmetry, every indication that the material has been handled with loving care. We also understand the desire for vitality and exuberance, and for a unity and course of development which impress us as being organic rather than mechanical. Our respect for these qualities is a way of assuring ourselves that we are dominated not by hatred but by love, not by dark destructive forces but by the desire to maintain and preserve life.

3

To relieve anxiety, to give pleasure, to make us see certain happenings in a given way—these are obviously large assignments, and yet it is doubtful if any mere description of them can suggest the difficulties which attend their achievement. Even if the task of making us see were as uncomplicated as it is sometimes conceived to be, if it involved nothing more than bringing everything clearly before us, it would require more skill than most people—indeed, than most writers—can summon. As I. A. Richards points out, it is difficult for the average person to describe another person so that a friend who has not seen him will gain a reasonably accurate impression of his physical appearance. "Unless A has remarkable gifts of description and B extraordinarily sensitive and discriminating receptive ability, their two experiences will tally at best but roughly. They may completely fail to tally without either being clearly aware of the fact." [15] It is only necessary to add that the description of the physical appearance of his characters is usually among the easiest of the tasks confronting the writer of fiction. He may have to give us an impression of a

[15] *Principles of Literary Criticism* (New York: Harcourt, Brace, 1934), p. 178.

battlefield, a brilliant party, or a country estate where many different events which are part of the action of a story are occurring at more or less the same time. He must be able to provide unerring reports of the intricate relationships among many people and of elusive subjective states. Most difficult of all, he must convey a sense of the constant imperceptible change taking place in everything he describes, capture the ebb and flow of life itself. Perhaps we accept such achievements as complacently as we do because the writer uses words, a medium of which we all flatter ourselves we are the master. In fact, words are a clumsy and recalcitrant medium for making us see an involved sequence of events with hallucinatory vividness. It is all the worse that they are used so frequently and, usually, so indifferently. "Defaced," in Conrad's phrase, "by ages of careless usage," their capacity to make us see freshly and vividly has been impaired.

Furthermore, the fiction writer cannot concentrate upon making us see, since certain perceptions would arouse anxiety and displeasure. He must define and pursue each of the objectives of form in such a way that the achievement of one does not jeopardize the achievement of the others. In the successful completed story, it has been said, the relationships among the objectives are harmonious, but many latent antagonisms must be resolved during the composition of the story to bring about this result. A heavy-handed attempt to give pleasure, like tactlessness about bringing certain facts into the foreground, is likely to mobilize anxiety. Preoccupation with the liquidation of anxiety may make a story grim and unprepossessing. The achievement of the ends of form requires not only many rare kinds of skill but an even rarer capacity to balance conflicting demands.

How much delicacy is required we can best appreciate by analyzing some of these conflicts in the more concrete terms in which they may present themselves to writers of fiction. The nub of the difficulty lies in the fact that all the conflicts must be dealt with at one and the same time. Rather than having to steer a frail craft through Scylla and Charybdis, or having to avoid a succession of such perils, a storyteller is in somewhat the position of a hostess uneasily aware of numerous sources of potential antagonism among her guests, to all of which she must be simultaneously alert if everything is to go well.

A storyteller must first of all capture our interest—upon the success of this everything else depends—and this task presents difficulties of the most perplexing sort. There is almost a paradox involved: to "interest" us a writer must appeal to us in terms of our interests, but those are the very interests he is asking us to cast aside in order to follow the careers of his imaginary characters. To be sure, he may appeal to us in terms of interests we are not able to gratify in our lives, but even here there is a difficulty: in many cases these are interests we are unwilling to acknowledge.

At least so far as this last difficulty is concerned, the reading situation itself eases things somewhat. As in sleep, we are immobile. We are neither acting nor laying plans for future action. Thus the ego is willing to relax its customary vigilance to a degree, and fantasies which might be quickly repudiated under other circumstances may be at least momentarily entertained. There is, after all, no "real"—that is, external—danger: no loved one to be hurt by our infidelities, no flesh to be lacerated by our blows, no neighbors to deceive, no police to elude or punishment to fear.

The storyteller intuitively knows, however, that he can place only limited reliance upon such advantages. There are forces in the reader which might react in the most violent way if lust and aggression were permitted to run riot. On the other hand, the necessity of arousing interest invisibly influences the writer to turn to "strong" material and to deal with it in extreme fashion. One reason we read fiction is to compensate for the deficiencies of our everyday lives. We not only want storytellers to offer us the experiences which fate denies us or we deny ourselves; we want them to restore to the experiences we permit ourselves the excitement of which they have been robbed by habit and prudential considerations. "Life is impoverished, it loses in interest," declares Freud, "when the highest stake in the game of living, life itself, may not be risked." [16] We know this well. We want fiction to show us our real nature—*what we would do if we were not inhibited by social conventions and fear.*

Once in a while a writer can satisfy this demand by the skill with which he treats quite bland material. Far more frequently he finds that he cannot escape the *risk* of causing offense. The necessity of interesting us compels him to create characters and situations which express our darkest impulses. He is driven also to heighten issues—to show us the ultimate implications and consequences of those impulses. The greatest narrative art shows us our desires, fears and conflicts writ large.

Writ large, they are almost certain to interest us, but the danger that they may arouse anxiety is very great. A whole battery of formal devices is called into play to prevent the anxiety from materializing. The writer displaces our lusts and hatreds onto others, the protagonists of his story, so that we can deny responsibility for them. He conceals and disguises the connections between the story and our own lives. By means of a device about which I shall have more to say in Chapter VII, he "distances" the story, creates the illusion, physical in its intensity, that the drama is being played out on a stage from which we are separated by a reassuring space. He is careful to orient our interest not toward action but toward perception and understanding.

4

All of these measures imply the presence of a basic quality of form which we may call mastery or control. This quality, it should be said at once, makes itself felt in all the techniques of form. Indeed, it is so pervasive that one may be momentarily inclined to equate it with form itself. However, form has other characteristics as well, and the influence of control—especially if we think of control in terms of tightness and rigidity—is not quite as powerful as it first appears. Its claims are contested by still other of our needs, and while the neces-

[16] "Thoughts for the Times on War and Death," *Collected Papers,* IV, 306.

sity of some degree of control is not disputed the decision as to how much is "right" in any given story is very much a matter for adjudication.

The basis of our demand for control is evident. Since the latent if not the manifest content of fiction is often concerned with the imaginary gratification of unsanctioned desires and the confrontation of terrible fears, we demand certain safeguards before giving the fantasies of fiction access to the unconscious. At best there is some danger. The ego of the reader is in somewhat the position of a householder examining a stranger who wishes to be admitted. Quite naturally, the householder scrutinizes the newcomer carefully: he wants to be certain that he will not be subjected to attack or any other form of unpleasantness. The quality of control provides such reassurance to the ego. It indicates not only that the ego's values are respected, but that *its work has been done*—that the dangerous material in the story has already been subjected to the kind of regulation the ego would exercise. The recognition of this encourages the ego to relax its own vigilance—to make the same kind of surrender of trust which is involved when one gives oneself in love. As will be developed in greater detail in Chapter VIII, this submission to the experience in prospect is an indispensable condition of both the understanding and enjoyment of fiction.

Evidence of control not only deprives a story of threat, thus quieting anxiety; it is a source of serenity and pleasure. As Wordsworth says in *The Prelude:*

> There are in our existence spots of time
> That with distinct pre-eminence retain
> A renovating virtue, whence . . . our minds
> Are nourished and invisibly repaired;

Part of the pleasure doubtless arises from the welcome release from anxiety, part from the clearer perception that release makes possible. But what we sometimes perceive when our anxiety is quieted is something broader than the body of experience organized by a particular story. We have the feeling, illusory perhaps to some extent but richly satisfying, of having reduced the chaos of our lives to momentary order, of having achieved both a deeper understanding of our situation and a larger measure of control over it. As Wordsworth declares a few lines later in *The Prelude:*

> This efficacious spirit chiefly lurks
> Among those passages of life that give
> Profoundest knowledge to what point, and how,
> The mind is lord and master—outward sense
> The obedient servant of her will.

Perhaps control gives us this sense of enhanced understanding and mastery of our own life because it stirs up memories of our own past triumphs of mind and will. It may recall the relief we experienced when a baffling problem was finally seen in clear perspective, the sense of mastery, pride and averted danger aroused in us by victory over rage or sexual excitation. Indeed, by suggesting that *it* will take care of everything, control may carry us back to a still earlier period, before the superego was instituted or could be relied upon, when we had the assurance of parental help in combatting impulses felt to be dangerous. In still another way control recalls the situation of childhood: it establishes limits upon everything, just as our parents once did. Furthermore, the limits serve the same purposes they did in childhood: they provide reassurance against the felt danger of running wild, of being overwhelmed by the instincts; and they provide a sanction for securing as much satisfaction as possible within the stipulated limits.

In part perhaps because control recalls these parental functions but more especially because the mastery of the material implied in control suggests the *powers* the young child attributes to the parents, control appears to have a great deal to do with the curious fact that our attitude in reading, when we are captivated, very closely resembles that of a small child watching some stunt being performed for his amusement by mother or father. Of the fact itself there can be no doubt. The degree of our absorption, the naive delight in the skill of the storyteller, the unquestioning acceptance of his scale of values,[17] and the complete absence of any competitive feeling, all suggest a relation to a parental figure.

The sources of our desire for control are numerous and deep-seated. However, wide variations in the amount of control evident in different narrative works, shifts from time to time in the amount of control a given reader finds desirable, and oscillations of taste in different ages between "romantic" and "classic" poles, all indicate that still other forces are at work, which should be identified.

We have a kind of sullen suspicion of control which impresses us as having been achieved too easily. We intuitively realize that control measures the ego's mastery of the unconscious tendencies struggling for expression. If the mastery is too complete, the tendencies, we reason, cannot have much force behind them, and we feel deprived. We want them to have force, an opportunity to develop with a certain freedom.[18] We are even pleased by the occasional introduction of the fortuitous. When mastery is too complete, we are also likely to feel that some kind of deception has been practiced

[17] Percy Lubbock offers an excellent example of this particular characteristic of the reading experience: Balzac's success in communicating his sense of the importance of the homes in which his characters live and the objects which surround them. Balzac does this, it might be remarked parenthetically, without dramatizing the information; he accomplishes it by "mere" description. "These descriptions are clear and business-like; they are offered as an essential preliminary to the story, a matter that must obviously be dealt with, once for all, before the story can proceed. And he communicates his certainty to the reader, he imposes his belief in the need for precision and fullness; Balzac is so sure that every detail must be known, down to the vases on the mantelpiece or the pots and pans in the cupboard, that his reader cannot begin to question it." *The Craft of Fiction*, pp. 220-21.

[18] Our desire that stories should unfold with a certain freedom may have physical as well as psychological determinants. Cf. A. H. B. Allen: "Our ordinary movements are constantly limited by the pull of gravitation and the friction of the earth's surface. Anything which enables us to overcome these impediments and to carry out swift gliding or swinging movements with the minimum of bodily effort gives us an exhilarating sense of freedom and power. Hence the fascination of mere speed in motoring, and of such exercises as tobogganing, skating, ski-ing." "A Psychological Theory of Aesthetic Values," *British Journal of Psychology*, XXVIII, 1937-38. Hence, too, Allen continues, the exhilaration certain patterns of music give us. But, "That music is usually judged the higher which in the midst of its freedom preserves a feeling of restraint and self-mastery."

upon us. Indeed, our protests are likely to emphasize this aspect of the matter; if a writer exhibits too much polish or organization, we will complain that his work is contrived and unrealistic. We know that our own experience is a mixture of the patterned and the unpredictable. While our personality structure dooms us to live within a certain range of possibilities and to experience certain types of situations over and over again, chance occurrences, such as wars and the decisions of people over whom we have no control, also play a part in shaping our lives. We do not expect fiction to duplicate this mixture—we want it to be more logical, more comprehensible, than our own experience—but a sound instinct warns us against stories in which everything falls out too pat.

Our deepest desire, evidently, is for a feeling of tension between the tendencies expressed in fiction and the forces which seek to hold them in leash.[19] The more dangerous the tendencies, the greater the need for control, but the amount of control should never be in excess of what the material actually requires.[20]

5

The fiction writer must also resolve a conflict, which to some extent overlaps the one just considered, between our desire for economy and our desire for fullness and even richness of development. The grounds, in both our physical and psychic life, for prizing economy are obvious and unassailable. Nor can the value of economy in art be challenged so long as its role is correctly defined. The claims made for economy

[19] This desire almost becomes visible in our response to the antics of acrobats, dancers and other performers who *almost* lose their balance, fall or whatever, then avoid the threatened disaster at the last second. What the performers are doing is arousing our anxiety about the adequacy of their skill, then liquidating the anxiety and giving us pleasure by showing us that their skill is, after all, sufficient.

[20] Cf. W. R. D. Fairbairn: "A further analogy between the work of art and the dream may be observed. In the case of the dream, the complexity of the dream-work depends upon the relative strength of the repressed urges and the factors responsible for repression. In the case of the work of art, the complexity of the art-work is similarly determined." "Prolegomena to a Psychology of Art."

can, however, be vulgarized, and that is what I believe has occurred in contemporary esthetic speculation, in which form is often equated with the kind of brevity and streamlining so highly esteemed in our commercial culture.

It seems certain that our demand for economy, so defined, is opposed by other wishes. If this were not the case, the visual arts would soon reduce themselves to mathematical forms —a tendency which, of course, does not lack advocates— and we would read only digests or summaries of stories. Our preference for the stories and our tendency—not itself altogether defensible—to place a higher value on long and complex stories than on short and simple ones show that still other forces are at work, however little recognition they may be accorded in theory.

"The arts are not algebra," wrote Eugene Delacroix in his *Journal*, "in which the abbreviation of the figures contributes to the success of the problem; success in the arts is by no means a matter of abridging but of amplifying, if possible, and prolonging the sensation by all possible means." [21] The large measure of truth in this claim is easy to demonstrate in narrative art. Witness, for example, the tendency of fiction to incorporate plot elements which will intensify, underscore or subtly enrich the emotional effect desired. Obvious examples are the kind of "doubling" to be found in *Hamlet* and *Lear*, where the main plot is echoed in a subplot, or the weaving together or juxtaposition of contrasting stories, as in *Vanity Fair* and *The Wild Palms*. The inclusion of the story of Levin and Kitty in *Anna Karenina* provides an even more interesting example, for the relevance of their story to Anna's and Vronsky's is not only subtle but partial: neither the parallels to be drawn between the two couples nor the parallels between the four characters as individuals would, of themselves, fully justify the fusion of the two tales. We do not demand this kind of logical justification. So long as the additional material is inherently interesting and at least tangentially relevant, we

[21] *The Journal of Eugene Delacroix*, translated by Walter Pach (New York: Crown, 1948), as quoted by Daniel E. Schneider in *The Psychoanalyst and the Artist* (New York: Farrar, Straus, 1950), p. 183.

are glad enough to have the canvas opened up to include it; and, of course, in a great novel such as *Anna Karenina* no plot element impresses us as having been inserted in this fashion. The point is simply that we welcome the large canvas, the symphony, the long novel: they promise a greater and a richer pleasure. Clearly the goal of economy does not dominate the *objectives* of art.

Even in the achievement of the objectives, it is evident that we are seldom solely concerned with making haste. Two conflicting tendencies can usually be discerned, one sweeping us along toward some predestined end, the other manifesting itself through delays and counter-movements and intent upon prolonging everything. To reach his goal the hero must overcome obstacles and inhibitions; before and after he reaches it, his plans are crossed by complications; even during the falling action there are developments suggesting that a conclusion becoming more and more visible can after all be avoided. In terms of our response to the content, the function of such developments is to satisfy our recessive desires: complications during the rising action satisfy the inhibitions which have to be overcome; complications during the falling action satisfy our sympathy wth the hero and sustain our hope that he can escape his doom. In terms of the objectives of form the retarding developments represent an attempt to augment pleasure by prolonging and postponing gratification.[22] From earliest childhood we often employ the same means to increase the pleasure we secure from satisfying physical needs. It is entirely possible that the artistic tendency derives from the primitive prototypes.

The quarrel between our desire for brevity and our desire

---

[22] I cannot resist conjecturing that the subtlety with which the greatest art satisfies our desires is also related to the tendency to enhance our pleasure by postponing fulfilment. Subtlety apparently suggests a qualitative consideration: it seems reasonable to suppose that a subtle satisfaction is simply the appropriate satisfaction of a refined desire. However, the distinction between qualitative and quantitative is not as absolute as it appears. We may tease a child by delaying before we give him something he wants or by giving him something different from what he wants but which we know he will like as well or even better. The two kinds of teasing do not seem discontinuous or even so very different.

for richness can be traced even in the language of fiction. Sometimes, for example, figures of speech are employed primarily for the speed with which they make us see. Usually, however, they serve some other purpose as well, and many of the figures we admire are majestic and leisurely, elaborately developed, clearly unconcerned with speed. Furthermore, the briefest metaphor may be followed by another, as in the following example from *Hamlet,* in which the subject happens to be speed:

> Haste me to know't, that I, with
>   wings as swift
> As meditation or the thoughts
>   of love,
> May sweep to my revenge.

Though in a sense "the thoughts of love" repeats "meditation," no one would maintain that it is redundant. It specifies, it introduces a sexual note, it perhaps recalls the connection already made (in I, 2, 153-157 and I, 2, 177-179) between haste and sexual gratification.

Taken together, the two metaphors represent an economical means of achieving a particular effect. In *this* sense the most elaborate figure and the most intricate plot complication may often be justified as economical. The party scene which opens "The Dead" is four times as long as the scene upon which the emotional impact of the story immediately depends, yet no perceptive reader is likely to feel that the first scene should be omitted or shortened. We value economy in narrative art, but by economy we mean the skill with which the storyteller selects and arranges his material to achieve his multifarious and often conflicting ends and not brevity per se.

Great narrative art contains little which is really irrelevant or redundant, and anything which is so is properly regarded as a defect. "Economy of expenditure of psychic energy in perception" deserves to be accepted not, as Joseph Weiss suggests,[23] as the sole source of "formal aesthetic pleasure" but

---

[23] In "A Psychological Theory of Formal Beauty," *Psychoanalytic Quarterly,* XVI, 1947.

as one of its important determinants. As Weiss himself recognizes, however, it is not ease of perception of itself which
gives us pleasure but, rather, a comparison of the ease with
which the artistic ends are attained with the difficulties we
would have had in reaching *the same ends* without the econo-
mies.

6

Two other conflicts must be resolved in achieving the ends
of form. The storyteller must work in terms of specifics—
tell us a concrete, particular story. Emotional force is invariably lost when fiction depends more than momentarily on a
general, expository form of statement or when the characters
are subordinated to some abstract intention, as in allegories.
But though the storyteller deals in specifics, we expect him to
spin a tale which impresses us as having wide significance and
validity. I do not think that D. H. Lawrence is correct when
he maintains that the beauty of the novel inheres in the fact
that "everything is true in its own relationship, and no further." [24] It is true that we do not expect fiction to offer us
generalizations of universal validity. On the other hand, we
would not be satisfied—we would not usually be interested—
if a story did not cast a shadow beyond itself, if it did not
possess a measure of general significance. A story need not tell
us how all men would act under all conditions, but it must
show us how men of a given psychological stamp would probably act under given conditions. The conditions themselves
must not appear unique. They need not have timeless validity,
impress us as a sample of what men in any age will experience
during their life—though the very greatest fiction manages to
do even this—but they must at least seem typical: the kind of
conditions which the characters described would be likely to
encounter.

The last of the formal problems we shall pause to consider
is by no means the least troublesome. We expect the storyteller, out of the mere stuff of words, to create a three-dimen-

[24] "The Novel," *The Later D. H. Lawrence* (New York: Knopf, 1952),
p. 196.

sional world so life-like or so much in accordance with certain psychological realities that we can deceive ourselves that we are living in it. At the same time we want him to make it clear that this world is no more than an illusion—a painted ship upon a painted ocean. We ask, that is, for the privilege of being at once participants in the action and detached spectators of it.

Although these demands may seem unreasonable, we are fully justified in making them. Except perhaps in response to comedy,[25] they must both be fulfilled if fiction is to give us pleasure. We cannot have the experiences for which we turn to fiction if what we read does not possess the momentary authority, the hallucinatory vividness, of our fondest dreams. It is essential, too, that the illusion be sustained: any jarring note will awaken us, return us to the "real" world, with its anxieties and frustrations. Yet we cannot have the experiences either unless we are aware that we are engaging in make-believe. Without this knowledge we would be too guilt-ridden and too frightened. We would know the terror as well as the exhilaration which accompany danger. We would experience neither pleasure nor the clear perception narrative art seeks to foster.[26]

A certain disassociation must be achieved in the reader. Chapter VII will take up some of the means by which the storyteller differentiates and distances his world from the one

[25] Cf. the discussions of comedy, Ch. VII and Ch. XI.

[26] Freud makes the same point in a little-known article, not presently available in book form in English: "The spectator . . . wants to feel, to act, to mould the world in the light of his desire—in short, to be a hero. And the playwright-actors make all this possible for him by giving him the opportunity to identify himself with a hero. But they must spare him something also; for the spectator is well aware that taking over the hero's role in his own person would involve such griefs, such sufferings and such frightful terrors as would almost nullify the pleasure therein; and he knows too that he has but one single life to live, and might perhaps perish in a single one of the hero's many battles with the Fates. Hence his enjoyment presupposes an illusion; it presupposes an attenuation of his suffering through the certainty that in the first place it is another than himself who acts and suffers upon the stage, and that in the second place it is only a play, whence no threat to his personal security can ever arise. . . ." "Psychopathic Characters on the Stage," *Psychoanalytic Quarterly*, XI, 1942.

we know, so that we will not be too fully enveloped in the spell he casts. To the means he employs to make his imaginary world convincing I shall not devote much space. They are the staple of most existing works about fiction—of discussions of "realism" and "naturalism," and treatises on dramatization, dialogue and the management of point of view. The last factor has perhaps been overemphasized in much recent criticism. In consequence, the impression is being unwittingly conveyed that our acceptance of a story depends largely if not entirely upon the skill with which an author handles this one technical factor—an example of the tendency to mistake aspects of the creative process about which writers are most articulate for the whole of the activity. In fact, of course, acceptance of a story depends upon the writer's skill in handling a dozen formal factors and, in equal measure, upon his mastery of his material. Even while considering form, we should not neglect the last factor. The writer's knowledge of the way people think, feel and behave does as much to establish his authority as any single thing, and nothing is so likely to disrupt our absorption in a story as an act or emotional response which does not ring true psychologically.

Chapter VI *The Language of Fiction*

In a Symbol . . . there is concealment and yet revelation.
CARLYLE

How are the objectives of form achieved? In this and the following chapter our focus will shift from ends to means. Since it would take a long volume to deal with all the weapons in form's arsenal, I shall deliberately concentrate on some which do not seem to me to have been accorded the attention they deserve.

Tardiness in recognizing the relief of anxiety as an important objective of form may have something to do with the scanty consideration given these devices. But there is a stranger explanation for the neglect of some of them: *they have simply been taken for granted.* Instead of being recognized as achievements requiring skill and effort, they have usually been regarded as generic attributes of fiction, characteristics which appear more or less automatically when one tells a story. In part this error is the result of circular reasoning. The characteristics in question *are* indispensable for successful storytelling and *are* regularly present in the fiction we admire. But they are there because they have been put there: in amateur work they are either absent or present in a faltering way which reveals how much talent and labor are required for their achievement.

The very writers who perform the labor, however, would usually explain the need for it on different grounds. It is the *differentiating* characteristics of various schools of fiction which excite attention and comment, and, on the part of aspiring writers, conscious imitation, adaptation or rejection. The qualities to be considered are so integral to fiction, and so omnipresent in the work on which each successive generation develops its conception of the story form, that writers, too, are likely to take them for granted.

The basic reason so little attention is paid to these qualities,

I believe, is that they seem so natural to us that it does not occur to us to isolate or explain them, much less associate them with labor. Certain formal qualities of fiction—the very language in which it is cast—closely parallel basic characteristics of the original language of our minds, what Freud calls "primary-process" thinking, the process which governs our unconscious psychic activity and triggers our fantasies and dreams. Our failure to take special note of the qualities is in some respects no more surprising than our failure to remark the fact that Shakespeare wrote in English. Perhaps, indeed, it is less surprising, for until Freud wrote *The Interpretation of Dreams* there was no key to the language with which fiction is in many essential ways to be compared.

In this chapter we shall note some of the parallels between fiction and primary-process thinking. It cannot be unimportant that fiction speaks to us in a language more natural to us, more intimate, more readily understood, than our native tongue. The achievement of all the objectives of form, and the entire process of response to fiction, hinges to some extent on this one fact.

2

In speaking of the language of fiction in this fashion, it is obvious that I am not referring to the words through which stories are ordinarily conveyed to us. Words, in fact, are used quite differently in fiction and in primary-process thinking and we shall take note of some of the differences later on.

What must have our attention first of all is that the words are largely used to create sense impressions—images or pictures, if we use those words quite loosely to embrace impressions which stir any of the senses and not sight alone. The impressions are, however, predominantly visual. Like our dreams and fantasies, fiction is really composed of a series of scenes, episodes, happenings. It shows us individual human beings doing specific things against a given background. Not all of these elements are necessarily particularized—a point to which we shall return in a moment—but, whether they be blurred or distinct, what we are given is a steady stream of sense impressions. The ultimate language of fiction is sensory and, to a quite astonishing degree, visual.

The tendency to translate everything into sense impressions is apparent in the smallest units of which fiction is composed. Individual words are often selected on the basis of their power to make us see or hear, feel, smell or taste. When direct discourse is used, the natural rhythms of speech are usually simulated, in part, of course, to achieve an effect of realism, but in part also to make it easier for the words to sound in our minds. When such things as abstract ideas and states of mind are to be conveyed, writers of prose fiction are almost as likely as poets to use similes and metaphors; they make perhaps more frequent use of concrete examples designed to visualize relatively abstract points. If on the whole writers of prose fiction use fewer figures of speech than poets, it is largely because so much of their material lends itself to other forms of sensory expression more indigenous to fiction.

I have referred to the fact that certain elements in the pictures offered us may be purposely left indistinct. There are a number of explanations. Too many details might distract our attention from the things it is essential we see clearly. In short stories, for example, a faint indication of the background may be all that is needed: fuller elaboration might impede the swift development of character and plot. Some writers, including Hawthorne, James and Kafka, prefer to keep the meaning of certain actions at least temporarily obscure. In many instances aspects of a story are left indefinite in order to stimulate the reader's imaginative activity. If a hero is not too precisely described, it may make it all the easier for us to slip into his place. If a heroine is described in vague or conventional terms, we may more readily picture her after our own desiring.[1]

---

[1] Certain things are also left vague, of course, to induce the reader to complete the psychological, as well as the physical, portrait of a character. Cf. Freud: "It is . . . a subtle economy of art in the poet not to permit his hero to give complete expression to all his secret springs of action. By this means he obliges us to supplement, he engages our intellectual activity, diverts it from critical reflections, and keeps us closely identified with his hero. A bungler in his place would deliberately express all that he wishes to

The reader may engage in still other kinds of supplementary visualizing. For example, I believe we often *see* as well as hear characters talk—picture the changes which take place in their expression, imagine them moving about and gesticulating. We may form impressions about what lies behind the words they speak, and recall the events which cause them to speak as they do or anticipate the developments their train of thought foretells. Besides making such interpolations when we read fiction, we do a great deal of what I call analogizing: we recall or invent episodes involving ourselves which parallel a story or various parts of it. So long as these memories and fantasies are controlled by the given structure of events, they should also be taken into account. They comprise a legitimate and important element in our response.

If we could photograph the way a story registers upon the mind of a reader—and we can do this to some extent by observing our own experience—we would be amazed, I believe, by the number of pictures, of sense-impressions of every kind, we would discover. It would not always be easy to distinguish between the impressions we had supplied and those conveyed to us in ready-made fashion, but even if we tried rigorously to confine ourselves to the latter, we would find that we had more pictures than we could readily count. Because of their number and the rapidity with which one image is followed by another the pictures would seldom be worked out in complete detail. As photographs they would strike us as being underdeveloped. The fact that the images succeed one another with extraordinary speed, so that they must be apprehended quickly and elliptically, is itself of the utmost importance, as we shall see. But first we should consider some of the results which flow from the fact that to an unappreciated extent fiction registers upon our minds in the picture-language of our fantasies and dreams.

---

reveal to us, and would then find himself confronted by our cool, untrammelled intelligence, which would preclude any great degree of illusion." "Some Character-Types Met With in Psycho-Analytic Work," *Collected Papers,* Vol. IV (London: Hogarth, 1948), p. 323.

3

Needless to say, not all of the advantages of the sensory language of fiction hinge upon its resemblance to primary-process thinking, nor have all the advantages gone unremarked. A number of storytellers have been explicitly aware of how much is gained in vividness, immediacy and emotional force from rendering material in concrete, sensuous terms. "It's by pictures, pictures . . . that one must get at you," Dostoevsky has one of his characters declare. As we shall see more in detail later on, "pictures" facilitate swift and easy communication, and most writers have been more or less consciously aware of this.

Probably writers have also sensed the fact that the concrete, sensory language of fiction is highly congenial to our minds, though so far as I know none has commented upon this. Actually, as Freud has pointed out, in transforming our thoughts into perceptual forms, the dream-work itself is obeying a regressive impulse: ". . . our thoughts originated in such perceptual forms; their earliest material and the first stages in their development consisted of sense-impressions, or, more accurately, of memory-pictures of these. It was later that words were attached to these pictures and then connected so as to form thoughts." [2] Insofar as fiction, too, casts things in concrete, sensory terms, it is bypassing ordinary symbolic modes of expression and bringing us as close as possible to the way in which experience originally registered, and to a considerable degree continues to register, upon our minds. It is in large measure because of the language it employs that fiction possesses something of the quality of actual experience.

It is obvious that the concrete language available to fiction is an ideal instrument for simulating the *events* of our lives—our actions and the things which befall us. The sensed recognition of its suitability may be partly responsible for the concept of literature as "an imitation of life." What has not been sufficiently appreciated is a fact to which the parallelism with

[2] *A General Introduction to Psychoanalysis* (New York: Garden City, 1938), p. 160.

primary-process thinking points: *the language of fiction is also an ideal instrument for objectifying and externalizing our desires, fears and inner conflicts.* It closely resembles the language we use for this purpose in our fantasies and dreams and, more soberly, in our conscious attempts to visualize the actions our desires imply and the consequences of those actions.

We already know that from the point of view of what it has to say fiction has certain advantages over these other forms of psychic activity. These advantages stem in large measure from its greater honesty, its refusal to misrepresent the human predicament in order to give us pleasure. Even our dreams and fantasies do not ignore reality considerations and the defenses we have developed against prohibited impulses, but, composed as they are under the sway of the pleasure principle, they seldom give them sufficient weight. It is scarcely surprising that they give us a less complete and trustworthy account of the world and of our own nature than does narrative art.

When we consciously try to understand the impulses which fret us and deal with the problems which arise in our lives, we, of course, aspire to complete honesty, but, as we are often aware, we seldom achieve it. Our anxieties thwart our desire to bring every consideration into the open and give each its just value. Even as we analyze an emotional problem, for example, we may be oppressed by the feeling that some possibilities for dealing with it are eluding us. Nor are we always able to consider the various solutions which suggest themselves without betraying bias. We may catch ourselves gliding over the difficulties of one course of action or dwelling on an advantage of another which is not likely to materialize while we ignore a consequence which is more probable. Almost always the complete and objective picture of the situation we consciously desire remains tantalizingly beyond our reach.

Two things enable narrative art to succeed where we so often fail: the basic tendency toward impartiality discussed in Chapter III and the formal tendency, first identified by Aristotle, to organize a story around some one action and to give the whole of that action. To give the whole, the writer of fiction must be more persistent than we ordinarily are ourselves in searching out whatever is relevant to the action and more rigorous than we are in excluding what is not. To make us appreciate the interrelationships among the events he selects, he must arrange them in a way which reveals or suggests their causal as well as their chronological connections; he must track down causes and trace consequences. From the flux of experience he must abstract something which has beginning, middle and end.

Fiction is driven, it almost appears, to strive for such virtues as completeness, unity and coherence. What makes us prize it, however, is not solely its capacity to see our problems more honestly and completely than we usually can ourselves but *its capacity to present what it sees in the very language in which we tend to formulate our problems*. It offers us something toward which a great deal of our own psychic activity is directed: a faithful, clear, readily-understood view of our actual experiences and the experiences which would be the natural expression of our proclivities. Fiction *objectifies* our problems: it translates what was internal and amorphous, or too close to us to be seen clearly, into something outside ourselves and easy to perceive: a series of images delineating a specific action, its causes and its consequences.

Since objectification necessarily involves the projection of our problems upon others—the fictional characters—and thus enables us to disown unwelcome impulses and concerns, it also contributes to the achievement of another goal of form, the minimization of anxiety. The very definiteness which is a by-product of successful objectification also contributes to this goal: it suggests a firm mastery of those forces which make it difficult for us to direct our lives in orderly fashion or even to formulate our problems clearly.[3]

[3] Cf. Yrjo Hirn: "The more therefore the work grows in definiteness in the thought and under the hand of the artist, the more it will repress and subdue the chaotic tumult of emotional excitement." "Art the Reliever," *A Modern Book of Esthetics*, Melvin M. Rader, editor (New York: Holt, 1935), p. 110. Perhaps the past tense would be preferable in the last part of Hirn's statement: the more a work grows in definiteness, the more it *has* subdued "the tumult of emotional excitement."

It is in connection with the objectification of our *inner* problems that the biggest *reductions* of anxiety are probably achieved. Fiction transforms what was internal, in all probability amorphous, but in any case terrifying because we could not know what form its discharge might take into a representation, in images, of a specific action. The fear aroused by such a representation is so much less than that produced by shapeless, mobile forces struggling for release that the change could be regarded as qualitative: what before caused a large amount of *anxiety* now produces a limited amount of *fear*.

Not even such a formulation does complete justice to the value of objectification, however. It indicates that our inner conflicts can be dealt with much more comfortably once they are objectified, but it fails to convey the fact that unless and until they are objectified in many cases they cannot be dealt with at all. Conflicts which arouse a great deal of anxiety are often repressed. Objectified, without being acknowledged they can be confronted—a gain of the utmost importance—and the fear they inspire can be cathartically relieved. Objectification provides the conditions which must be met for us to ventilate our most significant problems—a degree of detachment, a measure of security. It is the first and most essential step in the generally appreciated but dimly understood esthetic process called distancing.

Up to a point there is an analogy between objectification in fiction and symptom formation in the neuroses, especially in phobias. The development of a symptom suggests that a tangible external difficulty—even one involving inconvenience, loss and possibly pain—may be easier to tolerate than a tormenting inner conflict which we cannot understand or define. But symptoms are a device for evading our problems. Though objectification permits us to disown our problems, it sets the stage for us to examine them.

4

What I have called the language of fiction is only one of the factors which enables narrative art to objectify our problems. In still another way the concrete, sensory language of fiction single-handedly fosters the kind of anxiety-free perception toward which form strives: *it quickly and effectively transmits almost any kind of material without requiring the reader to put what he understands into words.* Though composed of words, so far as its reception is concerned the language of fiction is an instrument of non-discursive communication. The importance of this characteristic can scarcely be overemphasized. It plays a decisive part in achieving the objectives of form and in the entire process of response to narrative art.

We can quickly ascertain the extent to which fiction is composed of images by thumbing through some of our favorite stories. The first page and a half of Chekov's "On the Road" gives us more than a score of pictures and sense-impressions. We first get a distant view of a "tall, broad-shouldered man of forty," asleep with his elbows on a table. Then we see him close-up, so that his features become visible. Then our attention is directed to a bench where an eight-year-old girl sleeps, whom we later discover to be the man's daughter; she, too, is described in considerable detail: our eye takes in her thinness, her pallor, the semicircular comb cutting her cheek unbeknownst to her as she sleeps. Next we are shown around the room where the girl and her father lie sleeping and told how the room smells and made to hear the hiss of the fire. We are made aware of the storm raging outside, see the potboy enter the room, perform certain errands and leave. We hear the different ways in which the chimes of a church clock sound in the room, watch the little girl start and wake up. Still other images may flash through our minds as we take in the ones which are given. For example, we may add to Chekov's description of the girl and the man or speculate about them. Later in the story, if not at this point, we may imagine ourselves in the place of one or another of them or compose a story paralleling Chekov's, or some part of it, in which we have a role.

Only one thing needs to be added to make clear the nature of the communication process in fiction: for the most part

the images register upon our minds *as images.* Only occasionally is their meaning—or, at any rate, any considerable portion
of their meaning—transcribed into words. There is no need
for such transcriptions. Untranscribed, the images are not
only understandable, but possessed of more vividness and
immediacy than is usually attached to words. Nor is there
time for more than partial transcriptions, unless we choose to
read at an unnaturally slow pace. The images are often too
thick with meaning and they succeed one another too rapidly
to be anatomized. This is obviously the case when we watch
a motion picture or a play, but the situation is not so very
different when we read fiction: our desire to learn what happens next, to take in the entire story, reinforces our natural
tendency to depend upon our immediate, intuitive understanding.

Curiosity and our tendency to avoid unnecessary effort
exert a more or less constant influence in deterring us from
formulating the significance of each part of a story as it is
read. A third factor operates selectively. This is the censorship of the unconscious ego, which, out of its reluctance to
offend the superego and its desire to spare us pain, opposes the
conceptualization, and in general the conscious apprehension,
of those meanings of images which are likely to arouse revulsion and anxiety. As a result of the operation of the three
factors, we formulate no more than a small portion of what
we understand when we read fiction, and we are particularly
unlikely to formulate perceptions which would arouse anxiety
if made explicit. Obviously a language which lends itself to
this kind of partial and selective apprehension is an ideal one
for dealing with emotional problems. It encourages honesty
without jeopardizing security; it permits things to be said
and understood without being conceptualized and brought
to awareness.

5

The picture language of fiction has the further advantage
of being naturally ambiguous. This is so even if we tempo-

rarily leave aside the aspect of its ambiguity with which we are acquainted—the fact that a story, or any single episode or detail, may simultaneously mean many different things. The language of fiction may be ambiguous in at least two other senses: it may permit us to waver between two meanings which preclude one another, but seem equally tenable or almost so; and it may project an impression which is diffuse and broad rather than fixed and univocal.

"The Turn of the Screw" in its entirety provides an excellent illustration of the first type of ambiguity. We do not know whether the apparitions should be taken "straight" or regarded as projections of the governess who tells the story; almost every detail in the story can be interpreted in a double sense.[4] Here the two possible meanings do not support each other and give us a sense of something rich and overdetermined; on the contrary, they are incompatible with each other—as the governess herself realizes, she is heroic if the first interpretation is valid and guilty of terrible things if it is not.[5] The chance the story gives us to play back and forth between the two sensed possibilities is itself a source of pleasure—a pleasure which has as its prototype the solution of problems and especially puzzles or riddles.

This kind of ambiguity corresponds to what Abraham Kaplan and Ernst Kris call "disjunctive ambiguity." [6] The second type corresponds to what they call "additive ambiguity." An image is additively ambiguous "when it has several meanings differing only in degree of specificity, or in what they add to the common core of meaning. The word 'rich,' for example, may be interpreted in terms of 'abundance' or 'value' or 'excellence'; but the response clusters which these indicate are not fully distinct and exclusive, but overlap and merge into

[4] See Edmund Wilson, "The Ambiguity of Henry James," *The Triple Thinkers* (New York: Harcourt, Brace, 1938).

[5] The two meanings are, of course, compatible if one is taken to represent the governess' conscious, the other her unconscious attitude. However, the all-important question in connection with "The Turn of the Screw" is which of the attitudes is dominant.

[6] "Aesthetic Ambiguity," in Ernst Kris, *Psychoanalytic Explorations in Art* (New York: International Universities Press, 1952).

one another." [7] As the example suggests, almost any word *used in context* may be ambiguous in this sense to a certain extent.

Examples of additive ambiguity abound in fiction. In "On the Road" the detail that Liharev's daughter wore "a brown dress and long black stockings" gives us a picture and carries the implication that the girl is ill-dressed and poorly cared for. Perhaps it faintly suggests that she is without a mother's care; at any rate, it helps prepare us for this revelation. The snowstorm provides a far richer example; indeed, it is impossible to exhaust its significance. The core meaning is simple enough; the snowstorm represents nature or fate in its indifference and even hostility to man and his purposes, the thing against which man must exert himself if he is to live in the most meager and physical sense of the word. The storm is "frantic" and "wrathful"; it flings itself about the tavern "with the ferocity of a wild beast."

Other meanings radiate centrifugally from this one. For example, the strength of this adversary of man is developed: in the sound of the storm there is "angry misery . . . unsatisfied hate, and the mortified impatience of something accustomed to triumph." Curiously, the necessity of battling against such a foe makes man appear not heroic but puny. In the morning Liharev does not seem tall and broad-shouldered to Mlle. Ilovaisky but little, "just as the biggest steamer seems to us a little thing when we hear that it has crossed the ocean." At least one other meaning of the storm must be mentioned. At the end of the story we see that it is an adversary against which one must pit not only one's physical strength, but one's resources of mind, heart and spirit. It has offered Liharev the opportunity to know Mlle. Ilovaisky. Now it swallows her up again. As she disappears, it also swallows the beaten Liharev: the snowflakes settle "greedily" on his hair, his beard, his shoulders, signaling the end of what we feel to be his final opportunity to wrest a measure of warmth and happiness from life.

Still other images of fiction should perhaps not be called

[7] *Ibid.*, p. 246.

ambiguous but enigmatic: we feel that they have meaning, we may even feel we understand that meaning, but we find it difficult if not impossible to put what we understand into words. The large nose of Liharev's daughter, which stands out "as thick and ugly a lump as the man's," is an example of such an image. We feel the appropriateness of the detail, but cannot say what it means, any more than we can verbally define the meaning of a musical phrase. The communication process in fiction is often non-discursive because there is no incentive for us to state meanings in words or because some force inhibits us from making the attempt. In some instances, however, fiction is *inescapably* non-discursive: the meaning or full meaning of certain images cannot be reduced to conceptual terms.

In still other cases the images of fiction are ambiguous in a sense with which we are already familiar: they simultaneously mean a number of different things. Georgiana's birthmark, the court in *The Trial,* the white whale in *Moby Dick* —these are all examples of overdetermined images. "On the Road" furnishes us another such image: Liharev chatting gaily while wrapping Mlle. Ilovaisky in shawls, kerchiefs, scarves, pelisse and coat for the resumption of her journey. The deed has a natural place in the surface action of the story, but a reader would have to be inattentive indeed not to sense that it has deeper significance. It frames the story formally. It was as a shapeless, anonymous bundle that Mlle. Ilovaisky first appeared on the scene; she only gradually acquired a distinct physical appearance, identity, individuality. In restoring her to bundled anonymity Liharev is passing by or unconsciously rejecting the opportunity to react to her as a woman, an individual, a possible wife. The image even suggests the reason why he is doing this: it is because he himself is "wrapped up" in his problems and his posturing—and, more deeply, in his fears and feelings of guilt. Liharev wants to suffer; and he is afraid even to gamble for happiness—to commit himself to something once again, to risk rebuff and disappointment.

When the images of fiction have great richness of meaning,

it is customary to refer to them as symbols. By now it should be apparent that there is no sharp line of demarcation between a symbol and any other image. Though the designation of certain images of fiction as symbols represents a partial recognition of a highly significant resource of fiction, it is not without unfortunate consequences. It has tended to distract attention from the fact that *in general* the language of fiction functions symbolically.

The isolation of certain images as symbols may also lead us to think of them as somehow extraneous to the stories in which they appear—decorative or superimposed. In fact, the richest symbols are always an integral part of the background or action. Sometimes, to be sure, they may recur, like a motif in music or painting, and acquire additional meaning with each fresh use. The storm in "On the Road" has this characteristic, and Joyce's use of snow in "The Dead" is even more elaborately orchestrated. At the beginning of the story the snow is something to be scraped from Gabriel Conroy's galoshes as he enters the home of his aunts. As Joyce develops the image it is a way of informing us of certain aspects of Gabriel's character, above all of his narcissism. At the end of the story the snow is something larger than Gabriel, something which encompasses him and at the same time unites him with all humanity, with the living and the dead. The wrapping-up of Mlle. Ilovaisky also gains a measure of significance from the fact that it reverses the unwrapping ceremony which occurred upon her arrival. However, both actions, and all references to snowstorm or snow in "On the Road" and in "The Dead," have some immediate functional purpose. Some of the richest symbols in fiction, furthermore, are solitary incidents or other story elements which are nowhere echoed. "The Dead" contains an unsurpassable example of such a symbol—Gabriel Conroy standing in the dark, gazing up the staircase at his wife, only the lower part of whose body is visible, as she listens in rapt silence to some song he cannot hear. Many pages could be spent elucidating this scene, but the relevant point is that it does not impress us as being dragged in; it has a firm place in the texture of the story.

Certain images have many meanings for us, it should be remarked in passing, because they have many meanings for the writers who created them; genetically, too, they are over-determined, a single image simultaneously expressing a number of conscious or unconscious impulses and ideas. However, while an image formed in this fashion is particularly *likely* to evoke a rich response, there is no necessary relationship between the amount of significance an image possesses for an author and its effect upon us.[8] The image may or may not be readily communicable; in either case its impact also depends in part on the skill with which it is molded and used. Under the best of conditions I doubt if there is often an exact correspondence between the meaning an image possesses for author and reader. *Some* of the meanings the image had for the author will of course be communicated, but others may not be and still others may be added.

The resemblance between fiction and primary-process thinking is not limited to their common employment of a highly imagistic language. To mention only one other similarity, the transitions between images in fiction, and the relationship between background details and events, are often explicable, as in dreams, not so much on logical grounds as in terms of sensed emotional connections. We are told why Mlle. Ilovaisky moves away from Liharev after protesting his intention to accept employment in the coal mines—she is ashamed of the heat with which she has spoken. Our intuitive

---

[8] Cf. Abraham Kaplan and Ernst Kris: ". . . we may introduce the concept of the *potential* of a symbol as the obverse side of its overdetermination: a symbol has a high potential in the degree to which it may be construed as cause of multiple effects (rather than being taken as effect of multiple causes). While the two are obviously related to one another, potential does not *necessarily* correspond to overdetermination. The tyro may have an intense experience and employ for its communication symbols which—for him—are highly charged with multiple significance. But in fact this overdetermination may be purely private; . . . Conversely, symbols may have a higher potential for a particular audience than was involved in the artist's intent." "Esthetic Ambiguity," p. 255. Since the focus of *Fiction and the Unconscious* is on *response*, throughout it I have used the word "overdetermined" in the sense in which Kaplan and Kris use the word "potential"—to denote the power of an image or story to *evoke* more than one meaning.

comprehension of the physical basis of that heat helps us to understand why she walks toward the window and, without thinking, moves her fingers rapidly over the cold pane.

6

Though the particular similarities we have considered between fiction and products of primary-process thinking, such as dreams, have received relatively little attention, the fact that there should be certain similarities should occasion no surprise. Everything we know about the formation of dreams and the creative process leads us to expect them. As Dr. Gustav Bychowski has pointed out,[9] one of the terms Freud employed to describe a principle governing the dream-work—*regard for representability*—suggest an awareness on his part of a kinship between the dream and art. It should be remembered, too, that the last phase of the dream-work, secondary elaboration, occurs so near the point of waking that it has "practically the whole range of intellectual operations at [its] disposal." [10]

If within the limits imposed by the fact that the dreamer is asleep the dream strives for some of the effects we associate with art, it is even more obvious that creators of art try to tap the surging energies responsible for the formation of dreams. The fact that some writers drink or take drugs or employ special rituals to gain access to their unconscious provides dramatic proof of this, and from Plato to Yeats there are innumerable statements testifying to the important role unconscious thinking plays in creative activity. The very concept of "inspiration" attests to the same thing.[11] As Ernst Kris has emphasized, some degree of relaxation of the ego—of regression—is essential for significant artistic achievement. It is essential also in response—in the re-creation of the work by the individual reader—and many characteristics of fiction, including the imagistic language it employs, seek to induce such relaxation: to bring the reader, in Kris's terms, to a psy-

[9] "From Catharsis to Work of Art: The Making of an Artist," *Psychoanalysis and Culture*, George B. Wilbur and Warner Muensterberger, editors (New York: International Universities Press, 1951).

[10] Edwin Glover, *Freud or Jung* (New York: Norton, 1950), p. 111.

[11] See Ernst Kris, "On Inspiration," *Psychoanalytic Explorations in Art.*

chic level which corresponds to that of the artistic creator.

There is, of course, a decisive difference between the regression which is involved in artistic achievement and that which occurs during sleep: the former is usually deliberately sought, but sought or unsought it is *controlled*—it is in the service of the waking ego. The difference is all-important even when material erupted from unconscious sources is used unchanged in a work of art, for its use is a matter of choice; the material *could* be altered or rejected if it did not happen to suit the artist's purposes. In all artistic achievement there is an intricate interplay between two elements—free, spontaneous creativity and cool, critical reflection. The interplay is illustrated, as Kaplan and Kris suggest, by the tendency of painters to work for a while and then step back and examine their canvas.

The relaxation of the ego which takes place when we read fiction is also voluntary and controlled. There is a willing suspension of disbelief because we want to obtain the satisfactions which prompted us to read a given book. But our willingness to meet a book halfway must be requited: we are constantly judging and appraising, and if a work seems false or otherwise unworthy of our trust, we will become increasingly critical and less and less immersed in it. Our critical activity is, of course, effortless and automatic in comparison with the fiction writer's: we simply accept or reject or compare; he, if he is dissatisfied, must revise or rewrite. There is an analogy between the creative act and the reading experience but not an exact correspondence.

Since it is passed on and altered, even when it is not shaped, by the writer's waking intelligence, what I have called the language of fiction is, of course, not an exact replica of the language of fantasies and dreams. In the first place, the images of fiction are conveyed to us in words—a consideration to which we shall return—but they differ from the images of dreams also in being more intelligible: though their meaning cannot always be easily reduced to words they are more regularly and fully understandable than the hieroglyphic language of dreams. The dream is autistic; the artist is governed by the desire to communicate. Both in sifting the images his unconscious may suggest and in developing additional ones, he usually considers their communication potential. And often his work only begins with selection. He shapes, he defines, until his images have the particular range of meanings he wants them to have—consider the different use of snow made by Chekov in "On the Road" and Joyce in "The Dead." Like Chekov and Joyce also, he may orchestrate certain images so that they constantly grow in significance and emotional force. Even images which have a more or less fixed meaning in the unconscious may be treated in this fashion until their usual significance is extended, narrowed or even reversed. In "The Burrow," for example, Kafka uses what is fundamentally a womb symbol, which usually represents security (though sometimes death), to convey the frantic, almost incessant and yet invariably unsuccessful quest for security by the compulsive neurotic.

As we would expect, there is an analogous difference between fiction and dreams in their treatment of transitions between images and the connections between background details and events. Even in fiction, as has been mentioned, the rationale of transitions must often be intuitively grasped. But wherever necessary the writer explains and clarifies. In consequence, whereas dreams are characteristically jerky and disconnected, primarily because of the distortion the latent thoughts must undergo to pass the dream censorship, in a well-written story every detail falls into place and seems organically related to every other; every event flows logically and inevitably from what has preceded; background, characters and happenings all seem part of a coherent, comprehensible world.

Finally, we must take account of the differences in the way words are used in fiction and in primary-process thinking. Images are the primary medium for representing the impulses which seek expression in fantasies and dreams. Words, when they are employed at all, nearly always have a purely auxiliary role. In most cases the dream will strive to represent even such unlikely material as a chain of reasoning through images.

It is in part because of the lengths to which it may have to go to do this that certain dreams are so unintelligible.

In contrast, words are the primary raw material of fiction. I have emphasized the extent to which words are used to build up images. Easily, quickly and—in part at least—non-discursively understood, innately ambiguous and highly congenial to our minds, images are ideally adapted to the kind of pleasurable, anxiety-free perception toward which fiction strives. But it is obviously an advantage that fiction is not *compelled* to use images, that in dealing with material which does not lend itself to expression in concrete, sensory terms it can resort to ordinary conceptual discourse.

The basic aim of the dream is *expressive:* it strives for the hallucinatory gratification of impulses which threaten to disturb sleep. To be sure, in its use of words—even words which do not actually appear in the manifest content—the dream sometimes displays the same cleverness it manifests in constructing images. For example, a particular word may secure preference over others because it lends itself to visual representation, simultaneously represents two impulses struggling for expression, or facilitates a transition between one latent thought and another. It is true also that some of the words which intersperse dreams, like certain dream images, may be readily understood by others. But whether this occurs is purely a matter of chance. Words, like images, are selected because of their emotional significance for the dreamer and their capacity to express—not communicate—the latent dream content. As compared with the way they are used in rational discourse, words are ordinarily used quite carelessly in dreams.

In contrast, for most writers words qua words are objects of love. Good writers are sensitive to the slightest gradations of meaning among words, to their emotional connotations, the way they accommodate themselves to their neighbors, even to nuances of sound. There is, of course, a rational basis for their solicitude: the achievement of all of a writer's objectives is partly dependent on his skill in using words. As we would expect, the writer's concern for words and beauty of style also has unconscious determinants. We are already acquainted with the fact that excellence of form, to which, of course, beauty of language may make a large contribution, can serve to demonstrate one's innocence of destructive impulses, thus helping to ward off anxiety. Studies of creative people also indicate that in artistic achievement there is usually a displacement of narcissism from the creator *in propria persona* to the artistic work. Words qua words may become charged with significance for many reasons. They may be equated with milk, a connection to which many literary allusions attest.[12] They may appear to be a means of magically controlling and even appropriating the external reality to which they give shape. For writers for whom words have this significance they are a means of relieving anxiety; a successful description of an experience is equated with the mastery of the experience, and robs it of threat.

For readers, too, words are a source of more forms of satisfaction than we can pause to consider. Their very sound may give us pleasure. The cadences of good prose, like the rhythms of poetry, may help to induce that relaxation of the ego which is so indispensable for the enjoyment of fiction, acting, in Hazlitt's terms, "as a spell upon the hearer, and [disarming] the judgment." Finally, though not all the things which cause words to have value for a writer are necessarily communicated to the reader, mastery over words—a confident, triumphant style—inevitably has a powerful effect upon us. Unless we are compulsive neurotics, we are not likely to confuse the description of an experience with the conquest of it in reality. Nevertheless, articulateness does give us pleasure and a feeling of exhilaration and increased power. In part this may be because the writer's skill with words recalls some of that elation we experienced when we learned to speak. A sure style may also give us the feeling of extending our mastery of language; some of the writer's power seems to rub off on us. Beyond this there is in us some notion, which we are unable to down, of a connection between skill with words and mastery of ex-

[12] See Edmund Bergler, *The Writer and Psychoanalysis* (New York: Doubleday, 1950), Ch. III and *passim*.

ternal reality itself. Upon examination this idea, which we might hesitate to formulate, much less defend, proves to have some basis in fact. An accurate and complete description of a situation fosters as well as reflects understanding of it; and the understanding in turn may lead to an increased measure of control over the situation or facilitate adjustment to it. Genetically there are extremely close ties between the mastery of language and the formation of the ego and gradual extension of its authority. As Fenichel declares, "Tying up words and ideas makes thinking proper possible. The ego has now a better weapon in handling the external world as well as its own excitations. This is the rational content of the ancient magical belief that one can master what one can name." [13]

[13] *The Psychoanalytic Theory of Neurosis* (New York: Norton, 1945), p. 46.

Chapter VII *Movement and Other*
Resources of Form

. . . The process of writing a novel seems to be one of continual forestalling and anticipating; far more important than
the immediate page is the page to come, still in the distance,
on behalf of which this one is secretly working. The writer
makes a point and reserves it at the same time, creates an effect
and holds it back, till in due course it is appropriated and used
by the page for which it is intended.

PERCY LUBBOCK, *The Craft of Fiction*[1]

No matter what principle of organization it follows, a well-
told story flows as a river does; it never resembles a placid lake.
In part this characteristic, like so many others, derives from
the fact that a story centers upon a single action. In life our
eye is attracted now here, now there; our attention wanders
and spreads. Fiction not only focuses our attention on one
action, assembling everything necessary for understanding it
and rigorously excluding everything which is not; by mar-
shaling its events so that they at once satisfy and stimulate
curiosity it compels us to see them as parts of an emerging
pattern. It keeps our eyes hypnotically fixed on the skein of
plot as it unravels itself, on the moving tip of the story line.

In large part because it gives us a constant sense of movement, time seems to pass more rapidly—usually far more
rapidly—in fiction than it does in life itself. Fiction permits
us to gather experience economically. A novel we can read in
a few evenings or a short story we can read in one—Flaubert's
"A Simple Heart," for example, or Chekov's "The Darling"—
may sum up the significant events of an entire lifetime. Time,
of course, moves at different speeds in different works, and the
tempo of a single work of any length is seldom uniform. Time
may move sluggishly until the stage is set, gain momentum

[1] New York: Cape and Smith, 1929, pp. 234-35.

when the action starts, and finally rush irresistibly toward some destination, as though it had at last glimpsed a goal it had long sought. This is only one pattern among many, but fiction must be devoid of pattern—more specifically, it must be so inexpertly written that it does not appear to move—not to convey the impression of accelerating the flow of time. In the most densely written psychological novels, in apparently casual and unhurried stories like those of A. E. Coppard, as well as in tales of swift action, time flows more rapidly than it does in life itself.

Unless he is willing to rob his work of the quality of movement—and this is too high a price to pay for any end—the fiction writer is seldom able, even when he tries, to slow narrative time to the ordinary pace of life. It is all very well for Congreve to remark, "The time equal to that of the presentation." No evening of our life is ever so crowded with intrigue, deception, uproarious mix-ups and reversals of fortune as the one we spend watching or reading *The Way of the World*. In "soap operas," according to James Thurber, an attempt is sometimes made to make time pass more slowly than ordinary time in order to make it easier for the audience to follow the complicated goings-on.[2] Even here, according to my admittedly limited observation, the attempt is seldom successful. The instinct of the writers of these fables for workmanlike plotting, a habit of bringing in reports of all sorts of off-stage happenings, and an unacknowledged and perhaps unjustified faith in tumultuous action work against their humane impulse to give their listeners time to catch their breath, and perhaps even perform a few housewifely chores, between developments.

Narrative time glides by more effortlessly, as well as more rapidly, than the time allotted us in life. The movement of fiction lifts us to its breast and carries us along. Issues are posed and resolved, event follows upon event, and all the while nothing is asked of us: no action, no decision, not even, in any physical sense, any response. The very quality of the movement of fiction tends to make us spectators, to relieve us of the

[2] "Soapland," *The Beast in Me* (New York: Harcourt, Brace, n.d.)

feeling of responsibility which makes so much of our actual experience burdensome.

Like the special language of fiction, movement and the effects it gives rise to have received relatively little attention in literary criticism and esthetic theory. Yet no characteristic of narration is more influential in achieving the objectives of form. We are already acquainted with the way in which movement helps to minimize anxiety by keeping our attention fastened upon the manifest content of fiction. Before we have time to formulate the full meaning of an image—above all, before we are likely to bring its more disturbing implications to awareness—the image is succeeded by another. Movement works hand and glove with the concrete, sensory language of fiction to spare us anxiety.

The swift, easy and yet purposeful movement of fiction also relieves anxiety and gives us pleasure by helping us to escape or surmount the discontent we may feel because of the sluggishness with which time often seems to pass in life. Under the best of conditions—and no matter how rapidly it may seem to be "flying" in some respects—time seldom moves rapidly enough in bringing about the consummation of our desires; and the slowness with which it moves is sometimes more intolerable than the lack of whatever it is we seek.[3] What is most painful is the feeling that we are not moving at all, that we must expect nothing, or very little, from the days, weeks or months which loom ahead. Such a feeling may oppress us because some external obstacle—war, perhaps, or poverty, or the impossibility of marrying or, it may be, of securing a divorce —keeps us from progressing toward a desired goal. Or we may feel blocked, caught in an eddy, because we do not know what to ask of time. Because of some inner conflict we may

---

[3] Perhaps it should be added that, except when by recourse to art or some other means we escape what Schopenhauer called "the world of will," we are nearly always striving to satisfy some desire. Not even the fulfilment of our desires contents us more than momentarily, for "as soon as we attain to them they no longer appear the same, and therefore they soon grow stale, are forgotten, and though not openly disowned, are yet always thrown aside as vanished illusions." "The World as Will," *The Philosophy of Schopenhauer,* edited by Irwin Edman (New York: Modern Library, 1928), p. 134.

not know in what direction we should try to strike out; or, perhaps because some propensity is not being permitted to assert itself, we may feel bored and apathetic, without direction or aim. Particularly when we are in predicaments of this kind, the relatively swift movement of time in fiction is in itself a source of relief and pleasure.

The capacity of fiction to telescope time is of inestimable value in helping us to perceive and understand the human situation. We find it difficult to see our own life and the lives of others in clear perspective not only because they are confused but also because they pass so slowly. The patterns which may be present often emerge too gradually to be apprehended. At any given time much of the past experience which would help us to understand the present is unavailable to us; even the connections we have once traced between events may be forgotten. Because it obeys a compulsion to mold everything it represents into a coherent whole, fiction is more successful than we ordinarily are ourselves in discovering the patterns which underlie human experience. It is no less important that fiction is able to bring those patterns within the compass of our minds, so that they can be grasped, in a phrase of Maud Bodkin's, "within a single intuition."

In a sense the feat which fiction performs with time is comparable to that which cartographers perform with space by the device of scale. Just as a map helps us to visualize things our unaided eyes could never perceive—for example, the contours of a continent—so a story helps us to overcome the limitations of our eyes, minds and memories and see in a single instant the connections among events sprawling over decades of time. The map, however, is solely an aid to our intelligence. It is recognized as a mere representation of the space it helps make visible. Fiction compresses time and still manages to convey the "feel" of time itself, its relentlessness, its indifference to man and his purposes, even, when the occasion demands it, the tediousness with which it sometimes passes. Fiction helps us not only to perceive the changes which occur in time but to feel their poignance.

Often it performs a greater miracle than this. While it keeps part of us, the part that lusts for the experience the story offers, immersed in time, so that we feel the sadness of that element which, whether it fulfils or frustrates our hopes, carries us toward death, it permits another part of us, the part which watches the action and does not become involved, to escape time's dominion, to get outside and beyond time, to assume a spectator relationship toward it. Great fiction releases a part of the psyche and transports it to a high place, where, triumphant and god-like, it can behold everything that transpires and even observe the flow of time itself, the swath it cuts as it passes. Now if one can watch time, one is outside it and beyond its power, no longer compelled to experience it passively and to be subject to its inexorable disfigurement. One has escaped what Yeats would call the world of nature and Schopenhauer the world of will. And one has nothing to fear—not disappointment, disillusionment and the other vicissitudes of life, not even death itself. The tables have been turned: the watching ego has become invisible and immortal, and time corporeal and finite.

In a literary essay of exceptional brilliance[4] Joseph Frank describes some of the means modern literature employs to enable us to perceive the passage of time. The common denominator of these means is what Frank calls "reflexive reference." By a variety of devices the poet or novelist tries to inhibit our instinctive attempts to understand as we proceed, taking each word and idea in its given sequence, so that he can lay everything before us and "the entire pattern of internal references can be apprehended as a unity." Proust, for example, depends upon a "discontinuous presentation of character." "Instead of submerging the reader in the stream of time, that is, presenting him with characters that develop progressively . . . Proust confronts the reader with various snapshots of the characters . . . at different stages in their lives; and the reader in juxtaposing these images, experiences the effects of the passage of time. . . ." It is apparent that this is a particularly effective

<hr/>

[4] "Spatial Form in Modern Literature," *Criticism, The Foundations of Modern Literary Judgment*, edited by Mark Schorer, Josephine Miles and Gordon McKenzie (New York: Harcourt, Brace, 1948).

way of making time visible, but it is equally apparent that it is not entirely new. Such a conventional and now lightly regarded novelist as Thackeray utilizes very much the same method in *Vanity Fair*, and he succeeds, though perhaps not with the same poignance as Proust, in making us feel the flow of time and see his characters age. And the most determinedly chronological story can bring off the same miracle. As Frank would perhaps readily agree, what he describes as the spatialization of form is only one means of accomplishing a feat any great work of fiction can and does accomplish: the scaling of time to a dimension our minds can compass, and the appropriation of the very medium which ordinarily contains and restricts us.

2

Many aspects of form will have to be neglected simply because there is not world enough and time for examining them. However, a problem posed in Chapter V demands to be considered: how can fiction contrive to intensify issues and yet deal with them in a way which minimizes anxiety? Even here we shall have to proceed swiftly. Certain phases of the problem have been discussed by other writers or are referred to elsewhere in this book. It seems desirable, however, to gather together the scattered threads.

The problem does not arise, it should be said at once, in connection with one important segment of fiction, namely, comedy. Far from heightening issues, and thus incurring the danger of making us uneasy, comedy begins at once to reassure us. "Nothing is too important," it tells us with a smile, "and no matter how dark or confused things look at the moment, they'll turn out reasonably well in the end. You may have troubles, but what does that matter so long as you have the animal cunning and resilience you need to cope with them? Let's enjoy ourselves!" Comedy minimizes. It attempts to make us take the issues with which it deals more lightly than we ordinarily do.[5]

Perhaps in part because this is a peculiarly difficult attitude

[5] Cf. the longer discussion of comedy, Ch. XI.

to sustain, comedies comprise only a small portion of the entire body of fiction. Not only comedy's dark sister, tragedy, but most serious fiction takes the other tack: it raises, it heightens, it shows us the most dangerous implications of our actions and our desires. The starkness with which issues are characteristically posed in serious fiction is not entirely due to special efforts to raise and heighten. To some extent it is a by-product of narrative art's steadfast honesty, its refusal to do what we so often do in life, repress or side-step precisely those problems, or aspects of problems, which are painful and disagreeable. It might also be attributed to the tendency of fiction to show us the actions to which our propensities lead. In translating what was inner and perhaps nebulous and unacknowledged into a full-blown act, fiction inevitably invests it with a greater charge of energy. It partly reverses the process we follow when we think about something rather than do it. In proceeding in this fashion, however, fiction is probably complying with an impulse to heighten as much as it is adjusting to a kind of requirement of the narrative medium. The same impulse is in evidence when it deals with the external conflicts of our lives.

Indeed, when we think of fiction in terms of subject matter rather than form, the strength of its impulse to raise and heighten is very quickly disclosed. The heroes of many of the stories we have considered—Aylmer, Othello, Ahab—act like obsessed men. They are dominated by some emotion or torn by some conflict. They show us our own tendencies in extreme fashion. With what seems like inevitability such characters as these become involved in an action in which human life is eventually at stake. Even protagonists of a milder stamp tend to get themselves into critical predicaments. Crusoe is placed in a situation where he must exert himself to keep alive; Lieutenant Henry, in Hemingway's *A Farewell to Arms*, in a situation in which it appears he must fight single-handedly against the world to possess his beloved. Iona Potapov, in Chekov's "Grief," has no one in whom he can confide. The tendency toward heightening also reveals itself in the nature of the sorrow which possesses him. When a situation as originally given does not set off an issue sharply enough, special means may be employed to convey a sense of urgency. Often these involve the manipulation of time. In James's story, "The Beast in the Jungle," for example, May Bartram's impending death puts a limit on the time at John Marcher's disposal for profiting from the discovery of the unknown event he has spent his life awaiting.

Far from shunning the unpleasant and the dangerous, narrative art obeys a tendency to magnify everything. For example, *Oedipus the King* both lays bare the ultimate implications of our most sternly repressed desires and offers us intense representations of certain psychic experiences we have actually had in more attenuated form. The struggle about admitting repressed material to consciousness is one such experience.[6] As Dr. Mark Kanzer has pointed out, the play also represents the very process of repression. In gouging out his eyes, Oedipus is doing what countless children do in less intense and dramatic fashion: he is subjecting "the memory of the primal scene to . . . amnesia and to a dwelling-place in the unconscious. . . ."[7]

Heightening, of course, contributes to interest and to the clarification of issues, but it adds to the difficulty of combatting anxiety. How can fiction magnify material which is threatening even when shown in life-size and still not arouse painful anxiety? The problem is very real, and to cope with it fiction has developed a whole series of stratagems. The more dangerous the material, the more extensive the use of the stratagems; in tragedy the full potentialities of all of them are likely to be exploited. Before we turn to certain stratagems we have not yet considered, let us review those with which we are already acquainted.

3

If certain aspects of the subject matter of fiction tend to arouse anxiety, others tend to still it. Narrative art begins to

[6] Cf. the discussion of the play in Chapter IV.

[7] "The 'Passing of the Oedipus Complex' in Greek Drama," *International Journal of Psychoanalysis*, XXIX, 1948.

checkmate anxiety at its very source. It offers us gratifications of buried impulses, gratifications more extreme than we would be likely to fantasy for ourselves, much less act out, but at the same time it shows how inexorably such gratifications lead to punishment, and the punishments are terrible, too, scaled to the transgressions. Were it otherwise, fiction would indeed increase inner tension, both by arousing feelings of guilt and by making the impulses it released more clamorous and more difficult to control. In fact, as we shall see more in detail in Chapter X, the cathartic experience we have in reading fiction strengthens the hand of the ego in controlling repudiated impulses.

Other safeguards are necessary, however; the unleashing of warded-off tendencies is a dangerous affair. The additional safeguards are provided by form.

Form combats anxiety first of all by trying to reduce feelings of guilt—not only the guilt aroused by a particular story, but the guilt which hounds us always because of our unacceptable, and in particular our destructive, impulses. By its very nature form is committed to love and creation rather than hatred and destruction. It manifests an almost maternal determination to protect everything it treats from harm, to emphasize its wholeness, its vitality, its perfection. In responding to form we are protesting that we, too, are dominated by love, and at the same time are atoning for the rage and hatred which we cannot completely eradicate from our hearts even when we take refuge in the realm of art.

The solicitude form displays for everything it touches is only one of the means it employs to inform us that it respects the values of the ego and superego. One attribute of form, mastery or control, could be looked upon as an "objective correlative" of certain functions of the ego, those concerned with regulating the instincts and bringing them into harmony with the demands of conscience. Control is a kind of animal trainer in whose presence we feel safe no matter how great the ferocity of the animals which are brought forth. The analogy is apt, for it suggests the precise feeling a firmly controlled story

arouses in us—a feeling not so much of freedom from danger
as of security in the face of danger.

Of the already identified resources available to form for
combatting anxiety, we need remind ourselves of only one
more: its capacity to keep the most frightening implications of
its material from the attention of consciousness. Unpalatable
matters may be disguised, but we shall not pause to consider
the various means used to accomplish this. We are already
familiar with some of them, and the subject of disguise is discussed elsewhere.[8] Furthermore, if by disguise we mean the
deliberate, or even the pre-conscious or unconscious, *alteration*
of material so that its real significance will not be perceived,
though important it is far less important a device than was
originally thought. Fiction seldom has to go this far out of its
way to conceal anything. The language in which it is likely
to be conceived and cast from the start—a language so natural
to fiction that it has been accepted unthinkingly by generations of storytellers and readers alike—tends by its very nature
to inhibit the apprehension of anxiety-producing layers of
meaning in conceptual terms. Fiction speaks to us in a language which *effortlessly* conceals many things from conscious
awareness at the same time that it communicates them to the
unconscious with extraordinary vividness.

I am by no means sure that I have succeeded in conveying
the nature of this language or the extent to which fiction utilizes it. The concept of non-discursive communication is new
in esthetic theory, and may not seem applicable to the literary arts since their medium is words. But anyone can
quickly acquire an appreciation of the difference between the
language of fiction and ordinary conceptual discourse by un-
dertaking a simple and pleasant experiment. The experiment
I propose is to read in quick succession Freud's "The Most
Prevalent Form of Degradation in Erotic Life"[9] and D. H.
Lawrence's *Sons and Lovers*. By coincidence they were writ-

[8] See, for example, Marie Bonaparte, *The Life and Works of Edgar Allan
Poe* (London: Imago, 1949), especially pp. 642-48.

[9] *Collected Papers*, Vol. IV (London: Hogarth, 1948).

ten at about the same time and published within a year of one another—the paper in 1912, the novel in 1913. They have an almost schematic correspondence: they both explore the painful opposition which arises in some men between tender and sensual love—an opposition which may be so extreme that, "Where such men love they have no desire and where they desire they cannot love." [10] Both works show that the primary factor to which this opposition can be traced is the young boy's overattachment to the mother.

Despite the close relationship between the novel and the paper, which could be developed in greater detail, *one could read the former after reading the latter without becoming aware of it.* It is necessary to read the novel in a way quite different from that in which one ordinarily reads fiction—to have advance knowledge of the parallels and to be looking for them—to become aware of them during the act of reading. Is this because Lawrence learned of Freud's ideas, or by coincidence had precisely the same ideas, and then sought to embody them in a work of fiction which would at the same time conceal them from awareness? Almost certainly this is not the explanation. Lawrence may have never been aware of some of the ideas to be found in his novel; [11] and he was not primarily concerned with the ideas of which he was aware *as ideas,* as abstract generalities. He was concerned with telling a story— a story which grew out of his own experience and needs. He was concerned with Paul Morel (behind whom it is impossible not to discern Lawrence) and his mother and Miriam and Clara. His story represents an attempt to imagine how matters would have worked out among these people—and to some extent, of course, to re-experience actual occurrences. Whatever explanations are offered for his characters' conduct are

[10] *Ibid.,* p. 207.

[11] There is no evidence, for example, that he recognized the extent to which Paul's tie to his mother determined his very selection of Miriam and his failure to respond to either Miriam or Clara in a way which did justice to all their qualities. Lawrence did, however, recognize that Paul was fettered to his mother and that this made it difficult for him to establish a good relationship with any other woman. See *The Letters of D. H. Lawrence,* edited by Aldous Huxley (New York: Viking, 1932), p. 78.

intuitive, casual and fragmentary; very few generalizations are drawn.

It happens that the behavior of Lawrence's characters illustrates some of the very mechanisms Freud explains systematically in "The Most Prevalent Form of Degradation in Erotic Life." From Lawrence's novel the dissecting intelligence of the critic can abstract the main ideas Freud develops in his paper; and it is worthwhile to abstract them—doing so may help the critic to crystallize certain of his impressions of the book. But whereas Freud labored to bring his ideas before us as clearly as possible, it would not be an exaggeration to say that Lawrence was determined that we should *not* have "ideas," that we should not think conceptually, as we read his story. More accurately, he had a different objective: to engage us emotionally, to induce us to share the experiences of his characters; and he intuitively recognized that he could not achieve this objective if he spoke to the intellect alone. Lawrence himself, as Aldous Huxley has pointed out, "refused to know abstractly." [12] As man and as artist, he felt driven to render his story with as much concreteness, vividness and immediacy as he could muster. The scenes and incidents must speak for themselves, and they speak in a language which is vaguer but richer and more stirring than the language of intellectual discourse.

There is no word which will quite do justice to the way the language he employs is apprehended. Consider the scene where Paul, walking in his mother's garden at night, decides finally to give up Miriam. It is apparent enough that we do not formulate the meaning of this scene; how can one formulate the precise significance of the scent of a flower? Nor is it quite accurate to say that we *infer* what is going on in Paul; the word implies a more purposive kind of intellectual activity and a greater gulf between reader and character than actually obtains at this point. Even the word *sense* implies such a gulf. If we are absorbed in the novel, we are empathically linked with Paul, we feel what he feels, we are affected as he is affected by the sights, smells and sounds which assail him. It

[12] *Ibid.*, p. xv.

would be redundant and, we sense, a profanation to state what we feel in words.

In a sense it is foolish to compare paper and novel, they are incommensurate; but the reading of both in quick succession is likely to give us increased respect for the capacity of fiction to deal with potentially disturbing material without arousing anxiety. Freud's essay may make us squirm at times. There is some evidence that one of the statements his argument demanded caused him to recoil, despite his scientific detachment and long habit of confronting the facts about man's nature, however repugnant they might be. Though the novel gives us an experience of greater immediacy and intensity than the paper, it produces less of that disquiet which is a sign of inner anxiety. Of course, the sensory language of fiction, of which Lawrence was such a master, is only one of the factors responsible for this achievement.

4

As though not sure that the combined power of all the resources of form we have reviewed is sufficient to repulse so formidable a foe as anxiety, narrative art has developed two additional lines of defense. It seeks to "distance" the material it depicts, to separate it from us by a reassuring space, and it seeks to "bind" it, to keep it from affecting us too powerfully and personally as we read and from leaving us tense and anxious when we are done. Both distancing and binding attempt to foster a spectator attitude to the work of fiction. They try to keep our involvement from being too complete, to remind us that we are, after all, simply reading a story or viewing a play.

The sophisticated reader often finds it difficult to appreciate the need for such devices. We ordinarily discriminate clearly enough between reality and fiction; or at any rate we feel we do. We go to the theater, putting aside our everyday cares and settling down in our seats with the comfortable expectation of being entertained. It is evident enough, at least at first, that we are simply watching actors perform a made-up work. The setting, for example, particularly if it is an out-of-doors

one, is likely to be suggested rather than represented realistically. When we watch a drama performed on television, listen
to a radio play or read a book, the situation is very much the
same. We are in our own homes, but relaxed and immobile,
widely separated in most cases by space and often by time
from the drama unfolding before us, and often aware, at least
in the beginning, of the medium in which it is being presented,
be it pictures, sound or the printed word.

But fiction has more power than we know to overcome
these handicaps and spin a web of illusion which ensnares us.
Without realizing it, we may very quickly become involved in
the drama we are watching or reading. Normally, of course,
we do not completely forget that we are simply watching or
reading a story, but not only the joke about the legendary
backwoodsman who, on his first visit to the theater, shouts
out to warn the threatened heroine but a great deal of more
reliable evidence reminds us that the demarcation between
fiction and reality is sometimes obliterated. The reaction to
the 1938 Orson Welles radio dramatization of H. G. Wells's
War of the Worlds is a spectacular case in point.[13] Eleven
years later, another radio dramatization of the same novel
aroused a more tragic panic in Quito, Ecuador. Convinced
that strange creatures from Mars had landed nearby and were
heading for the city, people rushed into the streets in hysteri-
cal fear. When they finally became convinced that there was
no real danger, their fear turned into rage. They attacked and
burned the building which housed the offending radio station,
killing six persons and injuring fifteen others.[14]

The letters, telegrams and even packages which pour into
radio stations addressed to characters in "soap operas" or other
dramas, or sometimes to the actors who play them, also reveal
that unsophisticated people often confuse fiction and reality.
According to James Thurber, when Mrs. Donovan, a character in a folksy drama called "Just Plain Bill," was going to have

[13] For an interesting brief report of this broadcast and its repercussions,
see John Houseman, "The Men from Mars," *Harper's*, 197, 1948. See also
Hadley Cantril, Hazel Gaudet and Herta Herzog, *The Invasion from Mars*
(Princeton: Princeton University Press, 1940).
[14] The *New York Times*, February 14, 1949.

her first child, hundreds of gifts were sent to her. ". . . when, several years later, the child was killed in an automobile accident, thousands of messages of sympathy came in." [15]

In early childhood the line between fact and fantasy may be nonexistent. Even in pre-adolescence it is often shadowy. To be sure, it grows steadily more distinct as children mature, and adults do not ordinarily become so absorbed in fiction that they no longer recall that they are reading. We are concerned, however, not with the admittedly remote possibility that adults may *completely* forget that they are reading, but with the very real possibility that they may become so deeply and intimately engrossed that their own anxieties will be mobilized. Studies of audience response to radio and television programs provide empirical evidence that this does sometimes happen. For example, a study of a ranking television show by Social Research, Inc., revealed that its very success in cutting beneath certain conventions and pretensions, and revealing, for example, the hatred a husband and wife may feel for one another, made certain spectators "self-conscious and uncomfortable." Rather than attempting to distance or frame its material, this particular program reached out toward its audience, but it evidently achieved intimacy at the cost of arousing anxiety among some insecure spectators whom its material touched too closely.

Distancing tries to achieve and sustain a "spectator attitude," to keep the reader from feeling personally involved in the story, to remind him that he is just reading. It seeks the degree of detachment which is desirable for *esthetic* response. A work which is not likely to engage the reader deeply, or to arouse anxiety if it does, obviously requires a minimal amount of distancing. As Edward Bullough pointed out in the essay which promulgated the concept of psychical distance,[16] a work of art may be overdistanced as well as underdistanced. It is obviously impossible for the writer of fiction to estimate the exact amount of distancing a given work requires to be well received by everyone: the position of different readers in relation to the material varies too widely. For example, as Bullough suggests, despite all of Shakespeare's artistry, a reader of *Othello* who had reason to be jealous of a beloved wife might be unable to enjoy the play. While variations in response and occasional failures are thus unavoidable, the great writer of fiction intuitively divines the basic principle to be pursued: he must strive for the degree of distancing needed to contain the anxiety the particular material might arouse in the average reader. This means that he must achieve a certain disassociation between the problems with which he deals and the real-life problems of the reader. And he must orient the reader's interests toward perception rather than action.[17]

Objectification, as we know, is one of the measures on which the fiction writer relies to achieve the effect of distancing. We feel that we have achieved a degree of detachment toward our own problems when we are able to see them, as we say, "objectively"; that is, when we can picture to ourselves clearly and definitely the various things which *have* happened and the things which *may* happen, the alternative possibilities of solution. It is obviously an advantage that fiction can offer us representations of our problems in terms of clearly defined objective happenings.

Fiction, of course, does more: it displaces our problems onto others, the characters in the story, attempts to conceal the fact that the problems are ours or that we are involved in what it relates. More accurately, it attempts to conceal these connections from consciousness; it cannot, it would not want to, keep us from unconsciously recognizing them and identifying with characters who are like ourselves and bear our burdens. To achieve the illusion of detachment, to keep his readers from

[17] Technically, as Ernst Kris suggests, he must seek to regulate the amount and nature of the energy utilized in response. In cases of underdistancing, for example, it may be assumed "that not enough energy was neutralized or, alternatively, that neutralization was not complete enough; too much of libidinal and aggressive energy was at work: The function of the ego was too closely in the service of the id." *Psychoanalytic Explorations in Art* (New York: International Universities Press, 1952), p. 46.

being aware of the extent of their involvement, the fiction writer may also set his story in a milieu as different as possible from their own—in a faraway place, another historical period, or among a social class to which they do not belong. When the underlying issues with which a story deals are unusually anxiety-laden, we know, too, that fiction may seek to direct the reader's attention to other matters, to discussions of moral problems, for example, as in *The Brothers Karamazov* and *Billy Budd*.

Stylization, fiction's deliberate accentuation of its own artificiality, is its last important resource for achieving distance. The anxiety-potential of the material determines the amount of stylization which is desirable. Innocuous subject matter requires very little; tragedy, because it deals with our most rigorously repressed impulses, requires a great deal. Tragedy eschews "realism"; it strives for tidiness and perfection of organization, for an elevated and, it may be, even a polished and artificial style. By these and other devices it assures, it keeps assuring, its readers, "This is art, not life." [18]

In passing it may be observed that failure to achieve the right ratio between stylization and subject matter is probably the most common cause of dissatisfaction with fiction and inability to secure enjoyment from it. Because, as Bullough maintains, readers have a chronic tendency toward under-distancing, the bald treatment of "strong" material is especially likely to cause difficulty. Complaints may not reveal the source of the difficulty; they sometimes seem to be concerned entirely with subject matter or with style. But whether they are actually precipitated in many instances by either element separately is highly doubtful. I suspect that many of those who censure the style of naturalistic novels find a realistic style congenial; and, similarly, that many of those who object to particular themes would find those themes

[18] Cf. Bullough: "A general help towards Distance . . . is to be found in the 'unification of presentment' of all art-objects. By unification of presentment are meant such qualities as symmetry, opposition, proportion, balance, rhythmical distribution of parts . . . in fact all so-called 'formal' features, 'composition' in the widest sense." " 'Psychical Distance' as a Factor in Art and an Esthetic Principle," p. 339.

acceptable if they were handled differently. What really troubles most of those who raise criticisms, I believe, is a certain *combination* of subject matter and style: for example, the matter-of-factness (implying detachment and even hostility) with which some naturalistic novels treat the institutions, conventions and values on which many readers base their lives and about which, in some cases, they themselves feel insecure.

5

To enable us to participate imaginatively in the experiences it offers us, however hazardous they may be, narrative art has one additional resource: it "binds" the emotions it arouses so that they will neither reach disturbing proportions and conflict with esthetic response as we read nor leave us agitated or afraid when we are done.

A study of the way detective stories functioned in the life of a twelve-year-old analytic patient addicted to them reveals two of the mechanisms which may be utilized in binding.[19] First, the stories tended to confirm the little boy's belief that the satisfaction of certain of his impulses would lead inexorably to punishment. The fears aroused by the stories served to bind the very impulses they stimulated and satisfied.[20] Secondly, the identification with the always triumphant detective-hero not only helped to bind the anxiety aroused by a given story but at least temporarily allayed the boy's chronic anxiety. It provided reassurance against the criminal-killer, the feared reality figure who lurked behind him, and certain of the boy's own impulses of which he was afraid.

While fear of punishment serves to bind desire in nearly all fiction, including the very greatest, identification with a powerful hero is useful as a defense against fear, by and large, only in some little-esteemed categories of fiction in which the action is the dominant element. In more serious fiction, identification with the hero is itself likely to be a cause of anxiety,

[19] Edith Buxbaum, "The Role of Detective Stories in a Child's Analysis," *Psychoanalytic Quarterly*, X, 1941.
[20] It may be added that the vicarious satisfaction of the impulses itself contributed to this end by robbing the impulses of some of their intensity. Cf. the discussion of catharsis, Ch. X.

for whatever his virtues he himself may be an agent of chaos and destruction. It is interesting to observe how ruthless fiction is about annihilating characters who meet this description, however blameless they may appear and however deeply they may have engaged our sympathy, our admiration and our love; it appears to obey a compulsion to liquidate whatever terror these characters arouse. It annihilates even Hamlet and Lear. Anna is dead and Vronsky a ruined man, good only as a weapon or a target of one, at the end of *Anna Karenina*. At the end of *The Idiot* Myshkin, Rogozhin and Nastasya are all destroyed. At the end of *Moby Dick* not only Ahab, but all those who have let themselves be associated with his obsession for vengeance, even the Pequod itself, have been obliterated, swallowed in the sea. Only Ishmael survives, and he not as a principal in the action but as a reporter of it, like a fraction of our consciousness, itself invisible, first watching and then describing a turbulent dream.

To some extent, it is clear, binding is a function of content rather than form. But, as though uncertain of what content alone can accomplish, form also participates in binding. It tries to divert a portion of our attention from story elements especially likely to cause anxiety. And when, as in tragedy, fiction conjures up a particularly terrifying world, it is careful to "contain" that world, to surround it with a kind of frame, so that it will neither arouse a feeling of hopeless oppression as we read nor threaten to merge with our own world when we are done.

Robert Gorham Davis has identified some of the means used by form for the first of these achievements. By "a constant fulfilling of promises, a relieving of uncertainties and tensions, . . . the happy return of the expected and desired, . . . the predictable completion of patterns," and most especially by "the way it returns upon itself instead of merging with the world outside," [21] form seeks to fix our attention on the way a story unrolls itself, on the flow and sequence of

---

[21] "Art and Anxiety," *Partisan Review*, XII, 1945. Reprinted, in revised and expanded form, in *Art and Psychoanalysis*, edited by William Phillips (New York: Criterion, 1957).

developments. Form cannot, of course, completely distract our attention from content, for the pattern it unfolds is made up of story developments. It can, however, divert a *portion* of our attention to itself, and thus make it less likely that we will pause to fathom the latent significance of the content. And because its reference is entirely *internal*, because it winds back upon itself, form deters us from returning from the coherent, comprehensible world it opens to us to the more confusing and frightening real world, from consciously shuttling back and forth from the story to our own problems. In its comeliness and symmetry, form is the most seductive of the displacements by which fiction seeks to spare us anxiety. The spell form weaves can be easily broken, however. Any failure of form—a flaw in composition, an illogical development, an inconsistency of tone—may cause us to begin thinking critically about the story we are reading and break our absorption, compelling us to return to the anxiety-laden world of experience.

When fiction arouses very deep terror, it may also seek to enclose the terror in a kind of frame, to remind us that however powerful and triumphant evil may momentarily appear to be, its dominion is limited. Just beyond or outside this world of evil, fiction manages to inform us, there is a world of goodness, sanity and health, where the normal rhythms of life prevail and one does not have to remain forever on guard against danger and disaster. The knowledge is like a gift of space. It reminds us that *we* are beyond the reach of the forces which are so threatening. It re-establishes our spectator position.

In *Oedipus the King* the plague provides the frame. In itself it is terrible but it holds the promise that when the impurity is cleansed from the land—as it is with the discovery of Oedipus' guilt, his self-inflicted punishment and exile—health, quite literally, will be restored and women will once again begin to conceive and bear children in joy and security. In *Hamlet* the arrival of Fortinbras announces that terror has run its course. He is the representative of another, and, we have every reason to believe, a more wholesome, court. His ascension, we feel sure, will mean the end of the unnatural lust and ambition, fear, guilt and intrigue which are responsible for the feast of death that meets his eyes.

Still other of the worlds of evil Shakespeare created are hemmed by spatial rather than by temporal borders. The cruelty of child to parent which prevails in *Lear* could not be borne if it had gained sway everywhere. But it is confined to England. Across the channel, in France, where Cordelia goes for refuge and from which she comes to try to succor her father, there is a different and more normal world. In the same way, as Mark Van Doren has explained, England is a refuge against that world of horror Shakespeare has conjured up in *Macbeth*. Scotland is a land where "men must not walk too late," a land made dark and horrible by fear and sleeplessness and bloodshed.

. . . death and danger may claim the whole of that bleeding country; but there is another country to the south where a good king works miracles with his touch. . . . Shakespeare again has enclosed his evil within a universe of good, his storm center within wide areas of peace. And from this outer world Malcolm and Macduff will return to heal Scotland of its ills. . . . Blood will cease to flow, movement will recommence, fear will be forgotten, sleep will season every life, and the seeds of time will blossom in due order. The circle of safety which Shakespeare has drawn around his central horror is thinly drawn, but it is finely drawn and it holds.[22]

The contribution binding and distancing make to our security is evident enough. By making us feel secure these devices also encourage us to immerse ourselves in a story and secure whatever satisfaction or cathartic relief it happens to provide; and they contribute to that pleasurable, anxiety-free perception toward which form strives. As Schopenhauer has emphasized, when we are worried or absorbed in practical affairs, we either fail to see what is before our eyes, see only certain (e.g., the utilitarian) aspects of objects, or distort what we see; it is only when we are free of our everyday cares and anxieties that we may be said to see at all.

[22] *Shakespeare* (New York: Doubleday Anchor Books, 1953), pp. 229-30.

If . . . a man relinquishes the common way of looking at things, gives up tracing . . . their relations to each other, the final goal of which is always a relation to his own will; if he . . . looks simply and solely at the *what*; if, further, he does not allow abstract thought, the concepts of the reason, to take possession of his consciousness, but, instead of all this, gives the whole power of his mind to perception, . . . lets his whole consciousness be filled with the quiet contemplation of the natural object actually present, whether a landscape, a tree, a mountain, a building, or whatever it may be; inasmuch as he *loses* himself in this object . . . forgets even his individuality, his will, . . . and . . . can no longer separate the perceiver from the perception . . . because the whole consciousness is filled and occupied with one single sensuous picture; . . . then that which is so known is no longer the particular thing as such; but it is the *Idea*, the eternal form. . . .[23]

Only slight modifications are needed to make this statement acceptable even if one does not share Schopenhauer's Platonic orientation. It is the object itself, I should say, which becomes visible under the conditions Schopenhauer describes. That which we can only see in terms of our own needs, or which is veiled from us or covered by an ugly film when we are apprehensive or preoccupied with practical affairs, is revealed in the splendor and loveliness of its own being when, without abandoning our human interest in the object, whatever it may be, we achieve a measure of detachment toward it and a measure of freedom from care and fear.

It might be thought that binding and distancing, especially the latter, would tend to nullify that magnification of our problems, that raising and heightening of everything for which we turn to fiction. In fact, they help us to have it both ways. Instead of scaling down the heroic representations of our experience narrative art offers us, they labor to make it possible for us to accept them without fear.

[23] "The World as Idea," pp. 146-47.

Chapter VIII *The Processes of Response*

[In analysing *The Ancient Mariner*] . . . we saw how the compelling story of outer events, with its vivid detail, could carry the reader's attention from point to point, while, below the level of conscious attention, emotional forces combined in modes ancient and satisfying.

MAUD BODKIN [1]

The general nature of what occurs when we read fiction has already been suggested. We read, we have come to see, to satisfy needs of which we are largely unaware—and of which in many cases we must remain unaware if reading is to give us pleasure. We know at least some of the reasons why such a make-believe activity as reading can provide compensation for the limitations, deprivations and discontents of our actual experience, and we know with what discretion fiction fulfils the service for which we turn to it.

The discretion is the more extraordinary because great fiction is far more intrepid in its approach to life than we ordinarily are ourselves. It resolutely probes conflicts we hesitate to examine, seeking to uncover all the factors involved in them and the exact influence of each. As in that chapter of *The Scarlet Letter* called "A Flood of Sunshine," it shows the virtue and perhaps the beauty of impulses we either deny or gratify in a shamefaced way which robs them of dignity. At the same time, and with equal strictness, it shows us the results of our misdeeds and our mistakes, whether these take the form of yielding to our impulses, denying them, or satisfying them in covert or neurotic fashion: it forces us to see consequences to which we would prefer to close our eyes or which we believe by some magic can be averted. And it arranges, it almost points, to make us see that certain happenings *are* consequences. Unlike life, it has no use for irrelevant

[1] *Archetypal Patterns in Poetry* (London: Oxford, 1934), pp. 308-309.

developments which obscure connections or accidents which thwart the natural development of a given set of forces.

As we know, fiction contrives to give us these uncompromising images of our nature and our fate without permitting us to become aware of their personal relevance. It pretends, and we accept the pretense, that the characters whose affairs it chronicles are strangers in whom we have no reason to take a special interest. There is also a certain duplicity in the way it sets their affairs before us. Its light is like that furnished by those torches Hawthorne describes in "My Kinsman, Major Molineux," which conceal by their glare the very objects they illuminate. The light enables us to see without always being able to say precisely what it is we see, to understand without formulating our understanding.

Fiction accomplishes something more miraculous than this. It *involves* us in the events it puts before us, without permitting us to become aware of the nature and extent, or usually even the fact, of our involvement. The emotions fiction arouses in us are evidence of this: they are too powerful to be explained solely on the basis of our cognitive reactions, conscious and even unconscious. Normally, to be sure, even the emotions remain unnoticed, but sometimes they force themselves on our attention, occasionally by some visible sign, such as weeping.

We have already considered some of the characteristics of narrative art which enable it to speak simultaneously to mind and heart, to affect us deeply and personally. Now we turn to the process of response itself. Let us attempt to reconstruct the entire process—its unconscious as well as its conscious components.

The difficulties of such an endeavor are apparent. In a way it is comparable to the attempt to reconstruct the dream-work —the activity involved in transforming latent dream thoughts into a dream we may remember. In one way our endeavor is perhaps more difficult: at least after the latent dream thoughts have been reconstructed, it is only necessary to ask, "Why and how were they metamorphosed into the manifest dream?"

One is working between two relatively fixed points. In our endeavor, only the story is fixed, and not all observers will agree about its meaning and objective qualities. Response to the story radiates centrifugally, is in part unconscious and, if not inexhaustible, is likely to be so copious that it is impossible to recapture *in toto*. Furthermore, as we know, response varies widely from individual to individual.

But these difficulties are less formidable than they appear. It does not really matter either that there are individual variations in response or that one cannot recapture all the reactions of a single reader. All we are after is knowledge of the *kinds* of reactions which occur; from such knowledge, without too much difficulty, we can identify at least some of the processes of response. And, fortunately, we sometimes have direct access to reactions of which we are normally unaware and even to the unconscious processes of response. As a result of the mechanism Freud described as flexibility of the repressions, we can occasionally catch a glimpse of reactions which usually take place below the threshold of awareness. This may occur during reading or perhaps during a second or third, and unusually analytic, reading of a given work. Far more frequently, according to my experience, it occurs *after* reading, as one mulls over the effect a story has had upon one. Sometimes a stray thought which crosses one's mind weeks or months after reading a story makes one aware of a reaction to it one was unaware until then of having had. Such glimpses, whenever they occur, will make most fair-minded people willing to admit that when they read fiction they may have many reactions of which they are usually oblivious.

Empirical studies of response to fiction provide evidence of unconscious response and a great deal of information—though not, of course, necessarily complete information—about its nature. Reports supplied to me by psychoanalysts who have cooperated with this study also show that reactions to fiction are by no means entirely conscious, as is sometimes assumed.

Of the reality of unconscious response to fiction, therefore, I believe there is no basis for reasonable doubt. The evidence also permits us to identify some of the processes which take place below the threshold of awareness, and to describe them with a fair degree of assurance. When we go beyond this and try to reconstruct the entire process of response, it is necessary to depend to some extent on reasoning and conjecture. In the theory to be offered here there are possibilities for error which I do not wish to minimize. It is possible that mechanisms as important as any of those we know about have eluded identification. Since the mechanisms to be dealt with cannot be seen steadily and clearly, I may make mistakes in describing them. Mistakes are still more likely to occur when we try to trace the connections among the mechanisms and to surmise the contribution each makes to the total impact of fiction. The present attempt to reconstruct the process of response to fiction is likely to resemble one of those crude early maps which exaggerate the dimensions of certain territories, underestimate others, describe some geographic features mistakenly and omit others of considerable significance. However, even a map which shows what is now known, or can be conjectured, is not to be despised. If it is accurate in broad outline, it may be helpful to later explorers.

2

Let us begin with a kind of rough sketch which will orient us to the more significant features of the experience we are going to consider. Then, in later chapters, we can examine certain phases of the experience in closer detail and fill in some of the details we have omitted.

To facilitate matters let us leave to one side response to books which do not attempt to involve us in the events they relate or do not succeed in doing so. Most comedies belong in the former class. Like works of fiction in any other genre, they move us emotionally as well as intellectually, but they do so almost entirely by appealing to us as spectators; they seldom seek to entangle us in the events they put before us. Books may also fail to involve us because we do not permit ourselves to become immersed in them. We approach certain books in an attitude of "adult discount," with a resolute coolness and detachment. For example, stories of whose suitability for our children we want to make sure might be read in this spirit, or favorites of our youth to which we return with feelings of amused superiority. Far more frequently, we remain detached despite a willingness and desire to immerse ourselves in what we are reading. We find a book we had expected to enjoy contrived or juvenile—exaggeratedly and conscientiously lurid, let us say—and while we read on, perhaps with a certain fascinated horror at its badness, we remain on the outside, aloof and critical.

Our first concern must be to ascertain what occurs in us when a story ensnares us and tranports us to the special world it has created. The indispensable condition of such an experience, and the first stage of the experience itself, is a relaxation of the vigilance usually exercised by the ego. A willing suspension of disbelief, a receptive attitude, is essential not only to the enjoyment but even to the understanding of fiction. Since when we read or go to the theater it is because we are in search of the satisfactions fiction offers, it might be thought that the ego might be quite willing to relax, and no questions asked. And, indeed, there is ordinarily a certain willingness to let go, an impulse to loosen the reins somewhat. Actual reduction of control does not always follow immediately and automatically, however, any more than it does when we visit friends or engage in some other activity which promises to give us pleasure. Certain people simply cannot relax. Some basic personality difficulty, such as a weak ego organization and a consequent dread of fantasy, prevents it.[2] Since the fantasies embedded in fiction often involve a potential threat to the ego's authority, even people with a trustworthy ego organization usually demand that a story satisfy certain conditions before they surrender themselves to it.

These conditions are variable rather than fixed. Because of differences in personality structure, some people—let us say compulsives, used to screening any experience carefully —are much stricter in their demands than others. A given person will scrutinize fiction more carefully at one time than another. Even one's preconceptions about the potential dan-

[2] Cf. Ch. II.

gerousness of various genres, or individual works, may affect one's willingness to let go: standards are probably relatively high for tragedy, relatively low for musical comedy.

Because there are so many variables, it is difficult to make generalizations about the conditions governing relaxation. It appears, however, that the standards the average discriminating adult reader applies to serious fiction have to be characterized as rigorous rather than lax. While such a reader usually accepts, and even seems to welcome, departures from the literal facts about experience, he insists that the most airy fantasy, no less than a naturalistic novel, have some valid reference to psychological realities. As though distrustful of a work unwilling to abide by its own terms, he also insists that a work progress with a scrupulous regard for internal consistency. Finally, not only the discriminating reader but almost every reader tries to make sure that dangerous material is not handled in a way which is offensive. Though the judging activity of the ego becomes more automatic once its confidence has been won, it never ceases, and the ego will resume a vigilant attitude, and withdraw the trust it has provisionally granted, if a story transgresses against its standards. The conscious intelligence is not displaced in response to fiction because intense unconscious activity is also involved; there is work aplenty for all parts of the psychic apparatus.

It follows, incidentally, that there is no necessary quarrel between effortless, intuitive enjoyment of fiction and the close, careful reading for which some kinds of literary study equip one. There *may* be a quarrel, for the attempt to discover all the features and tendencies to which a student's attention has been directed may require him to read with a strained alertness, which is inimical to enjoyment. If in addition the student is under pressure to read at an unnaturally fast rate of speed, his reading is not likely to give him a great deal of pleasure. Fortunately, as it seems to me, pressures must be heavy and persistent to induce anyone to read fiction too alertly or too fast. To some extent at least the desire for pleasure may be counted upon to counteract the pressures, so that sooner or later, against one's resolve, one is likely to revert to a pace and a way of reading which are not incompatible with enjoyment.

Relaxation and enjoyment are impossible when a student, or anyone else, reads fiction which is really beyond him. But, again fortunately, only exceptional pressures, inner or outer, can induce one to do much reading of this character. Respectable motives, such as self-improvement, or less respectable ones, such as the desire to impress others, may make us ambitious to read certain works—usually "classics"—which we expect to find difficult, but we do not always "get around" to reading these works, nor finish them even if they are begun. As we shall see more in detail later in this chapter, we tend to search for fiction which is on our own plane of intellectual and emotional sensibility. Our distaste for books which we would have to tax ourselves to follow should not be attributed to mere laziness. It perhaps indicates an intuitive awareness of how much a relaxed attitude contributes to the enjoyment and understanding of fiction. It may also be an expression of a desire to conserve energy for the very intensive unconscious psychic activity involved in response.

A final condition of reduction of control by the ego is that the reading experience should not threaten to lead to immediate physical action. The ego will not stand idly by while decisions affecting conduct are being reached. The dangerous fantasies embodied in fiction are tolerated only on condition that, and only so long as, they are taken as fantasies.

As in dreaming and daydreaming, the immobility of the body provides a certain amount of reassurance. But the ego demands additional safeguards as well. It requires that fiction be approached with a certain detachment—more technically, with instinctual energy sufficiently neutralized so that what we read is disassociated from our experience, from either gratifying needs in actuality or laying plans to gratify them. It requires that one part of us remain aware of the make-believe character of the reading experience. The importance of the resources available to fiction for reminding us of this— for differentiating and distancing its events from the world of our experience—is apparent. A work which eschews these resources and incites us to some action, disregarding or even attempting to obliterate the division between fiction and reality, labors under grave and perhaps insuperable handicaps. Because it keeps us on guard, it cannot engage our emotions and accomplish its practical objective. It cannot give us pleasure. To some extent even fiction which seeks to foster a particular attitude shares these handicaps. It arouses resistance. It may open our eyes to an aspect of a situation to which we have been blind, and this must be regarded as a valuable service. But unless it transcends its own purpose, it cannot touch our hearts. It cannot promote that rounded, compassionate seeing which is possible only when we are not too close to a situation, and not too partisan in our view of it.

3.

Though even some of the "conscious" activities involved in response to fiction are sometimes quasi-automatic, they can be identified and described without too much difficulty. Basically the mind is occupied in following a story as it develops and in grasping its manifest meaning. Secondarily—incidentally rather than systematically—it is engaged in appraising: in judging such things as the honesty of a story, its relevance for the reader, the skill with which it is worked out. Both activities may involve "placing" a story—in terms of its period, tradition or genre, the previous work of the same author, or any other point of reference which facilitates understanding and judgment.

These activities can keep the conscious mind very busily employed. Even the task of following and interpreting the surface significance of a story often involves a great deal more than it may appear to. We feel impelled to read fiction at a fairly rapid speed. The events of a single story may be numerous, complex and intricately interrelated. Furthermore, they are not developed continuously; and certain things are left unexplained or are only partially explained. The storyteller requires the reader to make interpolations and draw inferences, to participate actively in the task of understanding his tale.

We could, of course, read only fiction which we can understand with an absolute minimum of effort. But we seem to avoid such fiction as instinctively as we avoid that which we would have to exert ourselves to understand. There is more than one reason—we shall return to some of the factors involved in our choice of fiction later in the chapter—but the immediately relevant consideration is that it seems essential for the enjoyment of fiction that the mind should be rather fully occupied. If it is not, it is likely to penetrate to meanings and appeals which would arouse disquiet, or even revulsion, if brought to light. The engagement of the conscious intelligence seems a necessary condition and cover for the unconscious activity involved in response.

Of one or two of the characteristics of unconscious response we can also speak with reasonable assurance. If only from glimpses we occasionally catch of the unconscious in operation, we know that it often works at lightning speed. We know, too, that it is unbelievably perceptive, and prodigal in supplying us with impressions and associations. Certain peculiarities of the unconscious processes facilitate speed and prodigality. The unconscious does not have to work out anything in detail either to reach or express understanding. Unconscious understanding is immediate, intuitive. In expressing understanding, the unconscious employs either words or images, whichever are most suitable for its purpose, without regard for consistency. Sometimes it eschews both, so that the only trace of its activity lies in the alteration of our feelings. Unburdened by the need to be coherent or consistent, employing the most slapdash kind of shorthand, the unconscious can easily outspeed and outproduce the painstaking conscious intelligence. Thus a few unconnected words which come to our lips unbidden may bespeak an understanding of some buried, abstruse meaning of a story to which our intellect could penetrate only with the utmost difficulty and express with tiresome effort.

In writing about unconscious responses, incidentally, it is almost impossible to do justice to their darting speed and largely non-verbal character. To make their nature and in-

fluence clear one is almost compelled to use terms which suggest that they are more carefully and coherently worked out
than in fact they are; indeed, one tends inevitably to describe
them on the analogy of conscious mental operations. To take
a simple example, a mother's acceptance of her son's relationship with a married woman (or some similar permissive plot
element) might contribute to reader acceptance of the affair.
In the reading experience a readier acceptance of the illicit
relationship might be the only indication that the unconscious
had been at work. A report of the experience, on the other
hand, could hardly avoid suggesting that the mother's attitude
had been singled out for special attention and its permissive
influence verbalized. In reading this and the following chapters it is necessary to allow for communication difficulties of
this kind.

4

Three unconscious processes can be distinguished in response to fiction. Of course, they do not occur in isolation,
but in admixture with one another and with conscious psychic
operations.

The first process is a part of our "spectator" reaction to
fiction. It is basically concerned with perception and understanding. "The heart has its reasons which the reason knows
not," and the unconscious can immediately and effortlessly
understand certain things which our conscious intelligence
would find puzzling and even inexplicable.

What kinds of things are likely to be unconsciously rather
than consciously apprehended? In answering, we should be
careful to exclude things which though ostensibly hidden are
really meant to be grasped by the intellect—for example, the
real motives for a certain action as contrasted with the explanation offered by a character blind to the forces driving
him, or dishonest reasons advanced to deceive someone. In
such cases as these, fiction writers want us to be aware of the
truth. The things which are meant to be apprehended unconsciously they are usually unaware of themselves—or, to be
more accurate, they are unaware of their unconscious signifi-

cance. Increasingly, however, now that knowledge of depth psychology is spreading, writers may consciously weave into their fiction things which they intend to be unconsciously understood. It seems safer to develop a definition in terms of the reader.

In general, it is things which would arouse anxiety, directly or indirectly, if consciously perceived which are likely to be apprehended unconsciously. It is not possible to specify the exact things, because these vary reader by reader. People differ widely in their ability to tolerate anxiety and in the things which cause them anxiety, and any given person may change in both respects at different times. "Economic" considerations complicate matters: isolated instances in which warded-off impulses secure gratification might be consciously observed, and accepted, because they mobilized relatively small amounts of anxiety. Yet these very things would be more likely to be unconsciously apprehended if they threatened to fit into an over-all interpretation which was inacceptable to the ego and a potential source of serious anxiety. A selective principle influences our understanding: we try to "repress," to keep from awareness, those perceptions which might cause us appreciable discomfort or pain. Of course, we are not always successful in doing so. An inexpert writer may compel us to take conscious note of things we would prefer to understand unconsciously.

Events or other aspects of fiction which have deep roots in the unconscious are especially likely to be unconsciously apprehended. In fiction, as in life, almost everything which happens is unconsciously determined to some extent. What is astonishing is the preoccupation of fiction with actions which are *decisively* determined by unconscious factors. The major actions of most of the stories we have considered, and of a large proportion of all the world's fiction, are so determined. Of course, unconscious springs of action are not always so hidden or so objectionable that they cannot be consciously apprehended; and in the relatively small body of fiction which appeals to us primarily as spectators even the perception of the ignoble motives animating the characters, from whom we feel disassociated, is ordinarily a source of pleasure. When we identify with the characters of a story, on the other hand, we are usually no more willing to acknowledge such motives than they are themselves.

Episodes which remind us of painful experiences or of aspects of our present situation about which we feel anxiety are also likely to be understood unconsciously. Empirical evidence indicates that such episodes also tend to be "forgotten" with comparative rapidity; in some cases, doubtless, they have not so much been thrust from the mind as denied the opportunity to register upon it. Story elements which come too close to some psychic sore spot may seem incomprehensible, or be distorted, by readers who intellectually are quite capable of understanding them. Dr. Martha Wolfenstein's study of reactions of four-, five- and six-year-old children and their mothers to a story called "Sally and the Baby and the Rampatan" illustrates this dramatically.[3] The children, for whom the story provided a covert and acceptable way of expressing and working through hostility toward an expected second child, understood the story's central fantasy better than their mothers, who, identifying with the pregnant fictional mother, felt threatened by the very emotions the story was intended to arouse. Clearly, we are willing to go to great lengths *not* to become consciously aware of meanings which would cause us pain. But the storyteller must cooperate: when he deals with potentially upsetting material, he must keep part of our minds in darkness of what he is about.

Frequently the connections among various actions and meanings which run through an entire story would also arouse anxiety if brought to awareness, and are left to the unconscious to apprehend. There can be no question that in response to fiction the unconscious engages in a kind of activity which we may think of as a prerogative of consciousness: it ferrets out connections, draws inferences and establishes connections; *it synthesizes its observations.* When we read *Ham-*

[3] "The Impact of a Children's Story on Mothers and Children," *Monographs of the Society for Research in Child Development*, No. 42, XI, 1946 (Washington, D.C.: National Research Council, 1947).

let, for example, it is the unconscious which is likely to take note of the contrast between the speed and sureness with which Hamlet acts on a half-dozen occasions and his power-lessness to proceed with that one action he has pledged him-self to perform; the contrast between his dilatoriness and the speed with which Laertes acts in a similar situation; and countless other things which betray the secret sources of Hamlet's inability to carry out his mission. By piecing to-gether and interpreting such observations the unconscious may penetrate to an entire level of meaning—or to numerous levels of meaning—to which, during reading at least, the con-scious mind is blind.

In our response to a story as a unified whole, no less than in our understanding of many of its component parts, uncon-scious perception plays an indispensable role. The things the unconscious perceives have to be communicated, or we miss the deepest sources of pleasure procurable through reading fiction. They have to be communicated unconsciously, or they will backfire and arouse painful anxiety.

5

The second and third kinds of unconscious response to fic-tion constitute a kind of activity, though, of course, the activity is psychic, not actual, and tolerated by the ego on that account. They are forms of response in which we are actors and not merely spectators. In the first of these "active" forms of response, we unconsciously participate in the stories we read; in the second, we compose stories structured upon the ones we read (or upon parts of them) which give us an op-portunity to relive or alter our actual experience or act out dramas revolving around our wishes and fears. The last-men-tioned kind of response, the creation of stories parallel to the ones we read in which we play a part, I call analogizing.

Whereas unconscious perception supplements the cognitive activity of consciousness, unconscious participation and analo-gizing may be said to comprise our "action" response to fic-tion. We are almost never conscious of becoming involved in the fiction we read. We maintain the illusion that we are simply watching a story unfold itself.

Sometimes, of course, we are doing no more than that. The storyteller may skillfully compel us to take a spectator role, or we may be too detached in our attitude toward a story to become involved in it. As has been said, however, the most frequent cause of our remaining outside the fiction we read is the failure of the storyteller to engage our interests deeply, despite his endeavor to do so and our willingness to be absorbed. Try as we may, we do not always succeed in finding fiction in which, as we sometimes put it, we can "lose ourselves." Some stories revolve around situations which do not interest us, or have characters who impress us as being precious or crude or in some other way are so foreign to us that we cannot identify with them. Even when we finish stories to which we have such negative reactions, we seldom become sufficiently engrossed in them for the participation responses to occur.

When we are engrossed, a great deal of evidence indicates, *we imaginatively experience the entire action, ourselves act out every role.* The experience is, of course, imaginary; it is elliptical in the extreme; it utilizes energy which is at least partly neutralized. Despite all of these provisos, the experience is "real" and, in view of its speed, astonishingly complete; it includes, for example, an understanding of the unconscious significance of the acts we perform.

We do not, of course, ordinarily experience all parts of the action of a given story with the same degree of intensity. As we would expect, there are differences, in accordance with our individual nature and needs, in the completeness with which we identify with different characters and the abandon with which we participate in different episodes. What is startling, however, is how encompassing our experience usually is when we are engrossed. Edith Buxbaum's analysis of a twelve-year-old addict of detective stories, referred to in Chapter VII, shows that the boy identified not only, as we would expect, with the invincible and invulnerable heroes of the stories, but, as well, with the unsympathetically presented villains, and even with the victims in their terror, suffering and death.[4] The boy secured the full measure of gratification, open or covert, which each of these roles afforded. Besides binding the anxiety the stories themselves aroused, the identification with the detectives served to make him more secure in the face of the terror his real-life situation inspired and to protect him against some of his own impulses. The identification with the villains satisfied his repressed but powerful hostile feelings toward his uncle, his mother and others; that with the victims, an even more deeply repressed wish to be overcome by the uncle and be the passive victim of love-making conceived as a sadistic assault.

Other studies of response to fiction also indicate that if we can understand and empathize with some of the characters in a story, with varying degrees of candor and completeness we can usually identify with them all. A superficial explanation is that the writer who possesses the magic to bring some of his characters to light can usually animate all of them. A more basic explanation is that all the characters are so many aspects, acknowledged or unacknowledged, lived-out or repressed, of the writer—and, if we respond to the writer, of ourselves. We know how many roles besides the one we play in life possess recognized attraction. Unconsciously, we may be sure, we desire to be many people besides that paltry thing we call our "self"; we long for many of the qualities we have crushed out in shaping that self.

In the fiction which engages us, characters who have the qualities we have stunted as well as those we have cultivated are both likely to be present. Indeed, many famous pairs of fictional characters are so closely linked that, like Dr. Jekyll and Mr. Hyde, they can be regarded as component parts of one person. They represent dominant and recessive, supplementary, conflicting, or conscious and unconscious aspects of one role. Myshkin and Rogozhin can be regarded in this way, as can Don Quixote and Sancho Panza, Lear and the

[4] Edith Buxbaum, "The Role of Detective Stories in a Child's Analysis," *Psychoanalytic Quarterly*, X, 1941.

Fool, possibly Macbeth and his Lady, and, as Dr. Mark
Kanzer has observed, the pursuer and the pursued in any
number of stories from *Les Misérables* and *Crime and Punish-*
ment to the tales of Sherlock Holmes. If we can understand
and identify with any one member of these pairs, we can
scarcely fail to identify with the other. However, one identification may be almost conscious, the other deeply buried.

All the empirical evidence I have been able to gather indicates that most people have a wide capacity for identification.
Correspondence between a reader and a fictional character
facilitates identification, but differences in situation, age and
sex do not preclude it. Nor do differences in personality
structure, unless they are so pronounced that a reader finds
the motivations and thought processes of a character incomprehensible.

In addition to participating vicariously in the stories in
which we become absorbed, we frequently create and imaginatively act out stories structured upon them. We analogize.
The stories we spin are, of course, highly elliptical. There
is neither time nor need to develop them systematically.

Analogizing may involve nothing more than the recognition of a similarity between a fictional event and something
which has happened to us, and a rapid reliving of the experience. Or it may involve some welcome alteration of past experience: as the long-suffering Dobbin tells off Amelia we
may imagine ourselves speaking in like vein to someone who,
we feel, has not sufficiently appreciated our merit and our
love. Still more frequently, in all probability, analogizing
takes the form of composing fantasies based upon our wishes
and fears rather than upon our experience.

Analogizing will be discussed further in Chapter X. Perhaps because it is so closely akin to daydreaming, of which
we feel vaguely ashamed, it is rarely mentioned in reports of
response to fiction. Yet few will doubt that such an activity
takes place: almost every reader of fiction has probably
caught himself engaging in it at one time or another. Again
because of the association with daydreaming, analogizing may
not be regarded as a legitimate part of the reading experience.

But analogizing should be distinguished from daydreaming. Whereas the latter uses a story only as a point of departure and gets farther and farther away from it, analogizing remains closely bound by the particular events which instigate it. It neither distracts our attention from what we read nor, so far as I have been able to ascertain, conflicts with any other form of response. Analogizing supplies additional evidence of the power of fiction to affect us simultaneously in many ways, and to engage us personally.

6

Although it will necessarily involve some repetition, it seems desirable to analyze response also from the point of view of the factors responsible for our reactions, conscious and unconscious. Such an analysis will help us to dovetail our knowledge of the processes of response with some of the things we know about fiction itself.

It is already evident that response to fiction is influenced, if not entirely determined, by three things—subject matter, form, and a third factor, as yet unnamed, the amount of difficulty a story offers, its plane of intellectual and emotional sensibility. Our choice of reading fare, which reflects our expectations of what will give us pleasure, is also influenced, though in somewhat different fashion, by the same three factors. Let us see the part each factor plays in selection and response.

Subject matter as it might be described in a book review, the manifest content of fiction, nearly always exerts a great deal of influence upon our decision of what we shall read. For example, we may decide to read a novel because it deals with some milieu which interests us—perhaps the community, or even the very neighborhood, in which we grew up, or some field in which we have worked or dreamed of working: the theater, let us say, or government, or journalism. Often, according to my experience and that of friends, we are disappointed in novels selected on such a basis. The milieux they describe, we find, are not the ones we knew, nor do the characters face the problems with which we expected them to be concerned.

The truth is that from one point of view our interests are so particular that only one novel—the one we intend to write ourselves but lazily seek in bookstores—will altogether satisfy it. From another point of view our interests are so broad that situation and setting tend to wash out as determinants of response. We want to know all places—the ones we have never visited as well as the ones we know. We want to know what it is like to be richer than we are and poorer: to know the world where people, we think, are more powerful and assured than we are and the world where they are more miserable and more desperate but have, we may suspect, certain secret and prized compensations. When we do become interested in the manifest content of a story, it may be for reasons quite different from those which prompted us to read it.

No matter what the source of our interest, it is essential, as we know, that we *be* interested. The waking intelligence must be pleasantly absorbed in order that still more important negotiations may go forward in the deeper chambers of the mind. Moreover, the intelligence must be satisfied with the internal consistency with which a story is worked out and the honesty and understanding with which it mirrors reality. It must be convinced that, in general, its values are being respected. Far from being unimportant, the characteristics of the manifest content have a significant influence upon response.

As we know, however, we turn to fiction primarily to satisfy desires inadequately gratified through our experience, desires which in most cases we do not acknowledge and are unaware we entertain. These desires are satisfied to a large extent through the latent content of fiction, the buried levels of meaning regularly found to be present in great narrative art. It would be difficult, I believe, to exaggerate the contribution the latent content makes to our enjoyment. To be sure, the gratifications it offers us must be firmly controlled, and harmonized with the demands of the regulating components of the psyche; they would be inacceptable if they were not. The essential point, however, is that the gratification of our most urgent strivings is a component of the experience great fiction offers us. Life itself involves the adjustment and reconciliation of various of our claims, but the adjustment arrived at is usually wasteful; it is achieved at the price of renunciations which may be unnecessary and to which we remain stubbornly unreconciled. Fiction strives for an equilibrium based upon maximum fulfilment.

As a rule, needs we would have no reason to disavow are satisfied through the manifest content of fiction, which is understood by the conscious mind; repudiated needs are satisfied through the latent levels of meaning, which are apprehended by the unconscious. But the relationships are not always as regular as this. Inacceptable needs are sometimes openly gratified. In at least incidental ways, the unconscious may participate in the assimilation of the manifest content, and the conscious mind is occasionally vouchsafed glimpses of buried levels of meaning.

If only because the reports from which we learn about books seldom tell us much about their formal qualities, considerations revolving around form do not often significantly influence our selection of books. The decision to read, however, is quite frequently influenced by the desire to secure certain satisfactions which are provided chiefly by form, above all by the desire to reduce feelings of anxiety and guilt and to escape to a more comprehensible world. Often the search for such satisfactions is of no more than supplementary importance, but at times it may be the decisive factor in impelling us to read.

In *response* to fiction there is no reason to suppose that form plays a role any less important than subject matter. Its role is, in part, auxiliary. One of the functions of form is to communicate a story's expressive content to us with the right degree of clarity. But if it does not achieve this right degree, and simultaneously solve a number of other problems which require consummate skill, we cannot enjoy a story, no matter how much we may be interested in its material.

Our apprehension of the formal qualities of fiction is probably unconscious to an even greater degree than our apprehension of content. We, of course, become aware of certain—usually rather external—formal features. We may be meant to become aware of them, as we are meant to focus our attention upon a story's manifest content. But by and large form strives to efface itself. It tries to give us direct access to the matter it puts before us. Form is abetted in making itself inconspicuous by the fact that many of its chief resources are not well known and are difficult to describe.

We are most likely to become aware of form when the storyteller is guilty of some failure, some deficiency of *expertise*. Even then we do not usually identify the formal problem which has been mishandled, unless it is one which is relatively superficial and specific, such as the management of chronology or point of view. We are aware of our dissatisfaction rather than the exact cause of it. Perhaps nothing is so likely to cause dissatisfaction as a disproportion of some kind between content and form. We are displeased if the expressive content is too laxly or too firmly controlled, if offensive elements are permitted to emerge too openly or innocuous ones are pointlessly concealed. A baldly told story may make us squirm with anxiety. A stylized, contrived story leaves us feeling frustrated and let down. In at least a general way we know what such a story withholds from us: libidinal content, passion, excitement—happenings that will satisfy our needs or purge us of our fears.

7

The third factor which influences our selection of fiction and our response to it could, strictly speaking, be regarded as in part an aspect of content, in part an aspect of form. But it deserves separate attention: it functions somewhat differently from the attributes of subject matter and form we have considered and cuts across the division between them. It refers to one specific thing: the crudity or subtlety with which a work is developed in all of its aspects, its general plane of intellectual and emotional sensibility. For want of a better word, let us designate this factor as *texture*.

Texture is of decisive importance in both our selection of books and response to them. If its influence receives little attention, it is because texture itself receives little. In the average book review, for example, the texture of the work discussed is even less likely to excite comment than its form. Texture is, of course, a difficult subject to say much about.

The influence expectations about texture exert upon selection can be inferred from our reactions to the appraisal of books made by others. No matter how highly a book is praised, and how much interest its subject matter appears to hold, we are not likely to want to read it if we feel that the taste, the general level of sensibility, of the person who recommends it is inferior to our own. In contrast, we may be willing to accept the recommendation of an admired friend even when he tells us very little about a story he has enjoyed. In part, of course, this is because we know his interests, but in larger part, I believe, it is because we know the texture of his mind. Whatever he likes, we unconsciously reason, will probably appeal to us also.

The influence of texture upon response is very easy to discern when we read fiction which is *not* on our own level of sensibility. Fortunately, that "level" covers a wide range of material; it should not be conceived as a particular point on a dial. A person may like Proust and Dashiell Hammett, Shakespeare and William Inge. Furthermore, the various factors involved in response interact upon one another, and we may be willing to read a subtler or simpler story than we normally enjoy if we feel it has something especially significant to say to us. But while the boundaries of our band of sensibility are fluid, we know very well when we have gone outside them. We are incapable of enjoying books above or below the band, and very often have strong negative feelings about them.

We may be aware of at least some of the factors responsible for those feelings. If we live in a world where good and evil seem intermixed, where we cannot even identify all the forces playing upon us, much less know which to trust and which to regard as suspect, we feel at once that a story which presents issues in black-and-white terms is false and worthless. Such a story may outrage our sensibilities to such an extent that we feel a need to disassociate ourselves from it. We are less likely to acknowledge that some works present a more complex vision of experience than we can readily understand and respond to, but we make accusations which suggest the source of our feelings: we call such works precious, or oversubtle, or overanalytical. There seems to be a certain correspondence between our attitude to books and to people we are considering as friends. Though we may admire people whose intelligence and emotional sensibility, we feel, exceeds our own, we may decide that friendship with them would involve too much effort and strain, or learn from experience that this is the case. On the other hand, people we do not respect will not do as friends. We do not feel that they understand us or our predicament. Sometimes our own words seem vulgarized and degraded in their mouths. We seek as friends people whose minds are textured as our own, who, whether or not they agree with us, or even share our particular interests, understand issues as we pose them; people, too, who, we believe, respond to things with as much feeling as we do ourselves.

Our analysis has already suggested one or two of the ways in which texture affects the unconscious processes of response. We know that the relaxation of control by the ego upon which everything else depends cannot occur when we read a story we must labor to understand or a story we find too simple. A story we find oversimple is likely to yield its secrets too easily to the conscious mind, or even permit unconscious processes of response to come to light. A story we find difficult and rarefied is unlikely to stimulate much pleasurable perception, conscious or unconscious. It would be an error to suppose that the unconscious mind would come to the aid of the intellect in achieving an understanding of a story beyond its particular range. The unconscious may perceive things hidden from consciousness for emotional reasons, but in no other respects are its powers of comprehension superior to those of the mind of which it is a part.

Texture plays a particularly important role in connection with the "active" unconscious processes of response. It is doubtful if we participate at all in the action of stories which impress us as being too simple or too complex: their characters and situations are likely to seem irrelevant, if not unreal. Texture may do more than either subject matter or form to foster participation. It is certain, in any case, that we can become deeply engrossed in stories which are on our plane of sensibility, even when our interest in their theme is remote or contingent. Of course, our participation is likely to be most complete and intense when a story appeals to us because of its content, texture and form.

Most evidently through the way it supplements the influence of subject matter, texture also helps to determine whether we will analogize on the basis of what we read, create fantasies related to our own experience, desires and fears. The content of an archetypal drama, such as *Macbeth*, is of potential interest to everyone. The play provides a frame for the enactment of almost any conflict in which the anarchistic part of the self wars with the forces, inner and outer, which seek to chasten it. But the play will actually instigate fantasies only if it is also on the reader's plane of sensibility.

Though here I am admittedly less sure of my ground, I believe that analogizing may also be stimulated by the very structure and texture of the events of a story, without regard to their content, except as that content, reduced to its most general and abstract terms (e.g., rise/fall), becomes indistinguishable from structure itself. In such cases, the fantasy activity should perhaps not be called analogizing, since it is not directed to the creation of some parallel legend. Rather, it is creating a legend which conforms to the formal and textural structure, flowing, as it were, where certain indentations have been made to facilitate its progress.[5]

[5] It is even more likely that some such process as this is involved in response to music. Little, if any, music has objective expressive content, and it

Behind everything which has been said about the effect of texture upon our selection of reading matter, an economic principle is clearly discernible. In accordance with a tendency which is pervasive in our psychic life, we seek to secure the satisfactions obtainable from fiction as effortlessly as possible. This does not mean, of course, that we search out the simplest fiction to be found; such fiction would not give us pleasure. It may be, however, that, rather than selecting only "what we have to stand on tiptoe to read," as Thoreau advised, we tend to read toward the bottom rather than toward the top of our particular band of interest, even though this entails the sacrifice of the richer satisfaction we could secure from somewhat more complex books. If this is the case, it suggests that education has an immediate as well as a long-range opportunity to improve reading taste. It can do everything possible to make students sensible of the pleasure they can obtain from fiction somewhat more complex than that which they normally tend to read, and make books which meet this description more readily available. If not carried to self-defeating lengths, such a measure can also make a contribution to a more gradual attempt to raise students' level of sensibility, so that they will develop an appetite for more mature and more rewarding fiction.

---

is inconceivable that music could move us as it does and yet be devoid of such content. The solution which suggests itself is that we *supply* the expressive content, following the patterns of rising and falling excitement, conflict and resolution, laid down for us.

Chapter IX *Conscious and Unconscious Perception*

> For purposes of instruction it is doubtless desirable that the poet's vision should be interpreted, . . . that the poetic beauty should be translated into the truth of reason. This of course is not at all necessary to the enjoyment of poetry, for the true reader of poetry reads, as the poet writes, with vision. . . . The translation is not necessary even for instruction, because the mind can receive the truth of the poem without interpretation, imaginatively and unconsciously, as the mind of the poet has imparted it; the thought need nowhere be formulated; the fable is instructive without the moral; and the parables of Christ were edifying even though they were not rationally comprehended.
>
> FREDERICK C. PRESCOTT [1]

The scene of Hawthorne's story "My Kinsman, Major Molineux" is a New England colony; the time, like the place, not too precisely fixed, a "moonlight" night during that period before the Revolution when Great Britain "had assumed the right of appointing the colonial governors."

To prepare us for certain occurrences in the story, Hawthorne tells us at once that those governors could not look forward with assurance to untroubled reigns. "The annals of Massachusetts Bay will inform us, that of six governors in the space of about forty years from the surrender of the old charter, under James II., two were imprisoned by a popular insurrection; a third . . . driven from the province by the whizzing of a musket-ball; a fourth . . . hastened to his grave by continual bickerings with the House of Representatives. . . ."

A young boy of eighteen, named Robin, has come to the capital to seek his relative, Major Molineux. The Major is

[1] *The Poetic Mind* (New York: Macmillan, 1922), p. 84.

either governor of the colony or a subordinate of high rank—just which is not made clear. The boy has good reasons for wanting to find him. He is the second son of a poor clergyman. His elder brother is destined to inherit the farm "which his father cultivated in the interval of sacred duties." The Major is not only rich and influential but childless, and, during a visit paid his cousin the clergyman a year or two before the story opens, has shown an interest in Robin and his brother and hinted he would be happy to establish one of them in life. Robin has been selected for the honor, handsomely fitted out in homespun, and, to cover the expenses of his journey, given half the remnant of his father's salary of the year before.

Just before reaching the town Robin has had to cross a river, and it occurs to him that he should have perhaps asked the ferryman to direct him to the home of his kinsman or perhaps even accompany him as a guide. But he reflects that the first person he meets will serve as well.

To his surprise, however, he experiences rebuff after rebuff, difficulty upon difficulty. He asks an elderly gentleman to direct him, but the man not only disclaims any knowledge of the Major; he rebukes Robin so angrily—the youth has impulsively gripped the old man's coat—that some people nearby roar with laughter. Robin now wanders through a maze of deserted streets near the waterfront. Coming to a still-open tavern, he decides to make inquiry there. He is at first cordially received, but as soon as he asks to be directed to his relative, the innkeeper begins to read the description of an escaped "bounden servant," looking at Robin in such a way as to suggest that the description fits him exactly. Robin leaves, derisive laughter ringing in his ears for the second time that night.

Now the youth loiters up and down a spacious street, looking at each man who passes by in the hope of finding the Major. Hearing sounds which betoken the approach of the elderly gentleman with whom he has had such an unpleasant encounter, he turns down a side street. He is now so tired and hungry that he begins to consider the wisdom of lifting his cudgel and compelling the first passerby he meets to direct him to his kinsman. While toying with this idea, he enters an empty and rather disreputable-looking street. Through the half-open door of the third house he passes he catches a glimpse of a lady wearing a scarlet petticoat and decides to address his inquiry to her. His appearance and voice are winning, and the lady steps outside to talk to him. She proves both attractive and hospitable. She assures the youth that the Major dwells there, but is asleep. Intimating that she is his housekeeper, she offers to welcome the youth in his stead. Though Robin only half believes her—he is not oblivious to the meanness of the house or the street—he is about to follow her when she is startled by the opening of a door in a nearby house and leaves him to run into her own.

A watchman now approaches, muttering sleepy threats. They are perfunctory, but sufficient to discourage Robin temporarily from inquiring for his kinsman. He shouts an inquiry just as the watchman is about to vanish around a corner, but receives no reply. Robin thinks he hears a sound of muffled laughter. He quite clearly hears a pleasant titter from an open window above his head, whence a round arm beckons him. Being a clergyman's son and a good youth, Robin flees.

He now roams through the town "desperately, and at random, . . . almost ready to believe that a spell was on him." In most of the houses of the town the lights are already out. Twice, however, Robin comes upon little parties of men, including some dressed in outlandish attire. In each case the men pause to address him, but saying nothing he finds intelligible and perceiving his inability to reply, they curse him and pass on.

Encountering a solitary passer-by in the shadow of a church steeple, Robin insists on being directed to the home of his kinsman. The passerby unmuffles his face. He proves to be a man Robin had noticed earlier at the tavern, but now half of his face has been painted a livid red, the other half black. Grinning at the surprised youth, the man tells him that his kinsman will pass that very spot within the hour.

Robin settles down on the church steps to wait. As he struggles against drowsiness, strange and extraordinarily vivid fantasies flit through his mind. He dozes but, hearing a man pass by, wakes and inquires, with unwarranted peevishness, if he must wait there all night for his kinsman, Major Molineux. Despite the rather objectionable way in which the stranger has been addressed, he stops and, seeing a country youth who is apparently homeless and without friends, offers to be of help. After hearing Robin's story he offers to keep the youth company until the Major appears.

Shortly a mighty stream of people come into view. Robin gradually makes out that some of them are applauding spectators, some participants in a curious procession. It is headed by a single horseman, who bears a drawn sword and whose face is painted red and black: he is the man who has told Robin that his kinsman would pass that way within the hour. Behind the horseman come a band of wind instruments, then men carrying torches, then "wild figures in the Indian dress, and many fantastic shapes without a model, giving the whole march a visionary air, as if a dream had broken forth from some feverish brain, and were sweeping visibly through the midnight streets."

Robin has a feeling that he is involved in this procession, a feeling which is quickly confirmed. As the torches approach him, the leader thunders a command, the parade stops, the tumult dies down.

Right before Robin's eyes was an uncovered cart. There the torches blazed the brightest, there the moon shone out like day, and there, in tar-and-feathery dignity, sat his kinsman, Major Molineux!

The Major is a large and majestic man, but now his face is pale, his forehead contracted in agony, and his body "agitated by a quick and continual tremor" he cannot quell. The encounter with Robin causes him to suffer still more deeply. He recognizes the youth on the instant.

Staring at his kinsman, Robin's knees shake and his hair bristles. Soon, however, a curious change sets in. The adventures of the night, his fatigue, the confusion of the spectacle, above all "the spectre of his kinsman reviled by that great

multitude . . . [affect] him with a sort of mental inebriety."
In the crowd he sees the watchman he has encountered earlier,
enjoying his amazement. A woman twitches his arm: it is the
minx of the scarlet petticoat. Among the noises he distinguishes the laugh of the initially courteous innkeeper. Finally,
from the balcony of the large house across from the church
comes a great, broad laugh which momentarily dominates
everything: it is the formidable old man of whom Robin made
his first inquiries and whom he later went out of his way to
avoid.

Then Robin seemed to hear the voices of . . . all who had made
sport of him that night. The contagion was spreading among the
multitude, when all at once, it seized upon Robin, and he sent
forth a shout of laughter that echoed through the street,—every
man shook his sides, every man emptied his lungs, but Robin's
shout was the loudest there.

When the laughter has momentarily spent its force, the
march of the procession is resumed. Robin asks the gentleman
who has been sitting beside him to direct him to the ferry.
The Major, the boy realizes, will scarcely desire to see his face
again. In the friendliest possible way the gentleman turns
down Robin's request. He tells the youth that he will speed
him on his journey in a few days if he still wants to leave. But
he suggests another possibility. " ' . . . if you prefer to remain with us, perhaps, as you are a shrewd youth, you may
rise in the world without the help of your kinsman, Major
Molineux.' "

2

"My Kinsman, Major Molineux" belongs, I believe, among
Hawthorne's half-dozen greatest short stories. But unexpected
difficulties arise when one attempts to account for the spell the
story casts. Although it seems clear enough as it is read, it
resists analysis. Above all, its climax is puzzling. "Mental inebriety" is hardly an adequate explanation for a youth's bare-
faced mockery of an elderly relative for whom he has been
searching, whose ill-treatment might have been expected to inspire feelings of compassion and anger.

Of the half-dozen critics who have discussed the story, surprisingly, no more than two seem aware that it presents any
difficulties. The rest accept Hawthorne's explanation at face
value. They regard "My Kinsman, Major Molineux" as the
story of an ignorant country youth who, happening to wander
upon the scene at an inopportune time, is first frustrated in
his search as a result of the preparations the colonists are making and then becomes a reluctant and confused spectator at
their humiliation of his kinsman. Such an interpretation not
only fails to explain many aspects of the story; it hardly suggests why the story should interest us. It is perhaps significant
that the critics who recognize that the story is by no means so
one-dimensional as this, Malcolm Cowley and Q. D. Leavis,
also show the keenest awareness of its greatness. Unfortunately, even these critics have not succeeded, in my opinion,
in penetrating to the story's richest veins of meaning.

Malcolm Cowley describes the story as "the legend of a
youth who achieves manhood through searching for a spiritual
father and finding that the object of his search is an impostor."
(Editor's Note to "Tales," *The Portable Hawthorne*.) Leaving
aside the question of whether Robin is searching for a spiritual
father, it may be said at once that there is no evidence that
Major Molineux is an impostor. The first paragraph of the
story tells us that the colonial servants appointed by Great
Britain were likely to be resented even when they carried out
instructions with some lenience; and we are later told that the
Major's head had "grown gray in honor."

Mrs. Leavis regards "My Kinsman, Major Molineux" as a
"prophetic forecast of . . . the rejection of England that was
to occur in fact much later." [2] This is by no means as farfetched a reading of the story as it may at first appear. It has
the merit of calling attention to a rebelliousness in Robin for
which, as we shall see, there is a great deal of evidence. But as
I think will become clear, Mrs. Leavis has perceived a secondary implication of that rebelliousness; it has a much more
intimate source and reference. To account for certain events

[2] "Hawthorne as Poet," *Sewanee Review*, 59, 1951.

in the story, furthermore, her interpretation would have to be painfully strained.

The remaining critics who have commented on "Major Molineux" have evidently based their remarks almost entirely on their conscious reactions to the story's manifest level of meaning. At best, I believe, such criticism is of limited value; in connection with such a work as this it is sometimes actually misleading. Like some other stories by Hawthorne and by such writers as Melville, Kafka, Dostoevsky and Shakespeare, "My Kinsman, Major Molineux" is Janus-faced. It says one thing to the conscious mind and whispers something quite different to the unconscious. The second level of meaning is *understood* readily enough, immediately and intuitively. Our acceptance of Robin's behavior—which, as we shall see, is bizarre not only during his ultimate encounter with his kinsman but throughout the story—is only explicable, I believe, on the assumption that we understand it without difficulty. To respond to the story, to find Robin's behavior not only "right" but satisfying, we must perceive a great many things which are nowhere explicitly developed. These hidden implications are not meant to come to our attention as we read; they would arouse anxiety if they did. Even to get at them after one has read the story requires a deliberate exertion of will. There is still another difficulty. To deal with these implications at all systematically, one is almost compelled to make some use of depth-psychology. This is a kind of knowledge most critics are curiously loath to employ.

3

As soon as we look at "My Kinsman, Major Molineux" more closely, we discover that it is only in part a story of baffled search: Robin is never so intent on finding his illustrious relative as he believes he is and as it appears. The story even tells us why this is so. To some extent we understand from the very beginning; the explanations offered serve basically to remind us of things we have experienced ourselves.

As Robin walks into the town, it will be remembered, he realizes that he should have probably asked the ferryman how

to get to the home of Major Molineux. Today we have scientific evidence for what Hawthorne, and we, understand
intuitively—the significance of such forgetting. In the paragraph before this we have been told something equally significant. Robin walks into the town "with as light a step as if his
day's journey had not already exceeded thirty miles, and with
as eager an eye as if he were entering London city, instead of
the little metropolis of a New England colony." This though
he has momentarily lost sight of the reason for his visit! As
early as this we begin to suspect that the town attracts the
youth for reasons which have nothing whatever to do with
finding his influential relative. The intimation does not surprise us. Robin is eighteen. The ferryman has surmised that
this is his first visit to town. In a general way we understand
why his eye is "eager."

Robin makes his first inquiry for his kinsman with reasonable alacrity. But a considerable time appears to elapse before
his second inquiry, at the tavern, and he is evidently spurred to
enter it as much by the odor of food, which reminds him of
his own hunger, as by any zeal to find the Major.

After his rebuff at the tavern it perhaps seems reasonable
enough that Robin should drop his inquiries and simply walk
through the streets looking for Major Molineux. If our critical faculties were not already somewhat relaxed, however, it
might occur to us at once that this is a singularly inefficient
way of looking for anyone. And Robin does not pursue his
impractical plan with any ardor. He stares at the young men
he encounters with as much interest as at the old ones; though
he notices the jaunty gait of others, he never increases his pace;
and there are many pauses "to examine the gorgeous display
of goods in the shop-windows."

Nor does his lack of success make him impatient. Only the
approach of the elderly gentleman he had first accosted causes
him to abandon his plan and turn down a side street. He is
now so tired and hungry that he *considers* demanding guid-
ance from the first solitary passerby he encounters. But while
this resolution is, as Hawthorne puts it, "gaining strength,"
what he actually does is enter "a street of mean appearance, on

either side of which a row of ill-built houses was straggling toward the harbor." It is of the utmost importance that Robin continues his "researches" on this less respectable street, although no one is visible along its entire extent. If we were not by now so completely immersed in the concealed story which is unfolding itself, we might begin to wonder consciously whether Robin is seriously searching for his kinsman.

The encounters with women which follow explain the attraction of the street. They show that unconsciously Robin is searching for sexual adventure. The strength of his desire is almost pathetically betrayed by his half-willingness to believe the cock-and-bull story of the pretty young "housekeeper." Here, if not before, we identify one of the specific forces which is inhibiting Robin in his search for his kinsman: he would like a greater measure of sexual freedom than it is reasonable to suppose he would enjoy in the home of a colonial official.

The encounter with the watchman furnishes additional evidence of Robin's ambivalence. The youth could scarcely hope to find a better person of whom to ask directions. It is likely that he is also held back in this case by guilt about what he has just been doing, but the ease with which he has permitted himself to be diverted from his search is probably one of the sources of that guilt.

After further wandering Robin finally detains the passer-by who tells him that the Major will pass that very spot within the hour. In talking with the kindly gentleman who joins him to await the arrival of the Major, Robin is unable to restrain himself from boasting of his shrewdness and grown-upness. These boasts help us to understand another of the forces which has been holding him back: he wants to succeed through his own efforts and his own merits. His departure from home has evidently caused him to dream of achieving economic as well as sexual independence. When at the end of the story the gentleman suggests that Robin may decide to stay in town and may prosper without the help of his kinsman, he is simply giving expression to the youth's unvoiced but readily discernible desire.

The gentleman has an opportunity to observe how half-hearted Robin is about finding his kinsman. When the sounds of the approaching procession become more clearly audible the youth comes to the conclusion that some kind of "prodigious merry-making" is going forward and suggests that he and his new-found friend step around the corner, to a point where he thinks everyone is hastening, and partake of their share of the fun. He has to be reminded by his companion that he is searching for his kinsman, who is supposed to pass by the place where they now are in a very short time. With insight and artistry to which any tribute is inadequate, Hawthorne spreads the evidence of Robin's irresoluteness of purpose from the very beginning of the story to the moment of Major Molineux's appearance; but so subtle is the evidence, so smoothly does it fit into the surface flow of the narrative, that its significance never obtrudes itself on our attention.

4

By this point in the story we unconsciously understand Robin's vacillation more completely than I have been able to suggest. We see that, unbeknown to himself, the youth has good reasons for *not* wanting to find Major Molineux: when he finds him, he will have to re-submit to the kind of authority from which, temporarily at least, he has just escaped. At some deep level the Major appears anything but a potential benefactor; he symbolizes just those aspects of the father from which the youth so urgently desires to be free. As an elderly relative of the father and an authority figure, he may be confused with the father. In any case, however undeservedly, he has now become the target of all the hostile and rebellious feelings which were originally directed against the father.

Hawthorne tells us these things, it is interesting to note, by means of just the kind of unconscious manifestations which twentieth-century psychology has found so significant. While Robin sits on the steps of the church, fighting his desire to sleep, he has a fantasy in which he imagines that his kinsman is already dead! And his very next thought is of his father's household. He wonders how "that evening of ambiguity and weariness" has been spent at home, and has a second fantasy of such hallucinatory vividness that he wonders if he is "here or there." Nor is this an idle question. His father and Major Molineux are so inextricably linked in his mind that in a sense the drama in which he is involved is being played out "there" —at home—as well as in the town where bodily he happens to be.

The climax of this drama, so puzzling to the conscious intellect, is immediately comprehensible to that portion of the mind which has been following the hidden course of developments. It is comprehensible although Hawthorne describes Robin's feelings, as is right, in vague terms. Robin never understands those feelings and the reader would find it disturbing if they were too plainly labeled.

The youth's initial reactions can, of course, be consciously understood. They express the emotions any decent young lad might be expected to have in the circumstances. Robin's knees shake and his hair bristles. He feels pity and terror and, it may be, an impulse to strike back at the tormentors of his elderly relative.

The feelings which then begin to assert themselves would probably never have secured open expression except under circumstances as out of the ordinary as those the story describes. But now everything conspires not simply to permit but to encourage Robin to give in to tendencies which, as we know, he was finding it difficult to control. To everyone present Major Molineux is overtly what he is to the youth on some dark and secret level—a symbol of restraint and unwelcome authority. He is this even to the elderly gentleman, the watchman, the man by his side—people whose disapproval of the crowd's behavior might have had a powerful effect upon him. Without a voice being raised in protest, the crowd is acting out the youth's repressed impulses and in effect urging him to act on them also. The joy the crowd takes in asserting its strength and the reappearance of the lady of the scarlet petticoat provide him with incentives for letting himself go.

And so Robin makes common cause with the crowd. He laughs—he laughs louder than anyone else. So long as he

himself did not know how he would act he had reason to fear
the crowd, and the relief he feels at the easing of the immediate situation is one of the sources of his laughter. But his
decision resolves still deeper and more vexing conflicts. The
relief he feels that he can vent his hostility for his kinsman and
abandon his search for him is the ultimate source of his "riot-
ous mirth." It is fueled by energy which until then was being
expended in repression and inner conflict.

Although Hawthorne uses figurative language which may
keep his meaning from being consciously noted, he is at pains
to let us know that murderous hate underlies the merriment of
the crowd of which Robin becomes a part. When the laughter momentarily dies down, the procession resumes its march.

On they went, like fiends that throng in mockery around some
dead potentate, mighty no more, but majestic still in his agony.
On they went, in counterfeited pomp, in senseless uproar, in
frenzied merriment, trampling all on an old man's heart.

Symbolically and to some extent actually the crowd has carried out the fantasy Robin had on the steps of the church.

To the conscious mind "My Kinsman, Major Molineux" is a
story of an ambitious youth's thwarted search for an influential relative he wants to find. To the unconscious, it is a story
of the youth's hostile and rebellious feelings for the relative—
and for the father—and his wish to be free of adult domina-
tion. To the conscious mind it is a story of a search which was
unsuccessful because of external difficulties. To the unconscious—like *Hamlet*, with which it has more than one point in
common—it is a story of a young man caught up in an enterprise for which he has no stomach and debarred from succeeding in it by internal inhibitions.

From one point of view the unacknowledged forces playing
upon the apparently simple and candid central character of
"My Kinsman, Major Molineux" are deeply abhorrent. Our
sympathy for the character should tell us, however, that there
is another side to the matter. The tendencies which assert
themselves in Robin exist in all men. What he is doing, unwittingly but flamboyantly, is something which every young

man does and must do, however gradually, prudently and in-
conspicuously: he is destroying an image of paternal authority
so that, freed from its restraining influence, he can begin life
as an adult.

5

"My Kinsman, Major Molineux" is one of a relatively small
but distinguished group of stories which would be incomprehensible, in part or in their entirety, on the basis of what we
understand consciously. In response to such stories it is evident that unconscious perception plays an indispensable role.
Though it is less evident, I believe that the unconscious plays
a role which is scarcely less important in response to many
stories which are intelligible on some level to the conscious
mind. For most, if not all, fiction—and certainly the greatest
fiction—has *additional* levels of meaning which must be communicated unconsciously. In many cases far more is communicated unconsciously than consciously. Even when this is
not the case, the meanings grasped below the threshold of
awareness may make a disproportionate contribution to the
pleasure we receive from reading fiction: they satisfy some of
our deepest and most urgent needs—needs which though unacknowledged are never relinquished.

It may be worthwhile to analyze a story which is perfectly
comprehensible to the intellect but has many further levels of
meaning. Let us glance, therefore, at Sherwood Anderson's
story, "I Want to Know Why." It has many interesting
points of similarity and contrast with "My Kinsman, Major
Molineux." And as it happens, the story has been analyzed by
Cleanth Brooks and Robert Penn Warren, so that once again
we have a jumping-off point for our own explorations.

I shall assume that my readers are familiar with the story,
and simply remind them of its chief events. It is narrated in
the first person by its fifteen-year-old hero, whose name we
never learn. A boy from Beckersville, Kentucky, a small
town evidently in the bluegrass region, he is "crazy about
thoroughbred horses"; to him they epitomize everything
which is "lovely and clean and full of spunk and honest." A

lump comes into his throat when he sees potential winners run. He knows he could capitalize on this physical reaction if he wanted to, but he has no desire to gamble; horses and racing represent something too important to him for that.

With three friends of about his own age, the boy runs away to attend the races at Saratoga. Bildad, a Negro from the same town who works at the tracks, feeds the boys, shows them a place to sleep and keeps still about them, which the hero seems to appreciate most of all.

The race the boys particularly want to see has two entries that give the hero a lump in his throat, and the night before it is run he is so excited he cannot sleep. He aches to watch the two horses run, but he dreads it too, for he hates to see either one beaten. The day of the race he goes to the paddocks to look at the horses. As soon as he sees one of them, Sunstreak, a nervous and beautiful stallion, who is "like a girl you think about sometimes but never see," the boy knows that it is his day. Watching, he experiences a mystical communion with the horse and the horse's trainer, a man named Jerry Tillford, also from Beckersville, who has befriended him many times. The experience is so central to understanding the story that it must be quoted at considerable length.

I was standing looking at that horse and aching. In some way, I can't tell how, I knew just how Sunstreak felt inside. . . . That horse wasn't thinking about running. . . . He was just thinking about holding himself back 'til the time for the running came. . . . He wasn't bragging or letting on much or prancing or making a fuss, but just waiting. I knew it and Jerry Tillford his trainer knew. I looked up and then that man and I looked into each other's eyes. Something happened to me. I guess I loved the man as much as I did the horse because he knew what I knew. Seemed to me there wasn't anything in the world but that man and the horse and me. I cried and Jerry Tillford had a shine in his eyes. . . .

Sunstreak does win the race and the other Beckersville entry, a gelding named Middlestride, finishes second. The hero of the story was so confident that it would work out this way that he is scarcely excited. All through the race he thinks about Jerry Tillford and of how happy he must be. "I liked him that afternoon even more than I ever liked my own father." Jerry, he knows, has worked with Sunstreak since the horse was a baby colt, and he imagines that while watching the race the trainer must feel "like a mother seeing her child do something brave or wonderful."

That night the boy "cuts out" from his companions because he feels an impulse to be near Jerry. He walks along a road which leads to a "rummy-looking farmhouse" because he has seen "Jerry and some other men go that way in an automobile." He doesn't expect to find them, but shortly after he gets there an automobile arrives with Jerry and five other men, several of them from Beckersville and known to the boy. All of them except the father of one of the boys who has accompanied the hero to Saratoga, a gambler named Rieback who quarrels with the others, enter the farmhouse, which proves to be "a place for bad women to stay in."

The boy telling the story creeps to a window and peers in. What he sees sickens and disgusts him. The women are mean-looking and, except for one who a little resembles the gelding Middlestride, "but [is] not clean like him" and has "a hard ugly mouth," they are not even attractive. The place smells rotten, and the talk is rotten, "the kind a kid hears around a livery stable in a town like Beckersville in the winter but don't ever expect to hear talked when there are women around."

Jerry Tillford boasts like a fool, taking credit for Sunstreak's qualities and the victory the horse has won that afternoon. Then the trainer looks at the woman who somewhat resembles Middlestride and his eyes begin to shine as they had when he had looked at the teller of the story and Sunstreak that afternoon. As the man weaves toward the woman, the boys begins to hate him. "I wanted to scream and rush in the room and kill him. . . . I was so mad . . . that I cried and my fists were doubled up so my fingernails cut my hands." When the man kisses the woman, the boy creeps away and returns to the tracks. That night he sleeps little. He tells his companions nothing of what he has seen, but the next morning he persuades them to start for home.

There he continues to live very much as before, but everything seems different.

At the tracks the air don't taste as good or smell as good. It's because a man like Jerry Tillford, who knows what he does, could see a horse like Sunstreak run, and kiss a woman like that the same day. . . . I keep thinking about it and it spoils looking at horses and smelling things and hearing niggers laugh and everything. Sometimes I'm so mad about it I want to fight someone. . . . What did he do it for? I want to know why.

6

"I Want to Know Why" certainly means something to the conscious intellect, and in *Understanding Fiction* Brooks and Warren give one interpretation of the story's manifest content to which I should not wish to offer more than one or two reservations. "I Want to Know Why," they declare, is an initiation story in which a boy "discovers something about the nature of evil, and tries to find some way of coming to terms with his discovery."

The boy knows that evil exists in the world. According to Brooks and Warren, what causes him to feel so much horror and disgust at Saratoga is the realization—pointed up by the parallelism of the scene at the paddocks and the scene at the rummy-looking farmhouse—that good and evil may be so closely linked, that they may coexist in the same person. He discovers, too, that virtue is a human, not an animal, quality. Unlike the horse, with which in other respects human beings are frequently compared, man has the capacity for choice. When he elects the bad, he is worse than the beasts.

It seems to me that the phrase "who knows what he does," on which Brooks and Warren base the last-mentioned observation, refers less to specific problems involving choice than to the willingness of a creature like man to come to terms with his propensity for evil. Nor can I assent to the claim that the boy *discovers*, at the climax of the story, that good and evil are closely joined. What he knows about Henry Rieback's father has already taught him that, if nothing else has. These are trifling qualifications, however. My real question is whether the interpretation offered by Brooks and Warren goes far to explain the impact of the story, even assuming the correctness of everything they say. They themselves seem a little uneasy on this score, for they write:

> . . . having extracted what may seem to be a moral "message," one should remind himself that the "message" is, as such, not the story. The story may be said to be the dramatization of the discovery. Now the message is something of which everyone is aware; it is a platitude. But the platitude ceases to be a platitude, it is revitalized and becomes meaningful again, when it is shown to be operating in terms of experience.

Here, again, there is little to which one can take exception. A very ordinary idea or event can be "revitalized" if dramatized successfully, and the fact that what we learn about Jerry Tillford is dramatized helps to account for its impact upon the boy at the farmhouse window and the reader looking over his shoulder. Even when dramatized, however, the knowledge that an adult is capable of good and evil is unlikely to have the powerful effect it has upon narrator and reader unless it has some special significance. Something about the nature of the narrator's relationship and experience with Jerry Tillford has eluded Brooks's and Warren's analysis.

7

It has eluded it, I believe, in part because they are so preoccupied with the moral values of the story that they have not asked the most important questions which must be answered if we are to account for the story's appeal.

A central question, as I have indicated, is why the climactic scene can arouse such pain, disgust and bitter disillusionment in the boy who tells the story. His discovery of the underside of Jerry Tillford evidently frustrates some yearning he can scarcely bear to renounce. Once we have gone this far, it is not too difficult to identify this yearning: it is for an ideal relationship with a man who is like his father but better than his father—less fallible, more sympathetic with the boy's interests and, what is at first glance a curious requirement, devoid of sexuality. His disappointment is the keener because, on the very afternoon of the experience at the farmhouse, the consummation of his desire seemed within reach—for an ecstatic moment had actually been achieved.

That the unnamed narrator of "I Want to Know Why" wanted to adopt Jerry Tillford as a kind of second father could not be more clear. Indeed, it could be maintained that the boy's feelings are sometimes too baldly revealed. They could be inferred from the few things he says about his father and various incidental remarks about the trainer. His father is "all right," and evidently extremely permissive, but he doesn't make much money and so can't buy his son things. The boy says he doesn't care—he's too old for that—but since he has just listed the kind of presents Henry Rieback is always getting from his father we doubt his statement. At a deeper level, we sense, the boy is disappointed because his father does not satisfy an immaterial need: he evidently does not share his son's interest in thoroughbreds and racing. Jerry Tillford, of course, is not only interested in these subjects but an authority upon them, and his job puts him in a position to befriend the boy in terms of his interests. He has let the boy walk right into the stalls to examine horses, and so on. These favors may have made the boy think of Jerry Tillford as a kind of father. In any case, the language the boy uses to describe the trainer's treatment of Sunstreak shows that he attributes parental kindliness to him. ("I knew he had been watching and working with Sunstreak since the horse was a baby colt. . . . I knew that for him it was like a mother seeing her child do something brave or wonderful.")

The various hints given us about the narrator's feelings for Jerry Tillford are confirmed by two explicit statements. The boy declares, it will be remembered, that on the afternoon of the race he liked the trainer even more than he ever liked his own father. He is equally frank about the feelings which prompted him to "ditch" his companions the night of the race in order to be near the trainer. "I was just lonesome to see Jerry, like wanting to see your father at night when you are a young kid."

What may require further explanation—although unconsciously we understand it very well—is why the boy's feelings are of such extraordinary strength and take the particular form they do. In part his hero worship of Jerry Tillford is a not uncommon outcome of an interrelated cluster of reactions to the parents which arise in children of both sexes during latency and early adolescence.[3] The fuller knowledge of reality children acquire at this stage of their development and the resentment they feel for rebuffs, imaginary or real, may cause them to become acutely aware of their parents' circumstances and limitations. Though they continue to love their parents, consciously or unconsciously they are likely to feel dissatisfied with them or even ashamed of them. Frequently these feelings cause children to replace their parents in fantasy —to imagine that their actual parents are mere pretenders to that honor and that their "real" parents are personages who are powerful, famous or wealthy, or the possessors of some other desired attributes. The children's disaffection may also impel them to establish relationships with adults who can easily be recognized as idealized replacements of one or the other parent.

In boys these feelings are powerfully reinforced by the changes which occur at puberty. The sudden upsurge of sexuality may reactivate the long-dormant Oedipal tendencies, jeopardizing and in some cases at least temporarily upsetting the still far from stable identification with the father. The wish to protect this identification against the reawakened competitiveness which threatens it is responsible for a curious secondary development—an attempt to deny the sexuality of the father and, by an inevitable chain of association, of the mother also. Misguided as such an attempt may appear, it has its own logic. Seen as a sexual being enjoying the favors of the mother, the father again becomes a person who arouses envy, hatred and fear. The knowledge of the sexual relations of the parents is inherently painful and, as Freud has explained, is usually conveyed to the child in a way which tends to belittle

[3] See Freud, "Family Romances," *Collected Papers*, Vol. V (London: Hogarth, 1950).

both his parents and himself. For this reason, too, the information is usually resisted.

The secret of sexual life is revealed to [the growing boy] . . . in coarse language, undisguisedly derogatory and hostile in intent, and the effect is to destroy the authority of adults, which is irreconcilable with these revelations about their sexual activities. The greatest impression on the child who is being initiated is made by the relation the information bears to his own parents, which is often instantly repudiated in some such words as these: "It may be true that your father and mother and other people do such things, but it is quite impossible that mine do." [4]

Now we are in a better position to approach the two contrasted scenes which do so much to make "I Want to Know Why" a compelling story. The scene at the paddocks depicts a fervently desired communion with an idealized and desexualized father, a father toward whom one need have no feelings of competitiveness and hostility. Moreover, it recalls just such a situation of innocence—it recalls the pre-Oedipal situation in which the feeling of father and son for the mother was a bond between them instead of the focus of rivalry, and father, mother and child were united in love. In this scene Sunstreak becomes the mother, and the boy and Jerry Tillford are brought together by their admiration and love for the stallion. (Sunstreak reminds the boy, it will be recalled, of "a girl you think about sometimes but never see.")

The scene at the rummy-looking farmhouse undoes the scene at the paddocks. Jerry's bragging, which is at the expense of Sunstreak, reveals that he has no real love for the stallion, and thus shows the boy that there was actually no foundation for the experience he thought he had had that afternoon. Because the boy identifies with the stallion, the trainer's boasts are also a blow to his self-esteem. Finally, the boasts show how unfit the trainer is to be the kind of parent the boy had desired.

The disclosure of Jerry's sexuality wounds the boy still more deeply. Even more than his bragging, it disqualifies the

[4] "A Special Type of Choice of Object Made by Men," *Collected Papers*, IV, 198.

trainer for the kind of relationship the boy had desired—a relationship which would be washed of all competitiveness and enmity. It is the source of a more encompassing disillusionment. It forces on the boy the unwelcome knowledge that this is a sexual, sinful world, in which he can nowhere hope to find the kind of communion he has sought or the perfection he once attributed to the parents and later hoped to find incarnated in others. The trainer's behavior, his very presence, at the whorehouse is also a particularly brutal and painful reminder of the sexuality of the parents—not only of the father, with whom Tillford is immediately associated, but of the mother as well. She is present in this scene also. She is the woman the trainer desires, the one, somewhat more attractive than the others, who resembles the gelding Middlestride. She is debased to a prostitute, a devaluation which almost always suggests itself—though, of course, it may be instantly repudiated—when an adolescent boy is compelled to take cognizance of the sexual relations of the parents. Freud describes the chain of reasoning in the same essay from which I have just quoted:

Along with this piece of "sexual enlightenment" there seldom fails to go, as a corollary, a further one about the existence of certain women who practice sexual intercourse as a means of livelihood and are universally despised in consequence. To the boy himself this contempt is necessarily quite foreign; as soon as he realizes that he too can be initiated by these unfortunates into that sexual life which he has hitherto regarded as the exclusive prerogative of "grown-ups," his feeling for them is only a mixture of longing and shuddering. Then, when he cannot any longer maintain the doubt that claims exception for his own parents from the ugly sexual behaviour of the rest of the world, he says to himself with cynical logic that the difference between his mother and a whore is after all not so very great, since at the bottom they both do the same thing.

On one level Jerry Tillford's behavior is wounding because it punctures an attempt to idealize him, to deny his sexuality and the parents'. On still another level it is wounding because it has the character of a sexual rejection and betrayal. To some extent the boy's feelings are those of an outraged lover.

Logically the two sets of reactions are incompatible with one another, but here, as is frequently the case, fiction is speaking to a part of the psyche which is not concerned with logic, a part of which can simultaneously accommodate divergent and even contradictory feelings.

The scene at the farmhouse gains additional poignance by stirring feelings originally experienced at different periods of time. Like the scene at the paddocks, it recalls an earlier situation heavily charged with emotion: it condenses the infantile and the adolescent discoveries of sexuality. On the immediate, realistic level the scene depicts something which befalls a fifteen-year-old boy, but in every essential respect it duplicates the "primal scene," the original investigation of the parents' sexual relations. The looking, the secrecy, the mixture of fascination and horror, the ambivalence about whether one will "find anything," the feeling of being alone and betrayed when one does find what underneath one did expect—all the characteristics of the prototype experience are echoed here.

Although only the unconscious is likely to perceive it, in the last analysis both "My Kinsman, Major Molineux" and "I Want to Know Why" are stories of a boy's relationship with his father. Both describe more or less universal phases of the process of growing up, although, as in great fiction generally, the actual events are so altered that they may not be consciously recognizable, and so telescoped and heightened that they arouse even profounder affects than the less dramatic and more gradual experiences they draw upon and evoke. "My Kinsman, Major Molineux" concentrates on the young man's rebellious and hostile feelings toward an authoritative image of the father—an image which must be destroyed in the course of achieving independent adulthood. "I Want to Know Why" describes the frustration of two dear but unfulfillable wishes of the adolescent boy. The first wish is to deny the sexuality of the parents in order to avoid competition with the father. This wish is incompatible with what one inevitably learns in growing up and on some deep level already knows. The second wish is for a love relationship with the father which, though idealized in some respects, is still so heavily cathected with libido that its satisfaction would involve both continued dependence upon the father and a proprietary right to his affection.

Although both stories refer ultimately to emotions felt by sons for their fathers, it is interesting that in each case the feelings are displaced onto surrogates. In "My Kinsman, Major Molineux" the advantage of the alteration is evident: it facilitates the expression of hostility. "I Want to Know Why" is probably both more realistic and more moving because the immediate object of the hero's feelings is just such a man as Jerry Tillford. By the time a boy is fifteen the feelings of affection for the actual father are usually too admixed with other elements, the disillusionment too advanced, to permit the sharp contrasts of hopes raised and abruptly deflated upon which the structure and impact of the story depend.

8

The nature of the conscious cognitive activity involved in response to fiction was outlined in Chapter VIII. If the importance of this activity has not been stressed, it is because it has long been emphasized in esthetic theory and is generally appreciated. Great fiction is the product of wise and finely adjusted minds. It is patterned: it shows us a given action in its entirety, furnishing us with all the information necessary for understanding it, excluding what is not, and tracing causal relationships. It is our experience filtered through an intelligence and made meaningful—like all art, a joy and a comfort to turn to when we are wearied by the confused face of reality. Entirely on the basis of what it has to say to the conscious intelligence, fiction is an unsurpassed medium for increasing our understanding of the human predicament and our own situation.

Even at the manifest level, however, fiction deals with our personal problems, and deals with them concretely. If only for this reason, our approach to it is seldom as dispassionate and objective as traditional esthetics has usually implied. Our conscious understanding of fiction is circumscribed and influenced at every turn by emotional considerations. We would not find it pleasurable to devote our attention to the issues raised in the greatest fiction if it were not for the power of form to quiet anxiety and conceal certain matters from our view. From first to last anxiety is the primary regulator of what we shall be permitted to perceive consciously. It also influences the accuracy with which we understand.

As the word itself would suggest if, like most words, it had not long since been emptied of much of its meaning, our very "interest" in fiction, at the most superficial level, is also primarily determined by emotional factors—by our interests, our situation, our desires and our fears. It would be a mistake to suppose either that we read with steady and even attention or that, like an indicator on a machine, our interest fluctuates entirely in accordance with the objective importance of what we read. Our interest is active and, in consequence, affected by subjective considerations and highly selective. While we read, among other reasons, to secure knowledge, as DeWitt H. Parker declares, "the interest in understanding invariably follows the track of some other desire. In pessimistic art, for example, it is ancillary to the need for an inner adjustment to a new and disillusioned vision of reality." [5] More generally, we can say that the extent to which the various interpretations of experience proffered by fiction are consulted, understood, enjoyed and accepted depends in no small measure upon the reader's emotional needs.

While the nature of the conscious cognitive activity which occurs in reading fiction has not always been correctly understood, the very existence of unconscious, intuitive understanding is usually overlooked or alluded to cursorily. Nor is this surprising, though the part the unconscious plays is large and crucially important. Until a half-century ago the very word "understanding" was usually associated with conscious mental operations. The unconscious processes involved in response are, of course, not meant to come to our attention, and until recently no tools existed for exploring them.

Even when their participation can be inferred beyond any

---

[5] "Wish Fulfilment and Intuition in Art," *A Modern Book of Esthetics*, edited by Melvin M. Rader (New York: Holt, 1935), p. 76.

possibility of doubt, furthermore, there are difficulties in the way of describing them with any precision. So far as I know, for example, there is no exact parallel for the kind of division of labor between the conscious and unconscious mind by means of which fiction, or imaginative literature of any kind, is understood. A somewhat similar disassociation takes place when we sustain a desultory conversation while furtively daydreaming of something else. But while the conversation and the daydream typically have little in common, conscious and unconscious response to fiction feed upon the same stimulus and go forward on parallel tracks. Response to humor provides a closer analogue, but the façade of a joke is very quickly pierced. In response to fiction we fall into a kind of long-sustained trance, a semi-hypnotic state in which the conscious mind focuses upon the more manifest meaning of developments while the unconscious penetrates to implication upon implication to which the intellect chooses to be blind.

The important part that unconscious understanding plays in response to fiction has already been authenticated by intensive studies of individual readers and small groups, and broader and more carefully controlled studies will follow in due course. But perhaps the most incontrovertible evidence of the existence of unconscious perception is our very ability to understand and enjoy such a story as "My Kinsman, Major Molineux." If we attempted to judge this story, or many other great works of fiction, solely on the basis of what we perceived consciously, we would almost certainly make the same mistake to which T. S. Eliot was driven when he overlooked the unconscious sources of Hamlet's behavior:[6] we would conclude that their heroes are dominated by emotions "in excess of the facts as they appear"—or stemming from quite different facts from those which appear—and that the works are, one and all, artistic failures. While our errors might be less evident, we would often be equally unfortunate in our evaluations of works which are intelligible on some level to the conscious mind, for, as I have tried to demonstrate

[6] "Hamlet and His Problems," *Selected Essays, 1917-1932* (New York: Harcourt, Brace, 1932).

by my analysis of "I Want to Know Why," our reactions to such stories are only explained in part—frequently only in small part—by what we understand of them consciously. Carefully analyzed, our response to any work of fiction would be found to depend to some extent on purely intuitive perceptions.

It is hoped that the discussion of "My Kinsman, Major Molineux" and "I Want to Know Why" will suggest not only how much may be unconsciously understood when we read fiction but the close bearing of what is unconsciously perceived upon our deepest and most tenacious concerns. We never cease to struggle against the hostile and rebellious impulses which were originally directed against the father. At some level we never cease to hope for the kind of love for which the boy in Anderson's story was searching. It is because fiction is so often concerned with such emotions as these that part of our response to it must take place below the threshold of awareness. We could not, without anxiety and guilt, confess that we share the secret impulses which motivate Robin and the unnamed narrator of "I Want to Know Why." But we can deal with those impulses, and secure the welcome release which comes from dealing with them, when we are unaware of what we are doing and can assure ourselves that we are engaged in so innocent and reputable an activity as reading fiction.

Chapter X *Participation and the*
Pathways to Satisfaction

Among the experiences which are by the nature of the case
hidden from observation are found almost all those with which
criticism is concerned.

I. A. RICHARDS [1]

Having gone as far as we have, it is difficult not to take
one additional step. Everything we know and feel about
fiction suggests that understanding is not its sole objective.
If it were, fiction would probably be less interested in particulars, it would certainly be more concerned with generalizations, than in fact it is. It would be more explicit. It would
be less intent on engaging the emotions as well as the mind.
The basic characteristics of fiction suggest that it usually
wants us not simply to see and understand but to participate
in the events it sets before us. It offers us not simply a spectacle but an experience.

Whenever the reading experience is successful, we may be
sure that fiction has achieved its double aim. The intensity
and sometimes the very nature of our emotional responses
indicate that in imagination we experience the events of which
we read. For example, as we shall see, neither catharsis nor the
esthetic experience can be satisfactorily explained except on
the assumption that we become actively involved in the fiction
which moves us. Empirical studies of response to fiction
furnish evidence of such involvement. Katherine M. Wolf's
and Marjorie Fiske's study of a hundred-odd young readers
of comic books declares: "So long as [the children] are read-

[1] *Principles of Literary Criticism* (New York: Harcourt, Brace, 1934),
p. 112.

238

ing Superman they not only become invincible, but they perform, vicariously, all of his remarkable feats." [2]

Reading fiction, we see, is not a completely innocent experience. As Kenneth Burke declares: "A tragedy is not profound unless the poet *imagines* the crime—and in thus imagining it, he symbolically commits it. Similarly, in so far as the audience participates in the imaginings, it also participates in the offense." [3] There is a sense in which we must accept responsibility for the fiction we enjoy, just as we accept responsibility for our fantasies and dreams. No less than our own psychic productions the reading of fiction permits us to deal with the past events of our lives and our hopes and fears for the future—and to deal with them actively, re-enacting troublesome experiences until the pain or other emotion they aroused has been assimilated; acting out, with such intensity that affects are discharged and tensions relieved, experiences which give shape to our wishes and dreams.

It makes surprisingly little difference that the fantasies embedded in fiction have been conceived by others. The explanation, of course, is that—in most cases quite blindly but none the less purposively and efficiently—we search out stories whose fantasies have relevance for us. Our absorption in a story may usually be taken as an indication that we have found something which we sought. Dr. Kate Friedlander's work indicates that at least in certain periods of childhood the central fantasies of the stories which are most enjoyed closely resemble the conscious or unconscious fantasies of the readers of those stories, though they, of course, do not become aware of this.[4]

In at least one respect our acceptance and fervent participation in the fantasies found in fiction is encouraged by the fact

[2] Katherine M. Wolf and Marjorie Fiske, "The Children Talk About Comics," *Communications Research, 1948-1949,* edited by Paul F. Lazarsfeld and Frank N. Stanton (New York: Harper, 1949), p. 11.

[3] *The Philosophy of Literary Form* (Baton Rouge, La.: Louisiana State, 1941), p. 48.

[4] "Children's Books and Their Function in Latency and Prepuberty," *American Imago,* 3, 1942.

that they do not appear to be our own. We can deny responsibility for them, and the discovery that others share our propensities reduces our feelings of guilt. It is helpful, too, that the fantasies underlying fiction are usually better disguised than our own, are far more likely to be curbed and controlled, and are woven into products which assuage guilt through their formal attributes.

Our participation in fiction is, of course, ordinarily less uniform and less complete than it is in our own fantasies, where every detail is determined and meaningful. The psychic organization of reader and writer seldom coincides in exact detail. Furthermore, a writer may have some deficiency of skill which prevents him from rendering some types of characters or situations as well as others. Some idiosyncrasy of the reader, or some factor in his immediate situation, may vitiate his response to certain aspects of a story though they be well handled. But such factors as these have far less influence than might be supposed. A well-told story is of a piece; if its main features interest us, no part of it is likely to lack a measure of appeal. While selective as compared with our participation in our own fantasies, our participation in the fiction we enjoy is nearly always broader and steadier, as well as deeper, than we realize.

A small minority of readers—usually, it appears, readers with an obsessive craving for a particular type of story and a particular type of satisfaction—react to fiction in quite different fashion from the way we experience dreams and fantasies. They respond to certain general characteristics of a story— or even to common characteristics of a series of stories or a genre—rather than to specific happenings. Thus some of the children studied by Misses Wolf and Fiske whose interest in comics was "patently violent and excessive" [5] paid little attention to the particular events of the endless series of Superman comics they devoured. What appealed to them were certain dependable common characteristics of the series—for example, the speed with which tensions are built up and dissolved and the victory of Superman and righting of all wrongs

[5] "The Children Talk About Comics," p. 22.

at the conclusion of each episode. "It is not the details of development, but rather the general aura which the child finds
fascinating. In this general aura he can re-experience his anxieties and yet know that the subject of the anxieties will be
overcome." [6] It may be conjectured that many addicts of
detective stories, adults as well as children, read in very similar
fashion, hardly attentive to details of development or stylistic
refinements in their compulsive search for certain primitive
satisfactions.

Even such readers appear to become involved in the fiction
they enjoy, although in selective and even inexact fashion.
More "normal" readers, there is every reason to believe, vicariously participate in the fiction they enjoy with the same completeness with which, consciously or unconsciously, they
understand it. The engrossed reader of "My Kinsman, Major
Molineux" and "I Want to Know Why" identifies with Robin
and the unnamed narrator of the Anderson story and acts out
their physical and psychical adventures—himself shares the
search for Major Molineux in all its ambivalence, himself experiences the flaming and extinction of desire for communion
with a man as dear and perfect as the father appeared when he
was most beloved.

2

Unconsciously and sometimes even consciously, it has been
stressed, we search for fiction which has some personal relevance for us. We ferret out stories which shed light on our
external problems or give form to our internal ones—in Eliot's famous phrase, provide an "objective correlative" for certain of our feelings. We may be sure that any story which
absorbs us satisfies some of our needs. The connections may
be subtle and difficult to trace, but in one way or another the
pattern of its events will be found to correspond to "configura-
tions of forces or tendencies within the responding mind." [7]

Since the fiction we enjoy has this close personal reference,

[6] *Ibid.*, p. 30.
[7] Maud Bodkin, *Archetypal Patterns in Poetry* (London: Oxford, 1948),
p. 70.

it is scarcely surprising that as we read we sometimes make comparisons between the events of a story and our own experience and even compose little episodes, modeled upon what we read, in which we are characters *in propria persona*. In these episodes we sometimes relive or alter the past and sometimes dream of the future, consummating desires and working through fears. These analogizing fantasies seldom become conscious. They are experienced with such extraordinary speed that they do not perceptibly slow the progress of our reading or interfere with any other responses. But our narcissism is warranty for the assumption that however fleeting and inconspicuous these responses may be they must add materially to our pleasure.

Fiction lends itself to analogizing because of the extreme connotativeness of its episodic language. As our examination of that language indicated, it is inherently, perhaps inescapably, symbolic. One episode may "stand for" some quite different experience—or simultaneously stand for many different things. This plasticity is highly appreciated by writers of fiction as well as by readers. They take advantage of it, for example, when they wish to utilize their own experience in altered form—whether because they desire to conceal the autobiographical significance of a story, are striving for perspective and detachment or feel that, unchanged, their experience is too internal, idiosyncratic, confused or undramatic to be suitable. In explaining how a truly creative writer might go about the task of finding material to represent such an unusable cluster of personal experiences and feelings, Clifford Odets has provided an ideal, though evidently imaginary, example of what I mean by analogizing:

. . . his drama, it is highly possible, may begin with him enviously watching strolling couples in the park. He feels alone, disconnected. Behind him there is, perhaps, an unhappy broken marriage; he has recently lost a good friend through a foolish misunderstanding; all his life he has wanted to be a good and true man, but recently has understood in himself an ignoble tendency to personal and selfish success. . . . His deepest belief has always been that men must work together, not apart; and now he feels that there is something in modern life (acutely and painfully reflected in himself) which makes this not only difficult but almost impossible.[8]

While in the grip of these feelings, the dramatist attends a string quartet concert, and the men on the stage, "who, by the very nature of their art must work together, dedicated, connected, humble and true" strike him as an image of everything he desires and does not possess. Perhaps to allay the guilt he feels because of his sense of alienation, he begins to muse on why so many quartets of other days have failed. His imagination quickens. He thinks of a quartet the members of which have worked and lived together happily for years. One of them marries. His wife, who is "young, beautiful and destructive," presently begins an affair with another member of the quartet; and she makes her husband feel that if he wants to keep her "he must leave the quartet and make more splash and money as a solo artist." End of the quartet, end of Eden, but for a troubled writer, at long last the emotionally compelling material he has been seeking for his new play.

Just as the play expresses experiences apparently not represented in its subject matter, so it may stimulate innumerable ideas, memories and fantasies which are analogous to its particulars rather than identical with them. It may remind many of those who see or read it of situations in their lives, quite different both from the one in the play and the one which gave the play birth, in which harmonious relationships which promised to endure forever were abruptly and senselessly ruined. It may stir feelings of alienation which had their source in some situation quite different from the one in the play though comparable to it in certain essential respects. Like some universally negotiable currency, the events of a well-told story may be converted effortlessly, immediately and without discount into the coinage of each reader's emotional life.

[3] "Two Approaches to the Writing of a Play," The *New York Times*, April 22, 1951.

3

The kind of stories which have been referred to in this book provide rich opportunities for analogizing. To take some fairly obvious examples, *Portrait of a Lady*, *The Ambassadors* and "The Beast in the Jungle," like many other stories by Henry James, provide ground plans for dealing with experiences of waste—with squandered opportunities for love, happiness and rich and rewarding experience. *The Trial* provides a frame for grappling with a particular kind of guilt—that clinging guilt which, like a parasite, feeds on us and destroys us, the pervasive guilt we cannot cast off though we do not know its source and may try to convince ourselves it has none. That portion of *Robinson Crusoe* which has captured the imagination of the Western world provides an image of the economic and spiritual predicament of modern man exerting himself indefatigably, in loneliness and insecurity, against a treacherous environment. The latter part of *Robinson Crusoe*, incidentally, which few people even remember, and *The Farther Adventures*, which few people even read, are good examples of the kind of fiction which does *not* encourage analogizing. They do not give us a sense of referring to any important experience or concern, and they are too cluttered with unrelated incidents to make a deep impression upon the mind.

Because analogizing usually proceeds unconsciously, we seldom catch ourselves engaging in it. But when others discuss their reactions to fiction with us, we can often see that *they* have analogized. Analysts cooperating with this study have reported several clear-cut instances of analogizing and the writings of people who have been in a position to observe or reflect upon the reading experiences of others contain a number of additional examples.

The first of these, though conjectural, is exceptionally interesting. Maud Bodkin believes that St. Augustine's reaction, recorded in his *Confessions*, to the Dido episode in the *Aeneid* is an example of what I have called analogizing. The episode moved him as it did, Miss Bodkin surmises, because the conflict in Aeneas' soul between his love and sense of obligation to the Queen and his feeling that it was the will of the gods that he should leave her paralleled the conflict in St. Augustine between his love for his chosen concubine, who had borne him a son, and his feeling that it was his duty to give her up and marry, as his mother urged. Aeneas' desertion of Dido would then have reactivated the anguish St. Augustine felt because of his abandonment of the concubine, an anguish which left his heart "torn and wounded and bleeding." If Miss Bodkin's surmise is correct, St. Augustine had no cause to reproach himself, as he did, for weeping for "Dido slain" rather than his own sins. Unbeknown to himself, he *was* weeping for those sins—for the suffering he had caused the nameless concubine and his failure to resolve his conflict in a way which left him at peace with himself.

Hanns Sachs had the opportunity to observe a patient whose reactions to a work of fiction must be attributed in large part to analogizing.[9] Searching for the source of the depression which had brought him into analysis, the patient recalled that when he was about five he and another boy had run away from home and become involved in a thinly veiled suicide attempt. The episode strongly suggested that, though the patient had been regarded as his mother's favorite, he had inwardly felt rejected and unloved. It also threw light on some material which had come up earlier in the analysis but until then had remained inexplicable. When the patient's mother died, during his adolescence, he had shown little sorrow. Yet about six months to a year later he attended a reading of Gerhart Hauptmann's play, *Little Joan's Ascension to Heaven,* which so moved him that he felt forced to leave. He went to a lonely beach, where he threw himself down and wept for more than an hour. Sachs had no doubt that this weeping, which had "a mysteriously pleasurable character," represented the delayed mourning for the mother.

It was evident that it was the play which had aroused, or rather unloosed, the boy's affects. Its central character is a little girl who tries to drown herself, is rescued, and in the delirium of fever which follows is granted all the things she had missed in real life—kindness, recognition, revenge on a cruel stepfather and love. Sachs felt sure that his patient had identified with the little girl and through the identification secured redress for his own grievances, real or fancied, so that at long last he could make his peace with his mother and grieve for her. Significantly, the play aroused no conscious recollection of either the patient's suicide attempt or the longings which had once dominated him as completely as they did Hauptmann's little heroine. It is clear that even when analogizing permits us to rehearse intense experiences, and is long drawn-out, it may remain unconscious.

Very frequently analogizing involves a longed-for correction of the experience which is its prototype. The example we have just considered involves such a correction, though the death of the little girl may obscure the fact for a minute. In their study of the movies Wolfenstein and Leites give a number of examples of such wish-dominated analogizing. For example, they believe that the recurrent situation in which the heroine promptly reveals her love for the hero while he keeps his love in suspense represents, among other things, "a rectification and reversal of the experience of American boys with their exacting mothers." [10] The situation provides compensation for the childhood experience of being constantly weighed and compared with others, of being accorded love only to the extent that one has proven one's worth and then only provisionally; and it may be surmised that in at least some cases it stimulates daydreams in which one turns the tables on one's mother or someone else who has been slow and niggardly about bestowing love.

Bruno Bettelheim also suggests how instinctively we analogize, in an article which reports the spontaneous comments made by a child to the animal stories which were read to him.[11] It is possible that children's response to animal stories—indeed, to all the fiction they enjoy—involves analogizing al-

[10] Martha Wolfenstein and Nathan Leites, *Movies, A Psychological Study* (Glencoe, Ill.: Free Press, 1950), p. 306.
[11] "Harry—A Study in Rehabilitation," *Journal of Abnormal Psychology*, 44, 1949.

most as often as it does identification and projection; Marie Briehl's study of the reactions of small children to fairy stories supports this conjecture.[12]

We sometimes analogize, it must be stressed, not only to the central legend of a story but to its component parts, down to the smallest elements. Ralph Touchett's deep and selfless adoration of Isabel Archer may remind a reader of his feeling for a beloved child. A portion of a sentence in *Robinson Crusoe*, "my desire to venture over for the main increased, rather than decreased, as the means for it seemed impossible," may recall an episode in which our longing for someone grew long after we became aware that she was too dear for our possessing. The passage in *The Ancient Mariner* describing the swift homeward flight of the ship made Maud Bodkin think of "moments of eager successful mental activity coming after periods of futile effort and strain." [13] Here the analogizing of author and reader may have coincided; there is reason to believe that this is one of the meanings the passage possessed for Coleridge himself.

Many additional illustrations might be given. Very frequently when we analogize we do little more than change quite inessential trappings. For example, Cressida's departure for the Greek camp, in Chaucer's *Troilus and Cressida*, may recall an incident in our own life where some separation from a loved one apparently dictated by circumstances unreasonably but stubbornly imposed itself upon our mind as a willful desertion, and filled us with ineradicable dread.

4

Now that we have a more complete notion of the various kinds of activities which take place in us as we read, we are

[12] "Die Rolle des Märchens in der Kleinkindererziehung." Though based on a lecture given in English, at the Walden School in New York City in 1933, Mrs. Briehl's paper originally appeared in the *Zeitschrift für psycho-analytische Pädagogik*, XI, 1937. I am grateful to Mrs. Briehl, a practicing child analyst now living in Hollywood, California, for having made available to me a revised English version of her paper, brought up to date for a lecture made to a Los Angeles study group in 1947.

[13] *Archetypal Patterns in Poetry*, p. 33.

in a better position to summarize what we have learned, or can surmise, about the principal ways in which fiction gives us pleasure and satisfaction. Most discussions of this subject have rested on an inadequate conception of the reading experience. With a few notable exceptions, such as Aristotle in antiquity and I. A. Richards in our own time, most critics have thought of response almost entirely in cognitive terms, and in many cases have conceived of cognition as being entirely conscious. In consequence, they have overlooked some of the most important satisfactions we secure through reading. Even their accounts of the ways in which fiction enlarges, clarifies and refines our knowledge often neglect the gains on which we set most value; usually, too, they slight the emotional basis and sometimes even the emotional repercussions of those gains, treating them like so many additions to our store of factual knowledge.

Upon analysis we discover that nearly all the satisfactions we secure from all forms of fiction save comedy are a product of our participant as well as our cognitive reactions. It should not be forgotten that at one time or another we are both spectators and actors in the fiction which engages us. Most of the time we are both simultaneously, but there are wide shifts in the extent to which we are involved and at various points— for example, at the very beginning, before we are captivated, and, as we shall see, sometimes at the very end—we are merely spectators. The converse is rarely true, at any rate for normal readers. No matter how absorbed we may become in a story, we seldom completely forget that we are "only reading." It is the knowledge that the world of fiction is a world of make-believe which emboldens us to plunge into it as participants.

The experience Aristotle described as catharsis, which is worth examining in some detail, evidently arises from an unnoticed shift of roles—a shift from a stage in which we are predominantly participants to one in which, predominantly or entirely, we are spectators. In reading a Shakespearean tragedy, or *Anna Karenina* or *The Idiot*, we identify with the principal protagonist and, as we know, in most cases with other characters as well, and covertly secure the full satisfaction the various roles provide. We err with the characters and vicariously secure the instinctual gratification their errors entail. We share the subsequent experiences to which their course commits them and the emotions aroused by those experiences.

We cling to our identification after the reversal of the hero's fortunes; we do not immediately abandon it when his doom becomes certain. At some point, however, we unobtrusively give it up. The particular point at which this occurs cannot be fixed with any exactness. Normally, however, it occurs very late, and it *must* occur late if we are to experience cathartic relief. The extraction of the emotional gratification a particular identification permits is the first constituent of the cathartic experience.

A perception of the consequences of the hero's conduct is the second constituent. The perception must be so unflinching that it amounts to a tacit acceptance of those consequences; there must be no disposition to question their justice and no idea that they can be escaped. Yet their inevitability and, above all, their actual approach, the imminence of the hero's death or destruction, tempt *us* to escape them—to abandon our identification with the doomed hero and watch his end in secure detachment, instead of vicariously experiencing it. Sometimes we cannot escape. Our immersion in a work of fiction is so profound, the ties that bind us to its protagonist are so strong, that they are not broken until we are released, as from a spell, at the very finish of the drama or even a moment after the curtain falls. We go down with the hero and do not adopt an outside, onlooker attitude toward him until later, when we begin to mull over what we have witnessed. Usually, however, the drop in emotional intensity which occurs toward the very end of a great novel or tragedy permits us to disengage ourself before the final phase of the hero's punishment.

Whenever it occurs, this shift of position toward the hero involves a very abrupt reversal, of crucial importance in understanding catharsis. We now act like a person who has narrowly escaped some catastrophe and is still in grave danger.

To reassure and safeguard ourself we emphasize our *separateness* from the tragic protagonist. We may become momentarily conscious of our own self and even of our body. We disassociate ourself from the hero and to some extent even repudiate him. Pharisaically, we congratulate ourself that *we* have not yielded to the impulses which have brought Othello or Macbeth, Anna Karenina or Myshkin to such tragic ends.

But, of course, the evidence of our previous involvement cannot be effaced. It is betrayed both by the very shift of position we have just examined and by the nature and intensity of our subsequent responses. Even when we slip into a spectator relationship toward the hero, we feel a deep sympathy for him, which we have no inclination to disavow. And our sympathy steadily increases; by the time the final blow falls we are overwhelmed by feelings of "pity and fear." We feel these emotions and are purged of them as spectators, but behind our solicitude for the hero it is not difficult to discern our concern about ourself. "There," we have every reason to know, "but for the grace of God go I."

Our earlier involvement is betrayed even more obviously by other aspects of the cathartic experience; it seems certain that it is more encompassing than Aristotle supposed. At the conclusion of a great Greek or Shakespearean tragedy we feel purged not only of pity and fear but of the desires to which the tragic hero has yielded and whose gratification is responsible for his suffering. This feeling is only explicable on the assumption that we, too, have vicariously satisfied those desires. Having done so, we now feel relieved and fulfilled, momentarily free of tension and anxiety.

Ironically, this very feeling of contentment supports the illusion that we have been no more than detached, although possibly sympathetic, spectators of the drama which has unfolded. The claim is certainly false, but so far as the present and future are concerned our protestations of innocence have a measure of justification. For somewhat the same reason that it is easier to repent a past indulgence than to forego a present temptation, we now feel free of the desires the tragic hero found so irresistible. They are quiescent, or at any rate less urgent, both because they have been vicariously satisfied and because we have just been vividly reminded of the punishment their satisfaction entails.

Though it rests upon the covert satisfaction of desire and upon fear, the relief we feel is very real. For a blessed moment tendencies which are usually a source of tension, anxiety and conflict are either not in evidence or so soft-spoken that they appear readily manageable. In addition to purging us of pity and fear, the experience we call catharsis "enables the ego to reëstablish the control which is threatened by dammed-up instinctual demands." [14]

It is in part because reading permits such convenient and imperceptible shifts of role as are involved in the cathartic experience that it provides combinations of satisfactions which are seldom possible in life itself. In our experience the pleasure we seek when we gratify some prohibited desire is nearly always marred and qualified by feelings of guilt. On the other hand, if we resist the desire, we usually continue to be plagued by tension and anxiety. For a time, at least, these may increase, condemning us to engage in a series of struggles, each fiercer than the last. Long after victory is finally won, and perhaps forgotten, we may be gnawed by a sense of deprivation. In reading fiction we secure the satisfactions we seek, in infinite variety, not only without guilt or undue anxiety but often with a positive sense of innocence. The satisfactions are, of course, only fantasied ones, but that is not so important a qualification as might be supposed. We discover in earliest childhood that fantasies, or activities involving fantasy, are an effective means of discharging and relieving very "real" feelings. We resort to fantasies for this purpose even during sleep.

5

Like that form of relief we call catharsis, most of the satisfactions we secure from fiction arise from the interplay of our participant and spectator responses. Some of the satisfactions

[14] Ernst Kris, *Psychoanalytic Explorations in Art* (New York: International Universities Press, 1952), p. 45.

we obtain from form appear to be exceptions, but I cannot resist the conjecture that not all of them are real ones. The apprehension of the formal qualities of fiction is particularly difficult to trace, but it is evident that the satisfaction we obtain from the fulfilment of aroused expectations is more intense when we are actually involved in the developments and experience as well as note the fulfilment. It may be that little-understood phenomena, such as empathy, play a part in our response to still other formal characteristics; it seems likely, for example, that we feel as well as recognize such a quality as control.

When we turn to the satisfactions in which the content of what we read is more obviously involved, we are on firmer ground. Most of those satisfactions can be shown to be due to the fact that we read on one level with a measure of detachment while on another we are so involved that we vicariously experience most developments.

Even the knowledge we acquire through reading must be regarded as a product of both sets of responses and not, as traditional esthetics has assumed, of our cognitive responses alone. Fiction does, of course, enlarge and extend our experience prodigiously through the things it asks us to apprehend as spectators. It shows us what life was like in ancient Egypt, Greece and Rome and what it is like in many milieux of our own society to which we do not have access. It helps us to appreciate the diversity of human nature. It reveals the wide variety of ways in which men may cope with a given problem or respond to a given event.

Fiction also deepens our understanding of experience through what it compels us to perceive as spectators. It endeavors to show us all aspects of any situation it puts before us, those we might be inclined to neglect as well as those we are better able to see. It excises irrelevancies and points up causal relationships. It distances everything to whatever extent is necessary to permit it to be easily observed. By these means and others it permits us to examine even shocking and painful events without undue anxiety and fear.

As we know, however, our interest in the material fiction

unfolds before us is seldom purely or predominantly objective; at the deepest level it is personal in the extreme. We are most likely to be interested, for example, when the events of a story represent experiences we would like to have or fear we may have to endure. Similarly, while we may be interested in fictional characters in their own right, this interest invariably has some narcissistic determinants, and we are most deeply interested when the characters represent aspects— usually unfulfilled aspects—of ourself. We read primarily to discover ourself—above all, perhaps, to discover what St. Augustine refers to as the dark corners of the heart. We want to know what we would be like if circumstances offered a particular propensity more scope, the form our life might take if we were less intimidated by prudential considerations, if we were more honest and more passionate, or possibly more cunning and predacious, than we are in our everyday life. We want to know how we would actually feel and behave if we were placed in this or that situation.

Such needs can be satisfied only to a very limited extent by observing others, even if we later compare ourself with them. To obtain the knowledge we most eagerly crave we are compelled to project ourself actively into what we read—to experience it, to imagine what we would feel and do under such-and-such conditions. It is as covert participants that we acquire much of the knowledge on which we set most store.

6

It is perhaps more obvious that our involvement as participants contributes to the other satisfactions we seek and secure through reading fiction. We read, as we know, not simply in search of knowledge, however broadly defined, but to secure pleasure or at any rate relief from painful tension and to assuage feelings of anxiety and guilt. It is difficult to believe that our spectator reactions to the things which befall imaginary characters are entirely responsible for such satisfactions as these, which involve complex emotional adjustments and the actual discharge of affects. These satisfactions are only explicable on the assumption that as we read, or sit in the theater and watch, we simultaneously engage in a kind of silent and immobile play. Out of the same impulse which leads a child to gallop about like a horse to find out what it would feel like to be one, we act out, of course in sublimated and truncated fashion, the roles and events which interest us.

The contribution made by such acting-out is perhaps most evident in connection with the instinctual gratification we secure from reading. When we secure pleasure from our reading, we rejoice with lovers when they wickedly enjoy one another, as St. Augustine confessed to having done when he attended the theater. We express the rage we are usually required to muffle and commit the aggressive acts conscience or fear compels us to forego. We do this, of course, only in imagination. The energy involved is partly neutralized. The words are spoken, the acts performed, under the supervision, if not the constant surveillance, of the ego. In part we remain spectators, our spectator responses serving to conceal our covert involvement. But the essential consideration is that in fantasy we do what we desire and secure emotional relief. Fiction functions, in a phrase of Marie Bonaparte's, as a safety valve for humanity's over-repressed instincts.[15] It permits a discharge of feeling which is very real though it is based upon imaginary fulfilment.

Fundamentally, admirable and poor fiction does not differ in the *way* in which it provides instinctual gratification. The difference lies in the nature and "texture" [16] of the gratification offered and the directness and rapidity with which it is made available. In contrast, fiction deals with anxiety by several methods which have little in common with one another. The difference between good and meretricious fiction is perhaps nowhere so pronounced as it is in the treatment— and indeed the very willingness to confront—painful aspects of experience. For the moment let us focus our attention on the fiction which seeks to relieve anxiety and tries to accom-

[15] *The Life and Works of Edgar Allan Poe* (London: Imago, 1949), p. 664. Simultaneously, fiction serves as a *social* safety valve, making people more willing to accept "the harness of their culture." See David Riesman, *The Lonely Crowd* (New Haven: Yale, 1950), p. 88.

[16] Cf. Ch. VIII.

plish this without shunning painful material or resorting to dishonesty. The relief we secure from such fiction stems from a highly complex interplay between our spectator and participant responses.

Our willingness, much less our eagerness, to read fiction which refuses to soft-pedal the painful may at first appear puzzling. And, of course, some people do avoid such fiction, or turn to it but rarely. But just as a criminal is said to want to return to the scene of his crime, our desire to escape anxiety may incline us to return, in imagination, to a situation which precipitated it. When the anxiety is intense, the inclination may amount to a compulsion. As in the traumatic neuroses, a person may return again and again to an event which caused him suffering and go over it in his mind and feelings until he has assimilated its pain and regained his stability. To some extent we often employ a similar mechanism to master the excitation caused by relatively minor upsets. Play is prized, among other reasons, because it provides propitious conditions for doing this and, as we shall see, fiction provides them too. By a quite logical extension of ideas people turn to both fiction and play to master not only past but possible future causes of anxiety—to deal in imagination with any situation which might cause pain, and thus strengthen their ability to cope with it.

One of the ways in which play encourages children to deal with painful situations is by permitting them to be reproduced in scaled-down form. Since mature adults would derive little satisfaction from a presentation of their problems which failed to do justice to their seriousness, great fiction spurns this particular device. As we know, it tends, rather, to magnify issues. It has other resources, many of which have no parallel in play, which permit it to do this and still "bind" the fearful issues it reproduces so that we will not be afraid to confront them.

Some of these resources are deployed to lower the general level of anxiety. Both the instinctual gratification provided by the content of fiction and the reduction of guilt in which form plays so large a part contribute to this achievement. The original source of anxiety, it should not be forgotten, is probably the fear of being overwhelmed by bad impulses with which we feel we do not have the strength to cope. By permitting us to "blow off steam" the reading experience mitigates this fear. It reduces the tension between the ego and the id. Once the psychic institutions are established, the fear of the superego's disapproval may be said to be the immediate cause of anxiety. The lavish satisfaction fiction offers the superego diminishes this fear. It persuades the superego to adopt a more tolerant attitude, to relax its pressure upon the ego. The reduction of tension between these two institutions of the mind relieves anxiety as well as guilt.

While the benefit of these intrapsychic changes accrues only gradually, we probably respond at once to fiction's *desire* to satisfy and balance the demands of the entire personality and thus reduce the tension which is felt as anxiety. We are promptly given, or promised, rich emotional satisfaction. At the same time we are made to feel that the values of the superego will be respected and that the most unruly forces which may be unloosed will be effectively contained and controlled. Our level of anxiety is quickly reduced to the point where we will not shy away from a depiction of the particular impulses, conflicts and fears which trouble us, so long as it is reasonably tactful.

As though aware of the danger inherent in its refusal to sidestep or minimize our anxieties, fiction proceeds in all other respects with the utmost tact. To begin with, it does not require that we become consciously aware of our most painful anxieties or the impulses which are most abhorrent to us. These it leaves hidden in the latent content, and while what is represented at the manifest level may be disquieting and disagreeable it is not beyond our capacity to bear.

Secondly, fiction is at pains to tell us that the fears and disavowed impulses which are shown are not "real" and are not our own. Everything is diligently "distanced." Our lusts and aggressions, and the fears they inspire, are displaced onto others, the fictional characters. And we are constantly reminded that the characters, and the difficulties in which they become involved, *are* merely fictional. Material which might arouse anxiety is heavily stylized to keep it distinct from our experience.

Another device involved in distancing, objectification, also makes a contribution of decisive importance in combatting anxiety. What is usually most intolerable about anxiety is its indeterminate, pervasive, "free-floating" character. It suffuses and surrounds one, it is inside and outside, everywhere and nowhere. There is enormous relief in turning from such a foe, as objectification may permit us to do, to a particular danger which is outside one and has definite shape and form. Something is gained when the danger remains amorphous, but is externalized or when it remains internal but is specified and defined.

Through these devices fiction so alters our anxieties, conflicts and inacceptable tendencies that we do not consciously recognize them as our own and can examine them without fear. Indeed, as spectators of our own difficulties, now projected upon others and distanced, we secure certain satisfactions, though they are not all of a kind we would be willing to acknowledge. The discovery or reminder that others feel the pull of the same urges which rack us, and sometimes yield to them, relieves feelings of guilt. Observation of the suffering and inner torment people must endure because of those urges provides consolation for our own unhappiness. The spectacle of the suffering of others also serves to confirm the knowledge, with which we sometimes seek to solace ourself, that this is a harsh world in which even good and courageous people—in whose company we usually include ourself—may be relentlessly buffeted. By watching others being buffeted we may also escape the desolate feeling that we ourself are a pawn in some sadistic game we cannot understand, much less control.

The spectator role has the final advantage of facilitating vicarious participation. But it is not yet completely clear why we should want to exercise the dubious privilege of involving ourselves in painful events. In some cases, as Marie Bonaparte has shown through her analysis of certain stories by Edgar Allan Poe, the pain is a price we are willing to pay for the satisfaction of some primitive and deeply repressed desire.[17] It may, indeed, be a bargain price: the anxiety we are asked to endure may be proportionate not to the primitive satisfaction we secretly obtain but to its ostensible source in the manifest content. But in a great deal of first-rate fiction matters are the other way around: the emphasis is upon the mental torment and suffering the hero must endure. The instinctual gratification he secures is slight and indicated by a few quick strokes; it may be assigned to a period before the action proper begins. Many stories depict the suffering man may have to bear through no fault of his own.

We are impelled to project ourselves into such fiction as this, I believe, not so much by the hope of pleasure as by the desire to secure relief and a measure of immunity from pain. We hope that the book we read will give us a somewhat better perspective on a tendency or situation which troubles us, permit us to work it through until we have assimilated some of the pain it causes, and perhaps make us better able to bear the rest. However, once we make the plunge and expose ourselves to a work which deals honestly with our fears, we may do better than we had expected. A great work of fiction may give us such a profound understanding of some situation which has troubled us and permit us to work it through with such completeness that the anxiety which it aroused is entirely liquidated.

Even when it is only abated, the satisfaction we experience is superior to the one we sought. The alleviation of anxiety gives us a kind of positive satisfaction, though it happens to be one which is difficult to describe. So far as I know there is no exact word in the language for what we feel. A subdued exhilaration—this is the best approximation I can achieve for the element which predominates. We may also experience a sense of strength and a feeling of quiet pride. The exhilaration is muffled because it seems unjustified and, as it were, illogical;

[17] See, for example, her analysis of "The Pit and the Pendulum," *The Life and Works of Edgar Allan Poe*, Chapter XLIII, and the further discussion pp. 662-63, where Dr. Bonaparte describes the discomfort which permits the satisfaction of the repressed desire as "a sort of *preliminary premium of anxiety*."

it is qualified by a continuing sense of the seriousness and painfulness of the human situation. But the exhilaration is there, and cannot be suppressed.

It arises, I believe, because we feel simultaneously liberated from a particular anxiety and strengthened for coping with anxiety in general. In very much the same fashion in which Mithridates' small doses of poison prepared him to tolerate the prescriptions of his enemies, the fictional encounter with anxiety, weathered, fortifies us for dealing with whatever perils the future holds. It gives us a feeling of being able to shoulder far heavier burdens than we have thus far been asked to assume, and the ones we have been carrying by comparison now seem light. The satisfaction we experience usually has a grim undertone, for the greatest fiction suggests that the new-found resources of courage and strength will probably be needed to meet the vicissitudes of life. But we exult because we feel that the resources are there, that if put to the test we will be able to say with Lear, "Pour on; I will endure."

The liquidation or even the alleviation of anxiety may also bring about what Sidney Tarachow has described as "a passive reconciliation with a feared object." [18] It may permit us to contemplate, not only without fear but with a tingling sense that we need not be afraid, some object, drive, situation or conflict from which we previously averted our eyes or could not see without distortion. Looking in this way, we sometimes find beauty in that which aroused terror before. This gain is perceptual and cognitive, but it is a product of our participant as well as our spectator responses. We must actually grapple with the things which cause us anxiety, prove our strength in combat, before we can confront them and acknowledge that attraction which is the ultimate source of our fear.

[18] "Remarks on the Comic Process and Beauty," *Psychoanalytic Quarterly*, XVIII, 1949. Cf. Maud Bodkin, ". . . when standing on some precipice edge, amongst peaks and chasms, one feels their lines overpowering and terrible through the suggested anguish of falling. That horror overcome adds a kind of emotional exaltation to the sight of actual mountain chasms; . . ." *Archetypal Patterns in Poetry*, p. 104.

7

Essentially, great fiction relieves anxiety by helping us to confront and work through the conflicts which arouse anxiety and our anxieties themselves. It permits us to do this in large part unconsciously, and in a dozen other ways seeks to minimize the painfulness of the experience. But it neither denies nor disparages the seriousness of the issues with which it deals; it does not attempt to eliminate pain. Rather, it requires that we temporarily experience a certain amount of anxiety, just as a vaccination gives us a small and controlled case of the disease it is meant to prevent.

However sound this approach may be—it is, of course, the only route to real and enduring relief—it involves too much discomfort to be attractive to everyone. What many people want is an immediate respite from anxiety—a narcotic which will enable them to forget the painful aspects of experience and their own troublesome drives and conflicts. A large body of fiction caters to the demands of such people. It seeks to transport its readers to a world where euphoria prevails— where there is no anxiety or a very minimum of it, where everyone rather promptly gets what he wants and, to facilitate this, by and large wants only what he can get. In such a world only pseudo-impediments thwart the consummation of desire, and they are present only so that the reader may have the pleasure of seeing them overcome or eliminated. No other outcome is permissible. Some foolish misunderstanding may have separated hero and heroine for a time, but it is mandatory that everything must work out happily in the end.

When such determinedly sunny fiction is successful, it does indeed offer a haven from anxiety. Unfortunately, to create such a haven, fiction must usually sidestep adult concerns and falsify the issues with which it deals. It is nearly always compelled to resort to some degree of falsification to make the issues susceptible of easy and happy solution. Similarly, it must falsify characters so as not to remind readers of their own divided nature. The poorest fiction paints only in black and white. Its characters are completely evil, wanting in any redeeming qualities, or so good that they are not vexed by lust and hatred, though they may, of course, feel righteous indignation and love of the more reputable sort.

Obviously, the kind of fiction of which I am speaking can comfort only those people who are blind to its shortcomings or so desperate for an anodyne they are willing to disregard them. Even the relief it offers such readers is ephemeral in the extreme. It may even be succeeded, as soon as they put down their novel or magazine, or walk out of the movie palace into the night, by a feeling of having been deceived. In any case the euphoria quickly vanishes. There is no carry-over relief or satisfaction of the kind we so often experience after reading serious fiction, no sense of understanding more or being better fortified to cope with one's problems.

Another large body of fiction, which includes most mystery and adventure stories, Westerns, animated cartoons and many other forms of popular art, is constantly engaged in generating and allaying anxiety. One might suppose that the conquest of anxiety was its primary concern. But one soon notes that, like the Pollyannaish fiction with which we have just been dealing, this fiction avoids the things which arouse anxiety in our everyday experience. It also disregards the fact that we do not always triumph over our difficulties and emerge unscathed from our conflicts with our fellows. One quickly realizes that the real purpose of this fiction also is to give us pleasure, to entertain. It has simply chosen another route to this end: it exploits the satisfaction we secure from dealing with anxiety under controlled conditions which assure its eventual liquidation. In this fiction anxiety is not generated naturally, as a by-product of the examination of painful aspects of the human predicament; it is blown up artificially so that we may have the pleasure of seeing it deflated. Our attention is distracted from our anxieties themselves to an enjoyable way of dealing with them.

The heroes of this kind of fiction have to face obstacles and danger; otherwise there will be no anxiety to wipe out. But the obstacles are robbed of much of their terror by the assurance—offered by the work or often a priori by the genre to which it belongs—that they will be overcome. A more formidable problem arises with respect to the nature of the problems and difficulties the hero will be asked to confront. Anxiety must be aroused, but the things which cause us anxiety in our everyday experience cannot be used to arouse it. They do not lend themselves to easy manipulation; they may get out of hand and generate more anxiety than this fiction knows how to cope with. The problem is solved ingeniously: the fiction bases itself upon some pseudo-fear, often conventionalized and nearly always external. Even when the fear has some real-life prototype, it is carefully distinguished from it. Thus the average mystery story does not invite us, as *Crime and Punishment* does, really to participate in the planning and execution of a murder. Its murders are pure make-believe, the victims bloodless. Everything is carefully set off from our experience; the fictional quality of the action is heavily accentuated. We are only asked what we might feel and do under certain quite hypothetical conditions.

The device is modeled upon one used in certain children's games—in "Peek-a-boo," for example, where the child does not really deal with his anxiety about being separated from the parents, but exposes himself to a more tolerable pretended fear, and does this for the pleasure he obtains from having the fear overcome. In precisely the same fashion the fiction I am describing really invites us to play a game. We sometimes agree to play and respond from old habit to the waxing and waning of tension, but even when we do so we remember that it is only a game and subject our responses, and the fiction which arouses them, to a heavy discount. Occasionally, to be sure, we may begin by playing a game and later become seriously involved. When this occurs we may be confident that the story we are reading is more serious than it pretends, and that on the latent if not the manifest level it has some reference to the real sources of our anxieties.

8

As we know, we also secure relief from guilt through reading fiction, and here again our responses as participants make a contribution, intensifying the relief we experience on the basis of certain things we perceive. In all probability, as we have seen, this is true with regard to some of the formal qualities which do so much to allay guilt. They are apprehended as spectators, but their effect is as powerful as it is because we also feel their impact as participants.

In our response to subject matter, things work out in very much the same way. As spectators we discover, or are reminded, that others share the tendencies of which we are ashamed—*many* others, not only the fictional characters and the writer who created them but, as we also sense, the faceless others who quicken to his work. If so many understand and share our weaknesses, we unconsciously reason, we are not so different from our fellows as we had supposed and we need not and should not judge ourself too severely. These cognitive reactions afford us a substantial measure of relief. But as secret participants in the action we obtain what is probably a still more potent form of reassurance—a sense that others have actually committed the prohibited acts with us; or, perhaps more accurately, that we have done no more than join forces with them. A remark which Otto Fenichel made about the drama holds for response to fiction generally: "In a good theatrical performance (as in ancient worship) actor and audience feel, 'We do it together.' " [19] It may be added that, as our discussion of catharsis indicated, the relief from guilt afforded by the punishment of the protagonist is also experienced by the reader, at least up to a point, and is undoubtedly more intense on that account.

Like the desire to be delivered from anxiety, the desire to escape the cancer of guilt invites certain abuses. A large body of fiction, not, of course, of a very responsible sort, tries to assure us that *we* have no reason to feel guilty. It offers us villains whose villainy is so unrelieved that without any difficulty we can disassociate ourself from them. As Edmund Wilson observed in writing of certain detective stories which resort to this device, it reassures us by making it plain that the murderer "is not, after all, a person like you or me." [20]

[19] "On Acting," *Psychoanalytic Quarterly*, XV, 1946.
[20] "Why Do People Read Detective Stories?" *Classics and Commercials* (New York: Farrar, Straus, 1950), p. 237.

Still other popular fiction adopts the somewhat more satisfactory device of permitting us to *establish* our innocence. It
invites us to identify with a hero who is apparently guilty of
wrongdoing but despite the difficulty of his position manages
to demonstrate that he is innocent. In doing so, as Wolfenstein and Leites have pointed out, he—and we—are really
trying to satisfy our conscience, of which the police and
others who must be convinced of our innocence may be regarded as projections.[21] We are trying to show that we would
not commit the transgressions in question, and are free of the
impulses which are the ultimate cause of guilt.

In sharp contrast to this fiction which tries to help us deny
guilt, certain stories are clearly intent on *satisfying* our consciousness of guilt, on making us feel guilty, on inducing us to
wallow in feelings of sinfulness and unworthiness. In such
fiction everything is inverted. One feels that the characters
have transgressed so that they can lacerate themselves for their
transgressions, so that they—and, of course, the responsive
reader—can indulge in what Sidney Tarachow has called "superego orgies." The abuse such characters heap upon themselves, and the punishment they are required to suffer, is
usually out of all proportion to their offense.

The need to satisfy feelings of guilt, to castigate and punish
oneself, is so obviously morbid that one's first tendency is to
condemn the entire category of fiction which appeals to it.
But as soon as one begins to think in terms of specific examples
one realizes that the category embraces works of undoubted
value; for instance, it includes a large part of the output of
Dostoevsky and Kafka. We do not shrink from the guilt-
ridden characters of these authors even when their guilt manifests itself in unattractive ways. We accept, I believe, even
such a character as Marmeladov (Sonia's father, in *Crime
and Punishment*), though his self-pity is unabashed, completely lacking in any saving quality, such as defiance. We
accept the unnamed narrator of *Notes from Underground*
though not only his self-abasement but his churlishness, which
also expresses his guilt, might be expected to repel us; to be

[21] *Movies, A Psychological Study*, pp. 176-77 and *passim*.

sure, he has certain redeeming qualities, such as honesty: we are impressed with his defense that at bottom others are as selfish and mean as he. To take a less equivocal example, we not only accept, we cannot withhold our admiration for Joseph K., the hero of *The Trial*. We know from the criticism this novel has received that for many discriminating readers K's gradual surrender to guilt possesses a perverse sort of dignity.

There is fiction at every level of value which seeks to mobilize guilt because there are people of every degree of complexity who are happy to acknowledge their unworthiness, and even endure suffering and punishment, in order to appease the superego and escape its still more intolerable threats. An inflamed sense of guilt is a pervasive illness in our culture. With some assurance we can assign a low rank to fiction which under cover of mobilizing guilt is really intent on gratifying aggressive impulses or arousing masochistically-tinged erotic feelings. But it must be confessed that fiction which attempts to do the latter cannot always be promptly distinguished from fiction which serves as an outlet for feelings of guilt. Whenever guilt is powerful enough to hold the center of the stage, we may be sure that it is libidinized to a degree.

9

What little empirical evidence is available suggests that our participant as well as our spectator responses have a hand in the satisfactions we secure from fiction. For example, Herta Herzog's investigation of the audience of daytime radio serials concluded that listeners obtain three forms of satisfaction from these programs.[22] First, they enjoy them as a means of emotional release. They like the opportunity to cry and to express various feelings, including aggressiveness. They like to compare their own troubles with those experienced by the characters in the serials. When their troubles are serious, they

[22] "What Do We Really Know About Daytime Serial Listeners?" *Radio Research, 1942-1943*, edited by Paul F. Lazarsfeld and Frank N. Stanton (New York: Duell, Sloan and Pearce, 1944). Reprinted in *Reader in Public Opinion and Communication*, edited by Bernard Berelson and Morris Janowitz (Glencoe, Ill.: Free Press, 1950).

secure a measure of consolation from the knowledge that others face difficulties too. When their problems are admittedly minor, they have a sense of conferring a borrowed dignity upon them, and upon themselves, by coupling them with the comparable but more serious concerns of the radio characters. Secondly, the listeners enjoy the serials because they provide opportunities for "wishful thinking"—for extending their own experience or compensating for their failures through identification with successful characters. Third, many listeners believe that they get useful knowledge, help and advice from the serials. " 'If you listen to these programs and something turns up in your own life, you would know what to do about it.' " [23] Much of the "help" the listeners thought they obtained, a relatively intensive study of some one hundred and fifty of them suggests, was of dubious value "if measured by the yardstick of real mastery of personal problems";[24] and in some cases the help stemmed from quite conscious cognitive responses. In most cases, however, the examples given by Miss Herzog suggest, the sense of being helped, like the first two satisfactions mentioned, was attributable in part to the listeners' involvement in the serials. It resulted from doing what was here discussed in terms of working through anxieties. "The overall formula for the help obtained from listening seems to be in terms of 'how to take it.' " [25]

As our analysis of the cathartic experience suggested, as one reads there are probably many shifts, gradual or even abrupt, in the extent to which one is involved. On the basis of the intensive study of the "Big Sister" radio program made by Warner and Henry,[26] it is possible to trace some of the shifts which are made to obtain the satisfactions offered by various roles. The purpose of the "Big Sister" program, Warner and Henry believe, is to help its audience (lower-

[23] *Ibid.*, p. 25.
[24] *Ibid.*, p. 32.
[25] *Ibid.*, p. 30.
[26] W. Lloyd Warner and William E. Henry, "The Radio Day Time Serial: A Symbolic Analysis," *Genetic Psychology Monographs*, 37, 1948. Reprinted in *Reader in Public Opinion.* . . .

middle-class married women) make an adjustment from a period of freedom—the courtship period when, within certain limits, impulse behavior was approved—to a period of restraint. The program confirms the values which, as wives and mothers, the listeners are trying to live by and, more important still, gives them an emotionally moving symbol of successful adjustment. This is Ruth, the heroine, who, it will be remembered, is the apotheosis of "restrained and non-impulsive goodness." [27] She has troubles, but regularly gets the better of them; she is happy and successful. Of course, such a character invites identification, but the satisfactions and rewards of her way of life are so heavily emphasized that beyond any question they are also perceived—often consciously perceived. In contrast, the foil to Ruth, an unmarried girl named Christine, is pictured as so giddy and so constantly beset by troubles that at the conscious level she is probably repudiated. But unconsciously the women perceive the advantages of her impulsiveness, of which with a part of their being they must be envious, and they identify with her and share her escapades. By different routes they obtain the satisfactions which proceed from being responsible and from being irresponsible.

10

The satisfactions we secure from reading fiction might, of course, have been described in different terms. For example, we might have employed an economic approach. As we know, fiction permits a relative saving in the amount of psychic energy required for understanding. It enables us to grasp whatever it sets before us as effortlessly as possible; it transports us to a world which is more comprehensible than the world of our everyday experience. Both by gratifying the instincts and thus making them less clamorous and by permitting the unconscious if not the conscious apprehension of what was before deeply buried, fiction also sharply reduces the amount of energy required for repression. It saves us energy by abating the pressure of anxiety and guilt; we know that these are

[27] Cf. Ch. II.

draining and wasteful, as well as oppressive, emotions. When, as in relieving anxiety, fiction simultaneously produces an energy saving and gives us a sense of increased strength, the disproportion between the energy suddenly put at our disposal and the demands upon us may be regarded as the source of our apparently "illogical" positive feeling of exhilaration and pleasure.

The satisfactions we secure might also have been analyzed structurally, in terms of the particular part of the psyche to which they appeal; some of the subject-matter satisfactions of fiction were considered in this fashion in Chapter IV. Finally, we might have put more emphasis on the contributions the satisfactions make to the achievement of intrapsychic harmony. It is evident enough that they reduce tension throughout the psychic apparatus, making the entire personality, in a beautiful phrase of Hanns Sachs's, "more coherent and continuous." [28] We shall return to this point when we consider the esthetic experience.

[28] *The Creative Unconscious*, p. 235.

Chapter XI   *Tragedy, Comedy and the Esthetic Experience*

> It is essential to recognize that in the full tragic experience there is no suppression. The mind does not shy away from anything, it does not protect itself with any illusion, it stands uncomforted, unintimidated, alone and self-reliant. The test of its success is whether it can face what is before it . . . without any of the innumerable subterfuges by which it ordinarily dodges the full development of experience. Suppressions and sublimations alike are devices by which we endeavor to avoid issues which might bewilder us. The essence of Tragedy is that it forces us to live for a moment without them.
>
> I. A. Richards [1]

We tend to use the word "esthetic" in two somewhat different senses. Most of the time we use it, rather loosely, to describe a satisfaction we characteristically obtain from art, a satisfaction we wish to differentiate from the sometimes keener, sometimes more attenuated but nearly always palpably different gratifications we secure from our everyday activities. Occasionally, however, we may speak of having "an esthetic experience." When we do this, I believe we are usually trying to characterize an experience of exceptional poignance, an experience so rare and ineffable that we feel a desire to distinguish it not only from most of the satisfactions life affords us but even from much of the satisfaction we obtain from art.

Once in a great while, as I shall try to show, our everyday experience may precipitate the consummate satisfaction we call esthetic in this second, highly honorific sense. But far more frequently the satisfaction is a product of our immersion in artistic objects, and, usually, objects of transcendental value; in the field of the literary arts, the satisfaction is most regularly

[1] *Principles of Literary Criticism* (New York: Harcourt, Brace, 1934), p. 246.

associated with tragedy. An examination of tragedy therefore seems one of the most promising ways of gaining an understanding of what we mean by an esthetic experience.

It is in tragedy that the aims toward which all fiction aspires are most fully and perfectly achieved. If we attempted to discuss tragedy exhaustively, therefore, we would have to retrace much of the ground we have already covered. To avoid this I propose that we concentrate on the characteristics of tragedy —I do not believe they are more than two—which appear to have most to do with its capacity to give us that supreme satisfaction we describe as an esthetic experience.

2

The first of the characteristics is singled out at the very beginning of Aristotle's celebrated definition of tragedy: it is seriousness. Tragedy pays man the simple but apparently difficult compliment of taking him seriously. It insists on regarding his life, his actions, his thoughts and his feelings as of supreme importance. "The Tragic Spirit proposes," writes Joseph Wood Krutch, "that man shall be judged as he judges himself. It defines him in Hamlet's terms—'a creature how infinite in faculties, in comprehension how like a God'—hence a creature whose every act is important and whose downfall is terrible. It attributes to him the dignity of intention and of bearing appropriate to a being for whom the whole universe was constructed, and it puts upon his passion the valuation which he, in the midst of a passion, attributes to it—treating love with the rapture of a man in love and death with the agony of a man about to die." [2] If so excellent a statement has any shortcoming, it is its failure to suggest the rarity of the attitude tragedy achieves and sustains. Even in moments of crisis, as Krutch himself emphasized in another work,[3] many people do not seem to attach any great importance to their acts or emotions or even to their lives. They creep from womb to grave without feeling, as tragedy compels us to feel, that human life is valuable and consequential beyond all reck-

[2] *Experience and Art* (New York: Smith and Haas, 1932), p. 59.
[3] *The Modern Temper* (New York: Harcourt, Brace, 1929).

oning in terms of gain or loss, or even happiness or pain, and without claiming for themselves the dignity which tragedy unhesitatingly confers upon its meanest creature.

If tragedy's attitude were not serious to the point of reverence, it could deal even with matters of life and death without making them appear consequential; the slick mystery stories and melodramas which pour from the presses by the hundreds demonstrate the truth of this. On the other hand, an attitude of high seriousness would seem inappropriate, forced and perhaps even absurd in an account of the ordinary doings of ordinary men. The substance of tragedy, no less than its attitude, reveals its seriousness. Its protagonists, and usually many of its principals, are people of heroic mold, and they become involved in large events. The action of tragedy, as Aristotle also observed, must possess "a certain magnitude." Tragic heroes are rent by desires the satisfaction of which requires the violation of the tabus on which human society rests. Parricide, incest, the murder of one's wife or one's sovereign, extreme cruelty of parent to child or child to parent —such are the deeds around which tragedy revolves.

It is from the contrast between the giant souls of its protagonists and the nature of the desires which thrust themselves into their minds that the poignance of tragedy derives. We are immediately made to feel the idealism and intelligence of Brutus, the still sharper mind and finer sensibility of Hamlet, the dignity and romanticism of Othello. What moves us to the core of our being is the discovery that such men as these are not immune from the same terrible desires against which we must struggle—that Brutus is so consumed by secret envy and ambition that he is willing to consider assassination; that Hamlet is paralyzed by guilty sympathy for the man who has killed his father and whored his mother; that Othello is so ready to believe Desdemona wanton and so swift to think of murdering her. It is by juxtaposing such strengths and such weaknesses that tragedy makes us feel the contradictions of our nature, in which god-like aspirations and bestial impulses dwell side by side.

In the way it poses issues also tragedy depends to a considerable extent on contrast: it offers its heroes no way of resolving or escaping their conflicts; it compels them to choose between extreme alternatives. Despite the gravity of the issues they are weighing, it does not even give them long to make up their minds. In most tragedies something happens very early which at once prods the protagonist to reach a decision and makes the decision which beckons more difficult. Caesar agrees to go to the Capitol, thus playing in with the plan of the conspirators, but he has thrice turned down the crown. Brutus must persuade himself both that Caesar will finally accept it and that this will change his nature—an outcome he knows to be conjectural. Duncan visits Inverness but his visit is another mark of his favor and imposes an additional obligation upon Macbeth to protect him. Because *Hamlet* is concerned with a failure to act, it may appear to be an exception but in fact it is not one. During the performance of the play within the play (Act III, Scene 2) Hamlet secures decisive and public proof of Claudius' guilt, and thus has an ideal opportunity to carry out his mission. After he fails to grasp it, it is perfectly clear to the reader—though not, of course, to Hamlet—that he will never be able to bring himself to avenge his father, and in fact he never does so. When he finally kills Claudius, it is to avenge his mother and himself.

The character, what today we might call the personality structure, of the tragic protagonist also dooms him to extreme choices. One and all, the heroes of tragedy are violent, impetuous and inflexible; as A. C. Bradley has observed, they are incapable of making compromises: they do not seek, and would probably disdain, "sensible" ways of resolving their problems. The rare person bold enough to urge a man of this stamp to be moderate is himself likely to incur his swift anger, and perhaps be banished, as Kent was. There is something frightening about the ease and speed with which tragic heroes succumb to the most intemperate impulses—about the suddenness with which Lear turns on his most dearly beloved daughter and Othello on his wife; about the ease with which the conspirators win Brutus to their party and Lady Macbeth overcomes her husband's scruples. One feels that the tragic hero does not really have to be persuaded, and in fact could probably not be dissuaded, from committing the act which has suggested itself; those who appear to persuade him can be regarded as usually repudiated but now ascendant aspects of himself. The protagonists of tragedy must have their desire, no matter what the consequences. In their willfulness they remind one of children during that stage of their development when they feel they can have whatever they want and attack with the full strength of their furious little bodies anyone who attempts to thwart them.

Consciously, of course, we condemn the rashness of the tragic hero, but there is another side to the matter. There is a portion of our own being which is importunate and un-reconciled to curbs.[4] Furthermore, the ease with which the tragic hero succumbs to the impulses which assail him helps to establish their urgency; it gives them a kind of sanction. It cannot be stressed too strongly that on some deep level we want the hero to yield to the impulses he feels and that we revel in his transgressions. Terrible as those impulses seem to us when they are abstracted and named, probably only the superego adopts an unreservedly censorious attitude toward them during the act of reading. The ego does not approve or even accept them, but it may be conjectured that it recognizes how inextricably interwoven they are with the other qualities of the characters and in particular with the very virtues which

---

[4] An unsubdued infant dwells within us all. Nor is this the only instance in which the infantile is involved in response to tragedy. Though our reaction to the high seriousness of tragedy rests upon a subliminal realization that we are engaging in reality testing and upon a conscious and mature recognition of the importance of the issues around which tragedies revolve, beyond any question the importance of those issues is sometimes exaggerated, willfully and arbitrarily. *Lear* will serve as a case in point. This overevaluation betrays the presence of unconscious factors. Cf. Ernest Jones: "To say that a later reaction to a situation is excessive is simply to say that contributions have been made to it by the unconscious, i.e., the still living infantile mind. Before humour and other aids to mental digestion make their appearance these aspects of the infant's mind are entirely tragic, and all the tragedies of poets are ultimately derived from them." *Hamlet and Oedipus* (Garden City, New York: Doubleday Anchor Books, 1955), p. 85.

cause us to admire them. They are, in fact, the price—perhaps the inescapable price—of those virtues, the other side of the characters' idealism and largeness of spirit.

Because they give this impression of existing in poised tension with one another, the strengths and weaknesses of the tragic hero confer dignity upon each other. Our concern for the hero is the greater because we perceive that he has defects which menace not only his position and continued happiness but usually his very life. The qualities which make the hero pre-eminent seem more precious and poignant, and perhaps even more lustrous, because they are juxtaposed to the weaknesses which imperil them; we fear—indeed, we sense—that these riches will be squandered. In turn, the virtues and stature of the hero extenuate and confer a momentary splendor on the weaknesses we share with them. Tragedy undoes some of the work of repression: it compels us to accept as part of our nature some of the tendencies we have tried to shunt from our sight.[5]

It is obvious that tragedy richly gratifies the instincts. It not only permits the vicarious fulfilment of some of our most urgent and stubborn—and *therefore* most strongly resisted— desires; it permits the satisfaction of those desires under conditions which momentarily re-establish their authority and invest them with a grandeur commensurate with their outrageousness. The satisfaction the events of tragedy offer the

[5] Cf. A. C. Bradley: ". . . tragedy portrays a self-division and self-waste of spirit, or a division of spirit involving conflict and waste. It is implied in this that on *both* sides in the conflict there is a spiritual value. The same idea may be expressed . . . by saying that the tragic conflict is one not merely of good with evil, but also, and more essentially, of good with good. Only, in saying this, we must be careful to observe that 'good' here means anything that has spiritual value, not moral goodness alone, and that 'evil' has a similarly wide sense . . . there is good on both sides . . . even where, as in Hamlet and Macbeth, the contest seems to lie, and for most purposes might conveniently be said to lie, between forces simply good and simply the reverse. This is not really so, and the tragic effect depends upon the fact. It depends on our feeling that the elements in the man's nature are so inextricably blended that the good in him, that which we admire, instead of simply opposing the evil, reinforces it. . . ." "Hegel's Theory of Tragedy," *Criticism, The Foundations of Modern Literary Judgment*, edited by Mark Schorer, Josephine Miles and Gordon McKenzie (New York: Harcourt, Brace, 1948), pp. 62-63.

superego is equally obvious and equally prodigal. Tragedy is as relentless as the superego itself in punishing wrongdoing and in discovering appropriate punishments. Indeed, as in *Oedipus the King*, where the messengers whose stories, separately considered, would be inconclusive by arriving at the same time furnish decisive proof of Oedipus' guilt, there is something deterministic about the way tragedy pursues and exacts retribution from its heroic but flawed protagonists. We are quick to feel that whatever transgression suggests itself will be committed, but there is something oppressive about the way the certainty of the tragic hero's downfall imposes itself upon our minds. At a certain point the world of tragedy begins almost visibly to shrink, to contract around the doomed hero like that chamber of horrors described by Poe in "The Pit and the Pendulum." The sense of fate that tragedy so frequently inspires is due in large part to the inexorable course of its falling action.

Though it is less apparent, I believe that the events of tragedy are also richly satisfying to the ego. It benefits from having the claims of the instincts specified and brought into the open. It benefits from having them symbolically gratified and made more amenable to its control. Above all, it benefits from letting desire and inhibition, id and superego, engage in a mock but violent battle under the strict terms which tragedy proposes. One may suppose that the ego sometimes becomes weary to the point of bitterness from its incessant efforts to moderate and reconcile the claims of its unreasonable psychic partners. "Very well," one can imagine it suggesting in such a mood, "within the framework laid down by tragedy let us have the pitched battle for which you both seem to be aching. Let us acknowledge our darkest and most carefully concealed desires. Let us see what acts they impel us to commit. And let us commit the acts. Let us see what kind of creatures we really are and fulfil our destiny no matter what the cost. Only let us agree now, the cost, however high, must be paid." It is easy to think of the events of any tragedy as having been selected to conform to the terms of some such confessional and cathartic proposal.

3

While immersed in the world of tragedy, we accept tragedy's high seriousness without question; we may temporarily forget that there are many other ways of looking at things. A single evening with tragedy's easygoing sister, comedy, will quickly remind us that the tragic attitude is in fact a quite special one—and perhaps make us feel that it is unnaturally and undesirably rigid.

The contrast between the tragic and the comic approach to life could scarcely be more sharp. Tragedy raises—more technically, it over-cathects—everything it touches. It depicts characters of heroic mold, involves them in large events, compels them to choose between extreme alternatives. It invites us to face and work through the aspects of our own nature and the human predicament which are most likely to arouse anxiety. In contrast, comedy tries to spare us anxiety and to dissipate whatever anxiety we may already feel. It minimizes and belittles. It tells us that everyone and everything, ourself included, is less important than we think. It focuses our attention upon characters who are either not large enough or not serious enough to commit the kind of offenses which shatter the lives of the protagonists of tragedy. To eat and drink well, have as much fun as possible and keep one's skin intact—these are the only goals to which most comic characters are likely to be firmly committed. Unlike the heroes of tragedy, they are usually quite willing to compromise.

To be sure, comic characters have their faults; some of them seem to be composed largely of faults. Comic characters may be indolent, unreliable, vain, hypocritical, frivolous, acquisitive or lascivious—and sometimes a single character has almost this entire roster of failings. But while such failings may arouse scorn, they do not excite fear. Particularly since they are usually buttressed by such qualities as cunning and resilience, they do not threaten to involve the characters in anything worse than the kind of scrapes from which, after a little squirming, we feel sure they will be able to extricate themselves. And the prospect of their having to suffer a certain amount of trouble is positively pleasing. Unlike other forms of fiction, comedy keeps us disassociated from its characters so that even when they are amiable we do not feel that we are debarred from having a certain amount of fun at their expense. We watch their antics in very much the same spirit in which we might observe the foolish behavior of small children, and while our mood would change instantly if they did something which put them in serious danger, so long as they do not we are unashamedly amused. When the characters are reprobates, comedy invites the kind of laughter which has some malice in it. Since we are not identified with the characters, nothing prevents us from laughing *at* them—from feeling scorn or some other emotion in which there is an element, sometimes a large element, of hostility. The emphasis on their weaknesses puts us in a good psychological position to entertain such feelings, for it causes our own weaknesses to sit more lightly upon us.

However, the pleasure we take in the misadventures of comic characters is not fully explained by the nature of their weaknesses, even when allowance is made for our comforting sense of disassociation. Objectively considered, in fact, those weaknesses are often not as insignificant as comedy pretends; and, because they are our own weaknesses, if treated in the wrong way they would arouse anxiety and guilt, so that we would feel obliged to take a disapproving attitude toward them as a way of asserting our innocence. Here, as in tragedy, attitude is of coordinate importance with substance. By one means or another comedy compels us to regard the weaknesses as of small consequence, and to judge them more leniently than we ordinarily do. It sets the tone for the response of its audience. The attitude of most comedies is that of an urbane and tolerant friend, amused rather than censorious about that blond he saw us out with the night before. In a world where such an attitude prevails, we sense that it would be unseemly and foolish to let ourselves become exercised by the spectacle of human frailty. Other comedies are caustic and the reverse of indulgent, but they suggest a scale of values against which the shortcomings and misdeeds of the characters seem trivial—

less important, in many cases, than the characters would like to think them. Human beings are errant knaves all, these more astringent comedies remind us, and, granted that the little people it sets before us are far from admirable, they, and by inference we ourselves, are no worse than anyone else.

Comedy also minimizes the seriousness of the situations in which its characters become involved. In most cases the characters cooperate: they do not take their affairs too seriously themselves. They quite cheerfully compromise, or even reverse their position, when that seems expedient. They do not permit themselves to get into extreme predicaments in which their very life may hang in the balance. When they stumble into trouble, and this they tend to do, they resort to any device which suggests itself, not excluding subterfuges which would be beneath the dignity of the tragic hero, in order to get out of it. Because they are flexible and resourceful, there always seem to be many possibilities open to them. For reasons we shall consider in a minute, even when comic characters are of a different stamp, and beset by innumerable troubles, they never give the impression of being trapped, isolated like a tragic hero whose doom is imminent in a small and contracting square of space. The world of comedy adjoins the one we know and is as spacious as that world appears when we are young.

When comedy deals with characters who take life seriously —and some of its characters, especially if they are youthful, may be guilty of this heresy—it is careful not to let the reader follow suit. Some comedies mercilessly expose the triviality and meretriciousness of the things to which the characters attach importance; they ask us to laugh at their scale of values as we laugh at everything else. Shakespeare and certain other writers feel too much affection for their characters to employ such an approach, but they also contrive to depreciate the importance of the matters which seem so momentous to the characters. They do this so caressingly that the very enthusiasm of the characters causes us to love them the more. Nevertheless, another attitude emerges, and prevails against theirs. Whereas tragedy may suggest that if necessary one should gladly risk life itself to win the woman one desires, and certain zealous comic characters espouse the same doctrine, comedy is likely to treat love as an engaging but irrational prejudice— "the delusion," in the words of H. L. Mencken's aphorism, "that one woman differs from another." The characterization typical of the kind of comedies of which I am speaking supports this attitude. Neither its Lysanders and Demetriuses, nor its Hermias and Helenas, are sharply enough differentiated to permit a bystander to suppose that it is a matter of world-shaking significance who mates with whom.

Not that comedy is unaccommodating. It is willing, and even desirous, that every Jack shall have his Jill. But it wants to tease Jack a bit first for our pleasure. It knows that in the end he will prize his Jill the more, and we will enjoy their union the more, if it is not brought about straightaway. The danger of this course is that we may also have to share the anxiety the characters experience during the more discouraging phases of their affairs. To prevent this from happening, comedy nearly always finds some means of letting the reader know that everything will work out well in the end. It may make us privy at once to the explanation of difficulties which perplex the characters. Shakespeare employs this device, for example, in *The Comedy of Errors* and *A Midsummer Night's Dream*.

In good time—when we have been sufficiently stimulated and before the characters are too discouraged—comedy begins to unravel the apparently hopeless snarl it has created. The task is never so difficult as it appears. Frequently the complications depend upon nothing more substantial than mistaken notions about what one or another of the characters has done or mix-ups of identity. The more hardened characters of comedy have manifest skill, and we would surmise experience, in extricating themselves from embarrassing predicaments; the more ingenuous ones at least have the virtue of persisting until matters can be straightened out. And comedy shows how good-natured it really is by the kind of help it now begins to furnish the artful and the innocent alike. Whereas tragedy appears to get more rigorous and deterministic as it proceeds, comedy usually becomes increasingly slack and haphazard. It utilizes whatever means seem handiest for setting matters straight, not shunning accidents, coincidences or supernatural intervention, and not troubling its carefree soul too greatly about plausibility; Voltaire unhesitatingly resurrects characters when that suits his purpose. The concluding phases of some comedies remind one of the kind of scurried tidying-up which may go on when a family has only a minute or two to prepare for the arrival of unexpected guests.

It is evident that comedy seeks to spare us anxiety and reduce feelings of guilt. Even when it is frenzied, and all but shouts with laughter about the foibles of humanity, it whispers its real message: "You foolish reader, with your small vanities and small vices, which you struggle so desperately to conceal and deny—relax, you're not so bad!" Comedy is by no means immoral. Implicitly if not explicitly it extols certain of the fundamental virtues, above all humaneness and honesty. But it suggests that to err is human, and—certain comedies such as *Gulliver's Travels* excepted—it minimizes the importance of our lapses from grace. Whether critical or compassionate, it views the foibles of human beings in somewhat the same perspective in which adults observe the shortcomings of children. It invites us to take weaknesses which are a source of shame and apprehension more lightly than we ordinarily do. The reduction of guilt and anxiety which ensues when we accept its invitation always produces a feeling of exhilaration, and when it is sudden and considerable may precipitate that outward sign of pleasure, laughter.

It could be urged that there is something irresponsible and even dishonest about the attitude of comedy. Its bookkeeping is often lax. The weaknesses it exposes sometimes involve us in difficulties which leave permanent scars. But there is something else to be said; if there were not, we would be unable to explain our respect for comedy, our feeling that it makes some contribution without which life would be infinitely more onerous. The respect is not adequately explained, in my opinion, by the common notion that what comedy supplies is escape, that it transports us to a pleasurable artificial world which has no relevance for our everyday existence. We value comedy, I believe, because it supplies us with an attitude which is important, perhaps indispensable, for our survival in the world in which we live and err and suffer, the only world we shall ever know. Without occasional recourse to that attitude, a creature like man, aspiring and god-like but also frail and fallible, might find it impossible to come to terms with himself. *Inter urinas et faeces nascimur*. If our standards are too high, how shall we find it possible to forgive ourselves for the compromises which we, no less than the characters of comedy, must continually make not only to succeed but to survive in a predatory and sinful world? The code of comedy is perhaps not literally defensible, but it is a necessary corrective to man's tendency to judge himself too pitilessly.

Apart from its utility, furthermore, there is something admirable about comedy. Even serious comedies do not confront the ugly and painful aspects of human life as unblinkingly as tragedy, but in their own way they not only deal with them, they attempt to wring pleasure out of them. It would be a serious mistake to equate comedy with the things it depicts. These, as we know, are often mean and paltry. What is wonderful about comedy is the way it treats even potentially depressing material, its equanimity and buoyance, the zest which manifests itself in pace and tone and style. Comedy's very resilience suggests that there is more to man than the rather soiled side of our nature it sometimes exposes. There is something tonic and redemptive about our ability to laugh at ourselves and perceive what a ridiculous figure we sometimes cut in a universe little impressed by our posturing or our accomplishments. An observation Freud made about humor applies without alteration to any masterpiece of comedy, such as *Candide:* "what is fine about [humour] is the triumph of narcissism, the ego's victorious assertion of its own invulnerability. It refuses to be hurt by the arrows of reality or to be compelled to suffer. It insists that it is impervious to wounds dealt by the outside world, in fact, that these are merely occasions for affording it pleasure. . . . Humour is not resigned;

it is rebellious. It signifies the triumph not only of the ego, but also of the pleasure principle, which is strong enough to assert itself here in the face of the adverse real circumstances." [6]

4

Tragedy commemorates a still more resplendent triumph of the ego, a triumph which does not depend upon pretense, denial or illusion of any kind. In tragedy the ego—the conscious ego of the protagonist—acknowledges its vulnerability: it does not attempt to minimize either the suffering it is already experiencing or that which lies ahead; it unshrinkingly accepts the prospect of its own annihilation. It also acknowledges its transgressions in all their seriousness and the justice of the punishment it is being called upon to bear. But it rejects the solace it could obtain by repenting those transgressions, by suing for peace with conscience or with secular or divine authority. The tragic hero appeals to no one. Simply by confronting his misfortunes and the mistakes or weaknesses responsible for them, by refusing to be intimidated, by facing the things from which at other times he might shy away, he gains the ascendancy over them.

The tragic hero's triumphant confrontation of his gravest defects and the most terrible penalties men or the gods can inflict upon him has no parallel in any other genre of fiction; it is the most stirring experience narrative art has to offer. The response it evokes is of cardinal importance in explaining tragedy's capacity to give us that exalted satisfaction we sometimes describe as an esthetic experience. This is the more remarkable because in certain respects confrontation accomplishes nothing. Furthermore, confrontation is often diffuse rather than dramatic—in *Lear* it spreads over almost the entire play. Even when it occurs at a precise point which can be fixed, as in *Oedipus the King* or *Othello*, it occupies too little space to warrant our calling it a structural stage of tragedy. Indeed, it is sometimes so fleeting, and so admixed with other things, that we may fail to single it out as a discrete phase of tragedy as we respond to it. It seldom leads to action, and

[6] "Humour," *Collected Papers*, Vol. V (London: Hogarth, 1950), p. 217.

when it does, as when Oedipus gouges out his eyes or Othello stabs himself, it is not the acts but what lies behind them which moves us. The acts seem foreordained. In what he does the hero by now seems no more than an agent of destiny. In what he thinks and feels, on the other hand, it is evident that he has attained a larger measure of freedom than ever before, and his thoughts and feelings consequently possess momentous signifi-cance. These thoughts and feelings must receive embodiment in soaring language, but confrontation is essentially a psychic experience.

Indeed, it is because it is too late for the tragic hero to act in any way which would significantly alter the course of de-velopments—and perhaps because he no longer has any dis-position to alter them—that he now finds himself capable of the kind of contemplation in which he engages. His folly or transgression is behind him. His doom is inescapable and imminent, its very shape visible or becoming so. But his powers of mind and spirit are unimpaired, and the very ex-tremity of his position prompts him to utilize them to secure an understanding of himself and his predicament. The same energy with which he previously tried to impose his will upon the world now flows into this psychic effort.[7] Some of the energy formerly consumed in repression is also available for the effort, for the tragic hero no longer has any motive to conceal anything from himself, to tell himself lies or comfort himself with false hopes. The dark aspects of his own soul have secured release, and the overwhelming legions the world has deployed to punish him for his misdeeds or his mistakes are already visible against the horizon.

And so he faces himself. With a determination, honesty and objectivity which would have been impossible before, he strives to understand himself and his destiny. In Santayana's words, "He sums himself up. . . . This I have been, says he,

[7] Cf. Santayana: ". . . impossibility of action is a great condition of the sub-lime. . . . While we think we can change the drama of history, and of our own lives, we are not awed by our destiny. But when the evil is irreparable, when our life is lived, a strong spirit has the sublime resource of standing at bay and of surveying almost from the other world the vicissitudes of this." *The Sense of Beauty* (New York: Scribner's, 1934), p. 178.

this I have done." [8] He does not always achieve complete insight, earnestly as he tries to. Othello is vouchsafed no more than a glimpse of the abysses of his nature which made him so easy a prey to Iago. Hamlet never becomes aware of the forces which keep him from proceeding with that one act he flagellates himself to perform. On the other hand, Oedipus and Lear achieve a large measure of understanding, and we feel that every tragic hero without exception continues to grow and never understands himself or his fellows so well as he does just before he dies. Basically, however, it is not the success or failure of the hero's effort to understand himself that matters. What stirs us is his very willingness to contemplate the darkest facets of his soul and the terrible fate awaiting him without evasion or dishonesty.

The tragic hero's resoluteness perhaps replenishes, as well as reveals, his courage: it may help him to summon the strength he needs to experience his fate without flinching. Somewhere he finds the strength; he goes to his death with a dignity which is difficult to convey in words. He does not protest the sentence which has been imposed upon him or seek to escape it. On the other hand, he does not "accept" his fate either, or become reconciled to it, if by these words something passive or supine is implied. Nor does he simply endure his fate, as an animal might. In some almost physical sense he rises to his fate, with his eyes open and his senses clear, and proves himself impervious to it. By his very demeanor as he is being destroyed he demonstrates that he is not "a pipe for fortune's finger to sound what stop she please."

As I have indicated, I believe that it is only in tragedy that one encounters the triumphant confrontation of the darkest impulses of the human heart and the most savage penalties society can devise to chasten these and punish us for our transgressions. In a great deal of fiction there is only a limited amount of self-exploration, or none at all. In *Remembrance of Things Past*, in many of James's novels and in Joyce's "The Dead" the characters face themselves and achieve deep insight, but what they contemplate is by no means so frightening as

[8] *Ibid.*, p. 180.

the things at which the heroes of tragedy unwaveringly gaze. It is perhaps significant that the heroes of Dostoevsky's three great novels, *The Brothers Karamazov, The Idiot* and *Crime and Punishment*, are all broken by their offenses, even when, as in the first two novels, they have been committed by proxy; they go mad or, like Raskolnikov, fall into a state between hysteria and illness; they are never able to look back without fear upon what they have done. Joseph K. is progressively possessed and overwhelmed by his guilt; he does not grapple with it and try to act against its dictates, he does not survey himself from the outside, as Hamlet does. Of the various heroes and heroines of fiction of whom I can think, only Anna Karenina faces the prospect of her own destruction, and the most shameful aspects of her own nature and of human nature in general, with the kind of remorseless honesty characteristic of the protagonists of tragedy. And Anna's confrontation is not triumphant. The wonderful poise we feel sure she still possessed in the early stages of her affair with Vronsky has long since deserted her; she rushes to her death, frenzied, disillusioned and embittered.

The kind of confrontation which occurs in tragedy is also rare in life itself. In one way or another—by repression, by lies, by denial—most people keep themselves from seeing the very things which at the end the tragic hero tries to see; this is the theme of Eugene O'Neill's little-understood and little-appreciated drama, *The Iceman Cometh*. In one way or another most people are also scarred and defeated by their weaknesses. For example, they may become brutal or cynical. They may find life tolerable only when they resort to drink or some other stupefaction, sacrificing the hope of ecstasy and innumerable mental and spiritual pleasures in order to win surcease from pain. When disaster strikes, even their customary props may prove ineffectual, and they may suffer some sort of mental or physical collapse which dooms them to function thereafter on a still lower level, going through the motions of life while awaiting death.

The tragic hero's steadfast confrontation of his predicament stirs us, I believe, because we sense it might save us from such defeats as these. Like the basic attitude of comedy, it supplies us with a stance important for our very survival. Because the tragic hero has become an instrument of destruction and must therefore be destroyed, the qualities he displays during his travail do not save him, but this may enhance rather than decrease their value: it gives them a wider and a deeper reference. When one faces a situation at all comparable to the tragic hero's, there is ordinarily very little that one can "do." And in general man is too puny to accomplish much through action, to make any significant alteration in that vast universe he inhabits such a brief and uncertain span of time; he has no control, or only a limited degree of control, over many of the things that befall him. He can, however, strive to understand and adjust to every vicissitude of experience, no matter how painful. When calamity strikes, he can summon resources he did not know until then he possessed—and perhaps until then did not possess—so that he can meet them without quailing. The confrontation phase of tragedy supplies an image of this kind of courage and dignity. It reminds us, even as the tragic hero perishes, of the indefeasible spirit of man.

Entirely on the basis of that high seriousness which is reflected in both its substance and its attitude, tragedy makes a deeper appeal than any other form of fiction to all of the psychic institutions. The confrontation phase offers the ego additional satisfactions of the richest sort. It exalts the ego. It shows it continuing its labor of reality-testing and reporting even when death or mutilation looms ahead. It shows it continuing and accelerating its efforts to integrate the personality under the most difficult conditions a man can be called upon to face. These efforts are successful. Before death the ego comes to terms with its intemperate psychic partners, and it does this not by repudiating or compromising their claims but by accepting them, by granting the legitimacy of their most extreme demands yet at the same time maintaining its own authority.

On occasion something more miraculous than this occurs. As the tragic protagonist takes stock of himself, chastened but not contrite, assenting to punishment but uncowed by it, his ego, and the ego of the responding spectator, appear to assimilate id and superego. For an instant the personality becomes not only more coherent and continuous but fully unified. The ego incorporates the dark, unruly forces it has tried so unremittingly to control. Even as it contemplates the irreparable damage they have caused, it accepts them and assumes full responsibility for them. At the same time, and in the same spirit, it replaces the superego. It not only agrees to the need for punishment but accepts responsibility for executing punishment should society prove laggard. And it does not do this, as one often does when one submits to punishment, so that, purged of guilt, it can sue for reconciliation with the superego and the parents and communal forces whose heir and representative it is. It asks nothing of the superego, not even forgiveness and love. It assimilates the superego just as it does the id: it assumes the right to judge itself. Without disputing the parental decree that one's anarchistic impulses must be disciplined and controlled—this is accepted along with certain apparently incompatible claims of the instincts themselves—in the confrontation phase of tragedy the ego asserts its independence of the parents. It stands on its own, fully mature, neither approving nor yet refusing to acknowledge its own unregenerate tendencies, erect, clear-eyed and self-sufficient, the parent of itself.

5

It is because tragedy so richly fulfils and harmonizes all the needs of our nature, from the most primitive to the most refined, from the basest to the most idealistic, that it so frequently gives us that supreme satisfaction we call an esthetic experience. For the esthetic experience can be nothing else but this—a feeling that all our claims, however contradictory, have been brought into balance and satisfied, a feeling of equilibrium based upon fulfilment rather than the denial of those needs which cannot be fitted into the more impoverished pattern of living we have developed for ourself, a feeling of wanting nothing, of having everything for which we could possibly ask.

The extent to which most available descriptions of the esthetic experience support this view of it is remarkable—particularly as the experience is so elusive that one might expect verbal accounts of it to vary widely. Like other intangible experiences, it probably takes a somewhat different form with every individual, and with any given individual on different occasions. Despite these difficulties certain words recur in most descriptions—contentment, peace, harmony, serenity, synthesis, equipoise, equilibrium. Certain omissions are perhaps also significant. Together with what is said, in any case, they make it clear that during the experience we are not disturbed by desire and longing. There is a complete absence of tension, anxiety and guilt, those indicators of disharmony and disequilibrium within the psyche. For an ecstatic moment we feel entirely satisfied and at one with ourself, free of the inner strain which makes life burdensome. The future is devoid of threat: we feel possessed of a key which will permit the free interplay and mutual accommodation of all our tendencies. Conflict is annulled, the cleavage between the various parts of the psyche obliterated. We feel healed and whole.

Another characteristic of the experience, perhaps a consequence of the efficient adjustment which has been achieved, is that we feel exhilarated and refreshed. We have no disposition to act, we feel content and still, but we have a tingling sense of vitality and power. Having no practical aim, the energy available to us flows into seeing and understanding: it seems that our eyes have never been so fully open and that we have never penetrated so deeply into the nature of things. The seeing is joyous and an end in itself; it is not an incitement to action any more than it is a symptom of restlessness; it is the kind of seeing celebrated by Marvell in "The Garden." We see clearly and, as it were, with our whole being, without either the selective singling out of certain details or the selective blindness which is inevitable when our eyes are fogged by anxiety or desire, habit or practical considerations. It is because we see in this manner, with our interest unaffected by our ordinary concerns and desires, that we sometimes have a sense of detachment, of "disinterestedness," of almost impersonal perception. We see truly and without haste: we know that we do not have to falsify our response out of a sense of what is expected of us or refuse to notice certain aspects of what lies before us or leave various implications unexplored.

Whenever we look in this fashion—whether at external reality or some "made object," an episode in a book or a story as a whole—what we perceive has a charm and loveliness, or an august splendor, we may feel we have never witnessed before —or have glimpsed briefly and then lost sight of, we had feared forever. We have a special word for the objects which permit this kind of seeing, which give us a sense of serenity and rich content: we call them beautiful.[9]

6

While tragedy is more likely than any other form of fiction to fulfil and reconcile the needs of the entire personality, every story which deserves the name, every story which meets the

[9] It will be apparent that the conception of the esthetic experience advanced here closely corresponds with what Ogden, Richards and Wood call "synaesthesis." (*The Foundations of Aesthetics*, New York: International, 1929.) My one reservation about their theory has already been suggested by what I have said about I. A. Richards (cf. p. 98, footnote 3), whose *Principles of Literary Criticism* is informed by a similar basic concept of the reconciliation of impulses: the concept is valuable and, I believe, unassailable, but somewhat vague; it does not help us to specify enough about the works of art which arouse the effects described.

I should also like to acknowledge my indebtedness to Hanns Sachs, who so far as I know was the first person to formulate a theory of the esthetic experience and of beauty on the basis of psychoanalytic concepts. (See *The Creative Unconscious* [Cambridge, Mass.: Sci-Art, 1942], especially Part Three.) Despite the many fine insights Sachs achieved, I believe that he confused the issue by introducing the concept of "death instinct." I cannot assent to his view that a feeling of sadness is a necessary constituent of the esthetic experience.

W. R. D. Fairbairn has also advanced a psychological theory of the esthetic experience which contains much of value. ("The Ultimate Basis of Aesthetic Experience," *British Journal of Psychology*, XXIX, 1938-39.) But in my judgment he puts far too much emphasis on destructive urges and the desire to make restitution for them. In brief, he maintains that, "The demands of the libido may be said to constitute the thesis [of art], the pressure of the destructive urges the antithesis, and restitution the synthesis." This seems too narrow a base for a theory of response in general or the esthetic experience in particular. To how many works can it be applied without some forcing?

minimum requirements of a work of art, labors toward the same end. The tension between content and form reveals that fiction tries to satisfy divergent and even discordant needs; and our separate analyses of content and form showed that each of them appeals individually to the several parts of the psyche, though leaving it to the other to supplement and balance its own accomplishments.

Since fiction has this characteristic, we may be sure that whenever the reading experience is successful, intrapsychic harmony is furthered to some extent. Sometimes—perhaps when important claims we had regarded as irreconcilable are adjusted and satisfied—we secure a satisfaction which seems qualitatively as well as quantitatively different from anything we ordinarily experience. It is this rare and deservedly prized satisfaction we call an esthetic experience. We are fully justified in regarding it as *sui generis* and giving it a special name, but we should not forget that it is continuous with a satisfaction we frequently experience. Nor should we forget that a novel or a short story—or a motion picture or musical comedy —may sometimes be the source of the more valuable satisfaction, and that tragedies do not always provide it.

The point requires stress because there is a persistent tendency to associate esthetic satisfaction exclusively with certain highly regarded artistic objects. It is sometimes even viewed as an attribute of those objects, and beauty is still more frequently looked upon as a property of things. Now in fact— as has been repeatedly pointed out since the eighteenth century, though it sometimes seems to no avail—there is a kind of shorthand involved when we speak of beauty in this way. Beauty really refers to the effect of an object upon a beholder. For the sake of convenience we may attribute the effect to the object which aroused it, but it is important that we remember that a beholder is also involved. Another beholder might pass by the object in question without noticing it; still another might find it ugly.

It is perhaps more obvious that when we speak of esthetic satisfaction we are referring to the effect of an object upon a beholder—in the context of our inquiry, of a story upon a reader. The reader's needs, his readiness for the satisfactions embodied in a particular work and his ability to perceive them, are all involved. The most perfunctory glance at any historical or sociological study of taste indicates that there may be great variations from period to period, country to country, and class to class, in the characteristics of the art works which are likely to be admired and a source of pleasure. The prestige of a given work, or of the whole body of work by a given author, may fluctuate widely through the centuries. This does not necessarily mean that all the elements affecting taste are in flux—some may be persistent and relatively stable—but some at least appear to shift, sometimes quite rapidly. The modal requirements of successive ages may vary sharply. One age may insist on strict adherence to classic norms, on mildness of content and smoothness of form, on the largest possible measure of control. The next age may contemptuously dismiss work with such characteristics as boring and flabby, landscape gardening for a generation or a social class afraid of nature and of life; it may demand *Sturm und Drang*, irregular contours, violent imagery, and forms which give the emotions as much play as possible. Furthermore, even in periods when the audience for art was evidently much more homogeneous than it is today, the work which achieved popularity varied widely in complexity and value. The point does not have to be labored. If we are adult our own taste has probably undergone enough mutations to teach us that the needs and capacities of the reader help to determine whether a given work will provide esthetic satisfaction or, for that matter, pleasure of any kind. The novel which thrilled us when we were eighteen may seem a piece of trumpery a decade later.

The tendency to disregard such facts as these and to claim that only certain works can provoke esthetic response is, however, understandable enough. Artistic works are bewildering in their number and diversity. It is natural that we should want to arrange them in some reassuring order of merit; natural, too, that we should put the works which most profoundly affect us at the pinnacle of the hierarchy. They may well belong there, but not even widespread concurrence about this will justify our appropriating the word *beauty* for them alone. All we are warranted in saying is that certain works seem more likely than others to provide esthetic delight and to be proclaimed beautiful. We may be sure that they will not be beautiful to all and that works we disdain will seem beautiful to some. The most gimcrack amusement-park prize may possess that wondrous quality for some of those who compete for it; and a story a student of fiction might find stereotyped and meretricious may arouse a response it would be priggish not to call esthetic in a reader hungry for the particular satisfactions it offers and blind to its defects. In view of such considerations as these, the futility of trying to anticipate precisely what will be regarded as beautiful in the future, and to prescribe rules for art, should be apparent. Because what pleased us yesterday palls today and new needs supplant old, there is necessarily something unpredictable about beauty.

Though the fact seems to disturb some estheticians, it seems certain that not only artistic objects of widely varying quality but things that we experience in our everyday life sometimes arouse esthetic satisfaction; from time to time we catch a glimpse of beauty during our ordinary activity. The occasions are infrequent enough. While immersed in affairs, we are usually too preoccupied with the practical aspects of things to see beauty though she be nearby. Our eyes may be blurred by habit or anxiety or desire, or we may be troubled because we have to choose between this satisfaction or that, or between gratification and a sense of guilt. But by various means, of which travel is a good example, we try to escape these handicaps, and sometimes, by design or chance, we succeed in escaping them. We find we can enjoy two experiences which we had thought were incompatible. Miraculously, inexplicably, a seascape, a city view, a humble natural object or some new perspective on our own life gives us a sense of fulfilment and inner peace. On such occasions the word *beauty* may come to our lips, and we have no more reason to doubt that we are in her presence than we feel when the word suggests itself at the theater. Despite the many differences between them, the world of art is not discontinuous with the world of our everyday experience.

Appendix *A Note on the Use of Scientific Psychological Knowledge in Literary Study*

To make use of empirical knowledge in a literary study seems automatically, in certain quarters, to touch off a kind of alarm system. The cry of "reduction" is immediately raised. Vigorous and sometimes angry voices are to be heard protesting that literature should not be assimilated to psychology, or economics or sociology.

Now, that the use of information in literary study does involve a danger I would be the first not simply to admit but to assert. Although I believe that literature is continuous with other aspects of our experience, I believe no less firmly that there are distinctively literary values and that it is the fundamental obligation of any literary study to concern itself with these. Experience shows that this is not easy. The things that distinguish literature as literature seem peculiarly difficult to isolate and focus upon; it seems easier to discuss almost anything else. Thus there is a very real danger that a novel, for example, may be treated as though it were a kind of case history, as though only its meaning mattered, or that it will be used to document some economic development or cultural trend. It is probably safe to say that most discussion of literature assimilates it to something else. In extreme cases, a body of knowledge first introduced to explicate literature may end by claiming the center of the stage. Literature is relegated to a supporting role; it does not so much speak as stand by to be pointed to when it can be of service in illustrating a statement about something else.

Whether I have been able to avoid this "reductive" danger, I do not know. I know that I have tried hard to. I have drawn upon other fields of knowledge, especially psychology, be-

cause I thought they would be helpful in abstracting and elucidating values which I believe lie close to the heart of fiction
as an art—values which are a function of what we call form
as well as of content. Because clear exposition would not permit any other course, I have often discussed formal and subject-matter values separately, but I hope I have nowhere
conveyed the impression that any work of fiction can be
reduced either to the various meanings to be found in it or,
alternatively, to its structure or form. It should be apparent
that a story, or any other work of art, affects us not only
because of "what" it says but because of the way it says it.
As we have seen, the two things are only analytically separable.[1] In reality there is no such thing as form and no such
thing as content; every work of art is an entity, and affects
us as an entity.

The danger which is involved in using information in literary study arises, it is worth insisting, in connection with any
and every kind of information. As I have already suggested,[2]
it arises in connection with bodies of information which are
usually an integral part of the study of English. And it arises
in connection with information and knowledge which fall
within the purview of other humanistic disciplines. Literature has probably been assimilated to cultural history more
frequently than to anything else. It has also often been assimilated to biography, to ethics and to various aspects of lin-
guistics. It has sometimes not simply been assimilated to, but
subordinated to, these subjects.

Despite this, the cry of reduction is raised in certain academic circles only when someone draws upon information
not presently embraced in the humanities; to borrow from the
social sciences seems to be regarded as a particularly offensive
breach of etiquette. I do not see how the kind of discrimination which asserts itself here can be defended. It is worth
remarking that it seems curiously unhumanistic. One would
suppose that the desirability of using a given body of informa-

[1] Cf. Chapter III.
[2] Cf. p. 17, footnote 9.

tion should be decided without preconceptions—and primarily on the basis of its value in terms of the nature and objectives of a particular study. I doubt if there is any sound basis for a general ban on the use of certain kinds of information; certainly the academic locus of the information should not be a decisive factor. Nor can it be justly claimed that certain kinds of information are more dangerous to handle than others; humanistic information can be misused as easily as any other kind.

In my opinion a great deal of harm has already been done by the attempt to excommunicate certain kinds of knowledge from the field of literary study. The attempt has not been wholly successful, but it has discouraged the use—above all, the scholarly and disciplined use—of many kinds of knowledge which might throw additional light upon literature. It has fostered parochialism at a point where counter-measures were needed to cope with the compartmentalization of knowledge and the already powerful pressures upon scholars to restrict themselves to a steadily narrowing field of specialization. It has provided a convenient excuse for neglecting other fields; and since we tend to be defensive about that about which we are ignorant, this neglect in turn has reinforced the all too human inclination to disparage other fields.

Opposition to the use of scientific psychological knowledge in literary study seems to me particularly indefensible and particularly unfortunate in its effects. For the fact is that one can scarcely discuss many literary issues without making some use of psychology. In particular, it is difficult to disregard psychology in intensive analyses of individual works. This is so even when one's approach is Aristotelian, even when one concentrates upon the way the parts of a literary work fit together and function internally. It is not possible to discuss, say, the way a particular episode contributes to a certain end, weigh its appropriateness, decide why it was used here rather than there, without either introducing psychological principles or depending upon them tacitly. How can one assert that three episodes in a story (or three quatrains of a sonnet) fall into a pattern of mounting intensity without some knowledge or assumptions about what affects human beings more and what less? [3]

Thus the real issue which confronts students of literature today is not *whether* to use psychology but what *kind* of psychology to use. They, or rather each student individually, must decide whether he should continue to depend upon a homespun, "common sense" psychology, however inadequate or even erroneous it may be, or whether he should avail himself of the more reliable—and, as it happens, more fertile—body of empirical knowledge which has been accumulated during the past half-century. Leaving to one side many of the objections which could be raised against the first-mentioned kind of psychology, one should be sufficient to decide the issue: no "common-sense" psychology yet employed in criticism has been helpful in exploring either the unconscious sources of the behavior of literary characters or the unconscious sources of literature's appeal.

2

To study the unconscious forces which play so important a part in literature and in our response to it, it is clear that one must employ some kind of dynamic depth-psychology, either Freudian psychoanalysis or one of its variants. Yet the resistance to introducing this kind of knowledge into literary study is especially intense—so intense as to make one suspect that *it* is partly determined by irrational considerations. I believe that it is worthwhile to identify some of these considerations, although I have no illusion that to do so will have any effect on those most swayed by them, those who want to believe that psychoanalysis is all nonsense or that, however useful it may be as, say, a system of therapy for treating neu-

[3] Furthermore, one can scarcely discuss the relationship of the parts intelligently without considering the ends toward which the work as a whole is moving. It is interesting to note that R. S. Crane defines a poem, for the purpose of the kind of Aristotelian analysis favored by the University of Chicago group of critics, as "a made object productive of definite effects upon our minds." (*Critics and Criticism, Ancient and Modern*, edited by R. S. Crane [Chicago: University of Chicago Press, 1952], p. 20.) It would seem that criticism based upon such a definition could not completely ignore psychology.

rotics, it is inconceivable that it should have any implications for the study of literature. I am addressing myself to students who have doubts about the desirability of using (or perhaps even familiarizing themselves with) psychoanalysis, but who are not rigidly "set" against the idea. Such readers may even realize that at bottom their hesitancy has an emotional basis. The identification of some of the irrational forces which may be playing upon them may help them to escape their influence.

I do not think that many readers will be inclined to question the fact that non-rational considerations often play a part in our readiness to accept ideas. A theory is likely to be well received when it confirms and refurbishes something which is already willingly accepted or, alternatively, when it provides a formulation for ideas toward which an age is groping and which it is not only ready to believe but desires to believe. It is quite otherwise with theories which produce uncertainty and discomfort—for example, theories which appear to threaten institutional arrangements in which its judges have a stake or which challenge convictions underlying their behavior and orientation to the world. Such theories may face an uphill battle even to secure a hearing. Indeed, it is frequently their fate to be rejected, for a time at least, on the basis of quite inaccurate notions of what they say.

Psychoanalysis evidently belongs with the theories which are found disturbing. From the beginning it has encountered the bitterest kind of opposition, condemnation and misrepresentation. Some of the less legitimate sources of the antagonism it has aroused have been discussed by Freud himself.

In a 1917 paper[4] Freud points out that certain analytic discoveries have wounded man's self-esteem in very much the same way that the discoveries of Copernicus and Darwin had wounded it earlier. By demonstrating that the earth was not the stationary center of the universe, Copernicus upset man's egocentric conception of his position in nature. The theory of evolution cast doubt on the belief that man is a creature of

[4] "One of the Difficulties of Psycho-Analysis," *Collected Papers*, Vol. IV (London: Hogarth, 1948).

divine descent, not continuous with the other animals who inhabit the earth. Psychoanalysis dealt man's narcissism a still more crushing blow. It revealed that the ego is not even master in its own house, the mind. The mind is frequently invaded by unwelcome ideas it can neither keep out nor easily cast out, and these ideas are recognizably the spawn of impulses the individual tried to turn his back on long before. The mind does not even have reliable knowledge about much that takes place in its own kingdom. An enormous amount of psychic activity goes forward almost incessantly of which it receives only belated, incomplete or distorted reports, or no report whatever.

In a 1925 paper,[5] Freud explained why this emphasis on the importance of the unconscious aroused the particular displeasure of philosophers—he might have written abstract thinkers in any field—who are used to exalting the supremacy of the conscious intellect. He also showed how analysis' emphasis on sexuality offended people individually and collectively: individually because it destroyed the myth of an asexual childhood and reminded everyone of phases of their development they go to great lengths to forget; collectively, because, though analysis never recommended the unfettering of the instincts, its suggestion that they be controlled somewhat less strictly and its exposure of the weaknesses of repression as a method of control appeared to threaten that regulation of the instincts which is one of the pillars on which civilization rests.

These same aspects of psychoanalysis may repel some of those to whom I am addressing myself not only individually and as members of society but quite specifically in their role as students of literature. Psychoanalysis has become associated with illness, abnormality and those dark aspects of human nature of which its therapeutic purposes compel it to take note. It does little good to point out that it investigates those aspects of our nature in order to make them better subject to understanding and control. Like a messenger who is blamed

[5] "The Resistances to Psycho-Analysis," *Collected Papers*, Vol. V (London: Hogarth, 1950).

for bringing bad news, psychoanalysis is reproached for the things with which it has been concerned, and in some curious way is even confused with them. At some deep level the application of ideas from such a field to something so highly revered as literature may seem a kind of profanation.

I also fear that some students of literature may be troubled by the emphasis in psychoanalysis, and in what has been said here, on the unconscious. By definition the things communicated to the unconscious through literature are not meant to come to our attention, at any rate during the act of reading. But I cannot believe that our unconscious perceptions, the unconscious bases of the appeal of literature, or unconscious processes of response are quite as inaccessible as the neglect of them in contemporary teaching and criticism would suggest. In reviewing one's impressions of, say, a novel, or in analyzing the reactions of others, as teachers are almost compelled to do, one or another of these unconscious elements frequently becomes visible.

I suspect that we prefer to believe that every aspect of literature and of our response to it is accessible to the conscious intellect and therefore subject to its control. The suggestion that this is not the case makes us uncomfortable. It appears to diminish the importance of the intellect, and this not only wounds us but makes us feel less secure. The recognition of unconscious influences may also seem to undermine modes of analyzing and teaching literature in which many people have an emotional, and even an economic, stake.

I am sure that most serious students of literature will not want their judgments of the truth or falsity of a theory to be influenced by the kind of fears and considerations I have mentioned. Furthermore, the fears are largely unfounded. The fact that literature is understood, in part, unconsciously in no way depreciates the importance of conscious intellectual responses. The notion that it does is comparable to the fallacious economic idea that the prosperity of one individual or group necessarily subtracts from that of others. As we have seen, the engagement of the conscious intellect is a necessary condition of the various unconscious processes involved in response to fiction. The greatest fiction occupies and rewards the entire psyche.

In my opinion, every mode of analyzing literature should take cognizance of the fact that literature speaks to the unconscious. But this is a requirement that most critical systems can meet simply by adding some kind of depth-psychology to the analytic devices now at their disposal. Depth-psychology should be looked upon as an auxiliary instrument; a less adequate set of psychological assumptions is the only thing it is likely to supplant.

I believe that some of the ideas developed in this book do have implications for the teaching of literature—more implications, indeed, than can be examined here—but so far as I myself can tell nothing which has been said suggests the need for radical changes. In the aggregate, it would seem to me, the ideas tend to support certain principles which already have strong advocates. For example, they point to the desirability of building the English program around books which are on students' level of sensibility and concerned with their deepest interests and problems; of seeking a proper balance between intensive and extensive reading; and of concentrating upon literature itself, using any and every kind of information which will help to illuminate it, but never letting the focus of attention shift to the information more than momentarily.

I hope that it will not be supposed that I advocate indiscriminate emphasis on the hidden levels of meaning often to be found in fiction. Nothing could be more injurious than to stimulate students to search for such meanings during their original reading of a story. Even in the discussion of works already read, these meanings should be touched on only when there is some positive reason for doing so—for example, when it is desirable to make students aware that there are closer connections than they appear to realize between "great" literature and their own problems and experience; or when they are puzzled by aspects of a story which can only be explained by taking account of unconscious sources of motivation. In dealing with hidden meanings, furthermore—hidden, it is to be remembered, because they might arouse anxiety if brought to light—it is evident that a teacher must employ the utmost tact. In particular, he must be alert to the reactions of his students, for their comments and demeanor are the best indicators of how far he should carry his explanations and of the kind of language in which they should be couched.

3

The extensive use I have made of psychoanalysis may provoke two specific objections. In some instances, I suspect, these objections will be parented by that irrational antipathy toward analysis we have just examined, but whether or not this is the case, they raise issues which seem to me to deserve consideration.

First of all, the wisdom of basing a literary study upon any particular psychology may be questioned. Students schooled in the humanities know that many psychological systems have had their hour of vogue and then been superseded. It is perhaps natural for them to suppose that psychoanalysis is likely to disappear from the scene in its turn.

In fact, however, there are more reasons than can be elaborated for believing that psychoanalysis represents the beginning of a true science of psychology, and that, though it will be subject to change, it will endure. Both the cultural climate in which analysis had its origin and the temperament and training of its founder favored its development along scientific lines. As Dr. E. Pumpian-Mindlin declares:

Historically it must not be forgotten that psychoanalysis derives from medicine. Its founder was a physician and remained within the medical sphere all his life. The starting point for the development of psychoanalysis lay in the fact that neurotic symptoms were unamenable to cure by any method then known. Even more important was the fact that they seemed meaningless, unpredictable, and inexplicable. No type of approach seemed to yield a satisfactory explanation of their existence. Freud entered the scientific scene at a time when the impact of the Darwinian evolutionary theory was tremendous. The bewildering chaos of animal life had suddenly become ordered, logical, coherent, rational. . . . If biologically man was a natural phenomenon, then perhaps psychologically he was also. In this intensely biological and rational atmosphere Freud approached the problem of the neuroses of man.[6]

From the beginning the hypotheses and constructs of psychoanalysis were based upon empirical observations, and the whole course of its development has been marked by that continual interplay between observation and the revision and extension of theory which is characteristic of science. Indeed, the growth of analysis has been fostered in a way which is sometimes overlooked by the richness, and in particular the breadth, of its data. Freud very early perceived that analysis need not confine its attention to the neuroses, that its proper field of exploration was the whole field of phenomena in which non rational factors play a significant part. In a single decade (1895-1905) he made intensive studies of such varied subjects as dreams, infantile sexual behavior, the parapraxes and wit. These studies shed light upon one another: what was obscure in one area of observation was often clearly defined in another. Furthermore, they revealed some of the general characteristics of unconscious processes. They provided excellent opportunities for the collation of data, for that continual process of confirmation and correction upon which science thrives. It should perhaps be added that Freud attracted a growing number of co-workers—there are today psychoanalytic societies in sixteen countries—and that analytic principles have been applied, and in effect tested, in many fields besides medicine. The body of hypotheses which may be said to constitute psychoanalysis at the present time is the product of the observation and conceptualizing activity of many hundreds of men and women, living in different lands and working at different tasks.

Thus psychoanalysis can hardly be dismissed as speculation, as just another psychology. This does not mean, of course, that present psychoanalytic propositions represent "the truth,"

[6] *Psychoanalysis as Science*, edited by E. Pumpian-Mindlin, M.D. (Stanford, Calif.: Stanford University Press, 1952), p. 126.

an ultimate and immutable codification of knowledge. On the contrary, they are still in process of evolution. They are all subject to change. Some may be completely overturned; a number are being sharply challenged at the present time. But such statements could be made about the propositions of most scientific fields. They do not justify any special skepticism toward analysis. The difficulty of investigating analytic propositions by means of controlled experiments is sometimes used to support the claim that it is not a science, but, of course, there are other kinds of objective evidence. Furthermore, there is more experimental evidence than is generally appreciated, and what there is tends, overwhelmingly, to support the validity of analytic hypotheses.[7]

I may add that the analytic concepts I have employed are by and large elementary ones, about which there is a minimum of controversy. They describe phenomena the reality of which could be substantiated if psychoanalysis were non-existent. Hypnosis shows, no less than analysis, that there is such a thing as the unconscious. Amnesia furnishes evidence of the mechanism of repression. On occasion, self-observation will show that there are warring factions within the self. Because of my own limitations I have built much of what I have to say on concepts covering such phenomena as these, and have dealt with only the more obvious implications of those concepts. Heuristically, I realize, this is disadvantageous even in such a preliminary study as this, but I believe it has had the effect of protecting much of what I do say (insofar as its truth is dependent upon the validity of analytic hypotheses) against anything short of a radical revision of theory.

I hope that the validity of at least some of the ideas I advance will be empirically investigated. Many statements can easily be converted into hypotheses which can be assessed by

[7] Cf. Ernest R. Hilgard: ". . . it has been possible to parallel many psychoanalytical phenomena in the laboratory. When this is done, the correspondence between predictions according to psychoanalytic theory and what is found is on the whole very satisfactory." *Psychoanalysis as Science*, p. 42. Anyone seriously interested in the problem of investigating analytic concepts, and in finding out what has already been done along these lines, will find this entire volume of interest.

some objective technique. For example, resourceful investigators should be able to ascertain whether when we read fiction we usually understand far more than we are aware of understanding; and whether, as I believe, anxiety is the principal regulator of what is unconsciously understood.[8] Simultaneously, the soundness of some of my interpretations of specific stories could also be determined.[9] While I, of course, believe that most of the propositions which are studied will be validated, I am reconciled to the possibility that some may be overturned and others found in need of amendment.

4

Objection may also be made to my occasional use of psychoanalytic terms. The introduction of these terms into a literary study seems destined to provoke the charge of "jargon." I suspect that this charge, too, sometimes conceals a bias; it is voiced by certain critics who do not keep their own writing free of jargon, and sometimes jargon of a peculiarly

[8] The following techniques, among others, might be employed in these investigations: (1) hypnosis—experiments modeled on those performed by Doctors Leslie Farber and Charles Fisher and reported in "An Experimental Approach to Dream Psychology through the Use of Hypnosis," *Psychoanalytic Quarterly*, XII, 1943; (2) depth interviews, ideally of subjects about whom a good deal is already known—for example, analysands or former analysands, or people who have been studied before by means of thematic apperception (or some other) tests; (3) "free association" statements designed to get at precisely the kind of reactions which might be screened out of the customary sort of student theme; (4) questionnaires designed, like some of those employed in the Eight Year Study of the Progressive Education Association, to elicit more information than the subjects are aware of divulging.

[9] I would not expect, I hasten to add, that all readers would find just what I have found in the various stories considered. On the contrary, as has been emphasized at various points, it is one of my basic assumptions that all but the shallowest works of fiction are overdetermined and admit of a number, often a large number, of correct interpretations. Allowance should also be made for the fact that subjects who did see the same things might express them in quite different fashion. Under most test conditions they could not be expected to work out the various levels of meaning of a story as completely and systematically as, in certain cases, I have endeavored to do here. I would feel that the soundness of an interpretation was supported if a reasonable proportion of the subjects studied saw the meanings I have declared to be present, no matter how differently and elliptically they phrased what they saw.

murky kind. However, the use of technical terms, and particularly terms from another field, does entail certain dangers,
and I feel that my decision to make some use of analytic terms
should be explained.

Perhaps the principal risk one faces in using terms is that
of overusing them, employing them where it might be possible
to find brisker, more vigorous and perhaps even more accurate
ways of expressing one's ideas. I have tried to guard against
this danger of letting my terms become crutches, frequently
avoiding analytic terms even when I was dealing with analytic
concepts. There is also the danger that terms from one field
will not be familiar to readers schooled in another, but this is
a danger that can be more easily circumvented. A term can be
defined when it is introduced, its meaning may be made clear
by its context, and so on. Some analytic terms labor under
another disadvantage, against which, I fear, no measures can
be taken: they may arouse unpleasant associations. For example, an analytically oriented critic could scarcely fail to
discern a quality in *Robinson Crusoe* for which the only completely accurate word is anal-erotic. Inevitably one feels
some hesitation about using such a word in a discussion of so
innocent and well-beloved a book. Nor can one plead that its
use is unavoidable. Without using the word Walter de la
Mare has identified the quality and written about it at length,
with disarming charm.[10]

I have decided to make some use of analytic terms, despite
these dangers and disadvantages, first of all, as I shall indicate
in a minute, because I feel that there are advantages which
outweigh them. But I was also influenced by the almost insuperable difficulties which would have arisen in attempting to
avoid all use of analytic terms in a study of this kind and this
length.

One example may make the nature of these difficulties clear.
The analytic term *ego* is a technical term for that highly organized portion of the psyche (not conceived as having ana-
tomical locus or reality) which is concerned with controlling

[10] *Desert Islands and Robinson Crusoe* (New York: Farrar and Rinehart,
1930).

the individual's behavior and adjustment to his environment. To perform its task it collects and organizes sense impressions and other kinds of information about the environment. It also keeps close tab on the internal stimuli which reveal the desires and demands of the other parts of the psyche. It attempts to mediate between conflicting demands, impulses pressing for fulfilment and the inner voices which say, "Thou shalt not." It tries to reconcile the total demands of the individual with the requirements of the external environment. In accomplishing this, it makes use of various highly effective unconscious processes as well as the conscious operations we associate with judgment and intelligence. For example, it may alter the form in which some internal impulses come to our attention, or deny them any access to consciousness. Now, it is evident, I believe, that it is difficult to find alternative ways of expressing such a concept as this which are not either inadequate or lengthy. One might devise enough to serve the purposes of a short paper, but the attempt to avoid the word *ego* throughout a book such as this would have almost certainly led to prolixity and other rhetorical offenses.

Furthermore, analytic terms have certain advantages which seem to me to make their use, in moderation, desirable. Like the word *ego*, they usually refer to something which has many dynamically interrelated characteristics. Thus the recognition of an analytic quality in a literary work may cause one to note many related manifestations of the quality one might otherwise have missed; or it may help to unify what at first appeared to be unrelated observations. The use of the term anal-erotic, for example, in a discussion of *Robinson Crusoe* may help to call attention to the connections between Crusoe's orderliness, his tendency to keep records, and his persistence; although these traits may seem diverse, they are in fact closely related.

In still another sense many analytic terms possess a desirable breadth of reference. They refer to qualities which may be found not only in literature but in many other subjects and phenomena and, most important of all, in ourselves. Besides identifying a quality in *Crusoe*, the word anal-erotic identifies a human characteristic which influences response to *Crusoe*. It also points to a characteristic of the culture which received the novel so enthusiastically—a characteristic, be it said, which is by no means extinct in the world of today. Thus analytic terms constantly suggest connections between literature and the human beings who read it, and between literature and other of our interests.

Index

SIMON O. LESSER has published literary articles, including portions of this book, in *Partisan Review, Psychiatry, College English, Modern Fiction Studies, American Imago,* and *Literature and Psychology.* He has also contributed to the *Nation,* the *Virginian Quarterly Review,* and the *American Scholar,* and is co-author, with George A. Works, of *Rural America Today: Its Schools and Community Life.*

Fiction and the Unconscious was written with the assistance of grants from the Humanities Division of the Rockefeller Foundation, while Mr. Lesser was a research associate at the University of Chicago and New York Psychoanalytic Institutes, and at the Washington School of Psychiatry. Mr. Lesser has taught English at New York University, has held editorial and information positions in both business and government, and has been a research associate at the Institute for Motivational Research, Croton-on-Hudson, New York.

THE TEXT *of this book was set on the Linotype in* Janson, *an excellent example of the influential and sturdy Dutch types that prevailed in England prior to the development by William Caslon of his own designs, which he evolved from these Dutch faces. Of Janson himself little is known except that he was a practicing typefounder in Leipzig during the years 1660 to 1687. Printed by* MURRAY PRINTING COMPANY, *Forge Village, Massachusetts and bound by* THE COLONIAL PRESS INC., *Clinton, Massachusetts. Cover design by* PAUL RAND.